The Social Studies and the Social Sciences

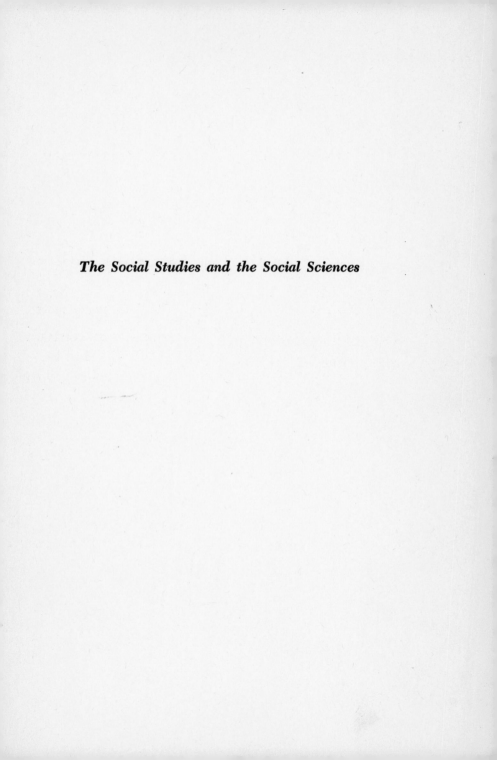

BERNARD BERELSON / PRESTON E. JAMES / HYMAN KUBLIN / BEN W. LEWIS / NORTON E. LONG / W. J. MC KEACHIE / DOUGLAS OLIVER / MICHAEL B. PETROVICH / JOSEPH R. STRAYER / GRESHAM M. SYKES / LEWIS PAUL TODD / GORDON B. TURNER

The Social Studies and the Social Sciences / *Sponsored by the American Council of Learned Societies and the National Council for the Social Studies*

HARCOURT, BRACE & WORLD, INC.
New York

B.10.63

LIBRARY OF CONGRESS CATALOG CARD NUMBER: 62-19583
PRINTED IN THE UNITED STATES OF AMERICA

Foreword

THE SOCIAL STUDIES in the schools are now in a state of ferment from which they are bound to emerge substantially altered. Scholars in the universities and teachers in the schools are joining in co-operative efforts to refashion the various segments of the curriculum in order to bring them into line with modern knowledge and current needs. History, which has traditionally been the core of the social studies, is about to be reviewed. Economics and geography are well on the road to revision, and other subjects are in various stages of development and redevelopment.

The essays that make up this book are intended to serve a related purpose, but they approach the problem of revision from a different and specific point of view. They assume that until basic objectives are formulated and substantial agreement is achieved about the aims of the several social studies, curriculum revision will produce less than satisfactory results. The social studies have not been static over the years; repeated attempts have been made to improve and update old courses and to introduce new ones. But in this generation no serious effort has been made to view the separate parts with reference to the whole, and, lacking a general framework within which to operate, the experts in the several disciplines have frequently worked at cross purposes. The American Council of Learned Societies and the National Council for the Social Studies have therefore jointly sponsored this book in the conviction that formulation of the general and content objectives of the social studies may prevent revisions of the separate parts from once again foundering for lack of a central rationale.

The social studies are, of course, of direct and primary concern to the NCSS and have been since the establishment of the Council. The interest of the ACLS developed more recently and peripherally as the result of a realization in the late 1950's that, as a federation of national organizations concerned with the humanities and the humanistic aspects of the social sciences, it had both a responsibility and an opportunity to direct the attention of scholars to curricular problems of the schools. The ACLS, therefore, established a Committee on the Secondary Schools, composed of teachers, scholars, and educational administrators, and in 1958, on the recommendation of this Committee, the ACLS sponsored a series of panel discussions on the secondary school curriculum in general. The panel on the social studies recommended that the primary need was for a thoroughgoing re-examination of the objectives of the social studies curriculum, and since that time the ACLS has been working closely with the NCSS to implement that recommendation.

Once agreement was reached between the two Councils on a method of procedure, the National Council for the Social Studies appointed a committee to draft a statement on the general objectives of the social studies, without specific reference to content, that would reflect the thinking of the secondary schools. This committee was composed of Jack Allen, George Peabody College for Teachers; Howard R. Anderson,

University of Washington; William H. Cartwright, Duke University; Dorothy McClure Fraser, College of the City of New York; John H. Haefner, State University of Iowa; and Samuel P. McCutchen, New York University. Its views were then prepared for publication in this volume by Lewis Paul Todd and appear in the Afterword.

Meanwhile the American Council of Learned Societies, with the advice of its constituent societies and other professional groups, commissioned one scholar from each of the relevant disciplines, as well as two representing area studies, to prepare statements on the content objectives of the social studies curriculum from the point of view of their particular fields of scholarship. These nine papers, therefore, as distinct from the NCSS paper, were designed to deal primarily with the content or scope of the social studies program, although it was understood that each author would set forth explicitly in an opening statement his assumptions about the general objectives of the social studies and of education more broadly defined. The latter was deemed essential for a full understanding of the subsequent comments about content that would comprise the body of each paper.

Before undertaking their assignments, the authors of the substantive papers met with representatives of the two Councils, and the following decisions were reached in the interest of uniformity:

1. It was agreed that the authors should discuss the kinds of concepts, knowledge, and techniques contributed by their areas and disciplines that are important for students to acquire by the end of their senior year in high school. The papers are not, therefore, concerned with specific course content nor with what should be taught in any particular grade, but only with curricular goals for the graduating senior.

2. It was agreed not to prepare separate sections for the terminal student and the college-preparatory student on the ground that once optimum objectives had been established, the individual schools would know best how much their ter-

minal student could cover. Similar reasoning dictated that no attempt should be made to deal with the problem of providing for the wide range of abilities that exists among students.

3. It was recognized that students should have an understanding of at least one culture other than their own, and that the schools would determine for themselves whether this should be African, Asian, Latin American, Near Eastern, or Slavic, or some combination thereof. The fact that this volume covers only Asian and Russian studies, therefore, should not be construed as a particular endorsement of these areas. They are included simply as samples, and are intended to answer questions that might apply to all areas; for example: Should they be studied primarily with reference to the cold war, or as points of reference and perspective for American history and traditions, or is the objective to give students an understanding of the contributions of different traditions to world history?

The types of questions to which the authors were asked to address themselves show that the aim of the volume is not to establish a uniform national curriculum but rather to provide general guidelines for reform. The questions are those with which curriculum planners have been grappling for years. Should the social studies be a vehicle for citizenship education? If so, to what extent should this be done by courses designed to develop in the student the ability to think critically, to reach conclusions, and to make his own decisions? In turn, to what extent should the curriculum deal with current problems as opposed to the basic historical, economic, and political factors that gave rise to them? Finally, does citizenship education as a general objective of the social studies preclude the possibility of making the social studies truly representative of the social sciences as they are practiced today? In other words, can the social studies program be designed simultaneously to provide knowledge about man and society and to make students aware of the general concepts and unity of social science?

Once drafted, most of these papers were reviewed by experts in the several fields; six were also the subject of prolonged discussion at a conference of social scientists and social studies teachers at Indiana University in the spring of 1961, and eight were placed on the program of the Annual Meeting of the National Council for the Social Studies the following fall for critical appraisal. The authors then met with Bernard Berelson, whose introductory chapter synthesizes the findings and recommendations of the group, and all of the substantive papers were then revised in light of the comments made.

Thus, although the chapters in this book are the responsibility of the individual authors, and no pretense is made that they represent a broad consensus of opinion about the objectives that the social studies should seek to achieve, they constitute a joint effort to view the social studies dispassionately, and it is hoped that they will serve as a useful guide to curriculum makers in the future.

It scarcely needs to be pointed out that a book of this nature is only a first step in the long and arduous process of revising and revitalizing the social studies program in the schools. Much work will have to be done by the teachers in the schools, assisted by the scholars in the universities, before the ideas presented here can be translated into practical results. New courses will have to be drafted, new materials will have to be written, and there must be experimentation, evaluation, and retraining of teachers. But the most fundamental decision of all, and one that will have to be faced by each school system on its own, pertains to selection and balance in the social studies curriculum. Time will not permit students to acquire knowledge in depth about all of the concepts and substantive ideas suggested in this volume. It is obvious, therefore, that a great deal of thought will have to be devoted to judicious selection of areas, disciplines, and subjects to be covered so that students will get a balanced education in the social studies. It is in this difficult realm of decisions that this book would serve the most useful purpose, and it is hoped that its publication will stimulate action on a broad front.

GORDON B. TURNER
American Council of Learned Societies

February 15, 1962

Contents

Foreword v
Gordon B. Turner / American Council of Learned Societies

Introduction 3
Bernard Berelson / The Population Council

History 20
Joseph R. Strayer / Princeton University

Geography 42
Preston E. James / Syracuse University

Political Science 88
Norton E. Long / Northwestern University

Economics 106
Ben W. Lewis / Oberlin College

The Social Studies and the Social Sciences

Introduction

Bernard Berelson / The Population Council

THE THOUGHTFUL and provocative papers contained in this symposium present an impressive cumulative picture of what the social studies curriculum might include. My purpose here is simply to pull the threads together into the emerging pattern. In doing so, I shall necessarily base my comments on these papers, and I shall simply try to bring out and underline some points they make in common.

To begin with, the need for detailed reconsideration of the social studies curriculum in the secondary school appears to be so clear that it hardly requires extended argument. Although the social studies is a sizable segment of the total, at the present time it is the only major segment not under systematic inquiry and development. In the past few years, the offerings in mathematics, in physics, in chemistry, in biology, in English, have all been put under intensive scrutiny. In most cases, revised programs not only have been put forward but have been put into effect. As for the importance of the social studies in the modern world, that needs only to be mentioned to be acknowledged. If anything, their importance will be even greater in the difficult years ahead, and especially for that half of the high school population that does not go on to college. Thus, the demands of modern life require an up-to-date version of the social studies curriculum.

So do the demands of the underlying intellectual disciplines. The present curriculum has been resting largely on the same fields for half a century, despite the dramatic development over that period of a whole body of scholarly and scientific material in the modern social and behavioral sciences. To a substantial extent, the social studies curriculum in the senior high school today is still based on the influential National Education Association report of 1916. Despite any number of local deviations, the general pattern includes civics or world geography in the ninth grade, world history in the tenth, United States history (usually by state law) in the eleventh, and an occasional Problems of Democracy in the twelfth. And despite several calls for reconsideration if not reform—most recently by a committee report to the National Council for the Social Studies in 1958 and an individual's "Call to Revolution in the Social Studies," by Charles R. Keller in the *College Board Review* of Spring 1961—there has not been a detailed national review of what the social studies curriculum ought to be.

This volume is perhaps the closest approximation, and it is intended only to open the discussion, not close it. For these papers were by their very nature not meant to be manuals or syllabi or course outlines; nor are they presented as necessarily representing a consensus of scholars in each field. They are offered simply as informed answers, by representative and qualified scholars, to the question: What ought a high school graduate know about my field? As such, they deserve serious consideration from each of the three educational groups interested in the best answer to such a question: teachers of the social studies in the schools; teachers of the social studies teachers, in the colleges and universities; and the disciplinary scholars themselves. Each has the right and the duty to be heard, and each has something to say that is worth hearing. This volume will serve its purpose if it starts a responsible discussion looking toward the first major reform of the social studies curriculum in fifty years.

In a way, it is surprising that the social studies are "left back" in the mid-twentieth century. If school programs are to be based on objective social needs on the one hand and the state of learning on the other, surely no field can make a stronger claim than the social studies.

In the past fifty years, the world has changed by a great order of magnitude. The major war in progress when the NEA report came out in 1916 now appears minor compared with the one we have had since, let alone the one we fear; the economic depression of the 1930's may be only a few pages of history to today's students but it was personally experienced by their teachers; developments in transportation and communication have pulled the world dramatically together while the national aspirations of newly emerging powers threaten in conflict to pull it apart. Certainly the least that can be said, by way of understatement, is that the high school student of today is going to be living in a far, far different world from that inhabited by the student of 1916.

Nor is the change in the scholarly disciplines themselves much less dramatic, as measured by their own yardsticks. History and geography and political science were mainstays of the social studies then, and are now, though all of them have undergone important developments in coverage and method since that time. But economics and the so-called behavioral sciences (anthropology, psychology, sociology) have risen over the intervening years to the position of major claimants for attention in their own right; and the emergence of the U.S.S.R., Asia, Africa, and Latin America have been accompanied by the greater attention given them in area programs in the universities (as only sampled here by the papers on the first two of them).

So, if one wished to characterize the situation for shorthand purposes, he could say with some justification that two current revolutions underline the reconsideration of the social studies curriculum: the revolution of rising expectations and national aspirations that will inform the rest of the twentieth century, and the scientific revolution that is here represented by recent developments in the social and behavioral sciences. How to take both into reasonable account in fashioning a realistic curriculum in the social studies—that is the issue.

Issues

Rather, there are a number of issues to which these papers speak, and it is worth considering them in turn. To begin with:

Should the social studies curriculum aim to produce good citizens, or knowledgeable students of the major fields of learning? At first glance, it would appear that there is a genuine difference of opinion on this matter among our authors, or certainly between some of them and the position of most social studies teachers. Lewis, for example, explicitly makes "responsible citizenship" the objective for teaching economics in the schools, yet Sykes from sociology seems to opt for disciplinary representation as such. Those who had the opportunity of hearing these papers discussed by school people know that this issue is close to their concern. At the least, if this is not a matter to debate, it is certainly a matter that needs clearing up.

My own impression is that this is largely a spurious issue that will go away if it is put in a different semantic frame. As a starter, suppose we were to say that we—all of us involved—want to give high school students the best introduction we can, within limits of practicality, to the best available knowledge from the social science disciplines *as a means to the end* of producing responsible citizens. That single sentence, which I think would be agreed to by many participants on all sides of the debate, may go a long way toward resolving the issue. That is, it will allow concrete, detailed planning to proceed. Indeed, that is essentially what Lewis himself goes on to say ("economics for citizenship means economics for understanding," etc., page 133); what Sykes argued in a related discussion of his paper ("ultimately, we all wish to produce responsible intelligent citizens . . . but this is best done by instilling a respect for objective knowledge," page 6 of a talk to NCSS, November 1961). It is what James seeks via his tripartite division of objectives in this field. So that does not seem itself to be a major obstacle to collaboration and to the development of a program; but there are a few more points that need to be made in this connection.

In the first place, the scholars are quite clear that "preparation for responsible citizenship" ought not be used as the facade for "how to do it" courses in the social studies —not on commercial education or business problems in economics (Lewis, page 131), not on personal adjustment in psychology (McKeachie, page 178), not on family living in sociology (Sykes, page 159), and in area studies not on the "trouble-spot approach" (Petrovich, page 247) but "primarily in terms of its intrinsic worth" (Kublin, page 197). In every case, the scholar would naturally prefer his subject to be presented for its own intellectual sake, in the spirit of the liberal arts; and he goes on to argue that that is indeed the best "preparation for responsible citizenship" so far as his field is concerned. Understanding, they feel, should precede and underlie application; and at this stage in education, the time available should be devoted to basic understandings, illustrated by their applications to past and present societies.

There are two additional reasons why this seems indicated. Both were noted above, but can bear emphasis here.

The first is that for a large proportion of high school students, this will be the last exposure to these fields in a formal educational program. Many will not go on to college at all, some will start in college but soon drop out, some will go on in fields that leave little opportunity for further work in the social sciences. So the social studies curriculum in the schools will have to serve not only as the introduction for those continuing in formal education but as all there is for the others—or, put another way, as the platform for adult education. Hence, the more representative of our best knowledge it can be, the better. If there is time for only a beginning, that beginning ought to be fundamental in nature, not peripheral.

The second reason takes us back to the objective of the social studies curriculum if stated as "responsible citizenship." In order to specify that condition for students in secondary schools, it is desirable if not necessary to look ahead, as well as we can. If there is one thing we know about the decades ahead in which today's high school students will be "responsible citizens"—perhaps the only thing we may know with some certainty—it is that they will be a time of change. Look back twenty-five or thirty-five years to the time when the authors of these papers were, on the average, high school students themselves. Who in 1925 could have foreseen the Depression, World War II, the space age, the cold war, the rise of the new nations throughout the world, not to mention the less dramatic, less eventful, but no less pervasive social problems that characterize our times? Look ahead the same period, and we are on the threshold of the twenty-first century. Who will now venture to say just what that time will bring in the way of specific, concrete demands upon "responsible citizenship"? The only safe prediction is that they will be sharply different from today's issues and conditions. Most of the students being trained in the high schools now will be participants in that world, and some of them will be the leaders of it. So we are training now for the twenty-first century. How can we do better for our students than to give them a fundamental, intellectual preparation that will last, rather than a vocational or utilitarian preparation geared to today's situations that will become outmoded so soon?

What would such preparation mean? In the first place, students would come to know, or at least be exposed to know, a number of things not now presented to them generally or systematically. If we were to follow only the suggestions set down in these papers—not that the authors thought that they were setting down prescriptions—here is just a sampling from the disciplines:

The regional concept, the geography of population, and the use of the culture concept, in geography
The biological bases of human behavior, perception, learning, and personality, from psychology
The nature of economizing and the market system, from economics
Socialization and social control, from sociology
Social function and structure, from anthropology
Political history and the development of governing institutions, from political science
Historical diversity and the great revolutions, from history

—not to mention a range of themes from the area programs. This is a tall order, and it remains so even when we recall that there is a certain amount of overlap among the illustrative recommendations made by our nine authors: between political science and history, for example, or between anthropology and history, or anthropology and the area programs, or psychology and sociology, or geography and history, or economics and political science. Such overlaps, incidentally, are encouraging instances of convergence that speak well for the prospects of putting together a coherent curriculum.

Before asking whether and how such a program could be put into effect, however, I wish to call attention to three special aspects of "what the social studies student should know" as they appear in these pages. Each of them, it seems to me, warrants a moment's extra look.

The first has to do with cultural diversity: explicit attention to differences among human ways of life. This theme appears in the papers on geography, on sociology, on anthropology, on history, and of course strongly in the case of the area programs. In each case, the author argues, it is of particular importance for the student to see himself and, in the literal sense, to appreciate himself in an objective relation to the rest of the world. Thus, Petrovich, just to take an example, argues against the presentation of world history as viewed from the White standpoint and again a few pages later against a presentation documenting our own virtue and superiority vis-à-vis others: "If the subject is taught primarily as a vehicle for drawing comparisons favorable to our way of life, this is bound to lead to a didactic tone, an air of self-righteousness, and an almost unavoidable tendency to stack the facts" (page 251).

The second point is closely related to the first; indeed, it may be the general point of which the first is a special case. That is the desirability of leading the student to an appreciation of what he thinks he knows that is not so. This point is made in connection with economics (there is an eloquent sentence on horse sense!) as well as sociology, geography, and psychology. Indeed, McKeachie's third and fourth "attitudinal goals" deal explicitly with this matter: "a critical attitude toward generalizations about human behavior" and "increased skepticism about the finality of our present state of knowledge." Certainly a sober appreciation of this point is the beginning of wisdom, and if this is soundly done, it could be among the most important consequences of the social studies curriculum.

And third, partly as a way of realizing that end, there is an emphasis in a few of the papers on the desirability of giving the student some familiarity and even experience with the research methods by which knowledge is gathered. Quite naturally perhaps, this point is made most strongly by the two disciplines most concerned with method, namely, psychology and sociology. This approach may be the channel for introducing the high school student to the kind of statistical reasoning and quantitative analysis that characterizes these fields, and that constitutes a great innovation in the study of man within the past several decades.

There remain a few issues that seem to be peculiar to the social studies. At any rate, they do not occur with similar force in such fields as physics, mathematics, biology, or even English.

The first has to do with the high school student's readiness for such a course of study. Is he sufficiently prepared by life experiences to seriously undertake an inquiry into economic, social, and psychological matters of the kind outlined in some of these papers? Can he appreciate what is involved? Will he unduly personalize psychology and sociology or make direct applications to himself and his environment that may not be justified? Ought such matters to be saved until he is more mature, until he has more background against which to evaluate this material? Now such questions do not typically arise in the impersonal case of mathematics or even in the case of biology, but they do in connection with the social studies. Are the students ready?

There is some difference of opinion among our authors on this score, but in general they believe that the students are readier than the teachers. Strayer remarks that "some of the concepts of the other social sciences are a little too abstract to be grasped by precollege students unless they are presented as a specific historical problem" (page 24), but McKeachie and Petrovich, for example, note (page 172 and page 275, respectively) that the problem of readiness is more serious among untrained instructors than immature youth. In general, our authors are willing to go cautiously ahead, to take it for granted that the students are indeed ready, and to focus on the central question of what they should be offered. Their assumption is that high school students can benefit from such material, that they can learn it in a scholarly way if it is properly taught, that they already do in the social-problems course as well as in experimental courses in anthropology and social psychology (plus, of course, the traditional historical, governmental, and geographical courses).

The second issue of peculiar importance to the social studies as compared, say, with mathematics or physics, is not unrelated to the first. It is that this field involves sensitive issues of social, political, economic, even personal policy. Behavioral norms are directly involved here in a sense that they are not in other fields, and that fact can lead to both practical and intellectual difficulties. Note, for example, only some of the problems that would come up and would require dispassionate attention and analysis: the Civil War in history, race differences in anthropology and certain area studies, child rearing and sex matters in psychology, the welfare state in economics, class differences in sociology, Communism in political science and the Soviet area, national aspirations in the Asian area. Beyond such matters, there are questions about the role of values in social studies—questions, incidentally, that the scholarly disciplines themselves are still debating, as witness the papers here by Sykes and Long.

Certainly such matters are necessarily involved in any proper course of social studies. What else, indeed, are they about if not the richness, the complexity, the controversy of human life? But where else can the student get a better introduction to such delicate yet important issues than in a classroom properly led by a teacher knowledgeable in the subject and dedicated to its objective analysis? As Lewis says, "insight and rationality are the hallmarks of objective scientific scholarship—the very antithesis of indoctrination in the classroom" (page 116).

But perhaps the concern over the matter of values has less to do with indoctrination of the students than with pressures from various minorities in the community. Here the high school teacher may feel somewhat vulnerable and exposed to attack, from whatever quarter does not sympathize with the particular point of view or even the particular fact presented: evolution decades ago, parts of the social studies today. Here, I suggest, the problem is not so great as it is customarily made out: the infrequent examples get much more attention than their number or importance warrants. Moreover, the entire academic community needs to stand together on this issue so that the normal protection of academic freedom can be extended to the faculties of secondary schools as now to the colleges and universities. Certainly one ought not to dismiss the seriousness of this issue for the proper organization of the social studies curriculum in the secondary schools; at the same time, one ought not to be immobilized into a hopeless frustration about improving the present situation. In a sense, it is the very controversiality of many parts of the social studies that requires some systematic attention in the schools for the health of the society.

The third issue centers on the organization of the social studies curriculum. In a sense, it is a political issue, what a friendly observer has characterized as "the League of Nations problem," in that the disciplinary claims for inclusion are as many and profound as the countering pressures of time. In other cases, like physics or mathematics or chemistry or English, the disciplinary remodelers of the secondary school curriculum have only themselves to take into account, to satisfy or to please: their own subject, their own criteria of truth and of importance, their own method of inquiry, their own personnel to judge. In the social studies, on the other hand, psychologists must somehow come to terms with political scientists, sociologists with historians, area specialists with geographers, economists with anthropologists. It is not an easy prospect, though in view of the agreed-upon urgency of the goal, it is by no means an impossible one either.

There are, naturally, differences of opinion as to how the secondary school curriculum in the social studies should be organized, given this diversity. No one, naturally, wants to see his own discipline slighted; as the reader will quickly see, each of our authors believes that he represents a field with a substantial claim upon the student's attention, and no doubt a good case can be made for each position. The fact remains that, given other claims for attention, the social studies curriculum can at most be allocated a course a year for all high school students and will probably have to do with less: the present average for high school graduates, across the country, appears to be about two and a half, or a little more.

How should the curriculum be organized, then? An answer is that there are several ways and the need is to experiment with various of them. At least four major segments can readily be identified: world areas (history, geography, cultures), American history and government, political economy (economics, economic geography, governmental relations to the economy), and the behavioral sciences (anthropology, psychology, sociology). Such segments can be put together in various sequences, or in various ways: an historical stream, à la Strayer; a geographic theme, à la James; anthropology at the service of other fields, à la the first part of Oliver; etc., etc. This is not the place to speculate about the matter: it is far too complex and it requires a collaborative approach of groups other than the scholars represented here. Furthermore, this arrangement is based only on a four-year sequence. If the junior high school curriculum is brought into consideration too, then the further flexibility of a six-year program is gained. The only point that needs to be made here, however, is that such enriching reorganizations are possible and now require considerable thought, ingenuity, and especially experimentation. The degrees of freedom are many, and the efforts to reorganize will almost certainly find several good ways to proceed rather than one best way. At this stage, at any rate, that approach to multiple outcomes is less likely to lead to bad mistakes.

In this connection, there are two more important points on which our authors appear to agree. The first is that if the social studies must choose between coverage and thoroughness—and given the practicalities of the situation, that choice is probably built in—it should choose thoroughness. As Strayer says, "there is always a temptation to try to do too much, and thus to do nothing very well" (page 21), and he advocates within history what is required even more in the wider program, namely, "judicious sampling" (page 25). This is a hard choice to make, but a necessary one if an ambitious curriculum is not to thin itself out to the vanishing point.

The other agreement is that the secondary school curriculum should and must stand on its own feet. It is not to be considered as a watered-down version of the college curriculum nor as necessarily having the same objectives—any more than the colleges would consider that their purposes were subordinate to those of the graduate and professional schools. This is not to say that a revised social studies curriculum would not have implications, and even repercussions, upon the work of the college and the graduate school; but the social studies program should be determined by its own demands, its own ends. At least one of our authors hopes that it would provide a generalist approach that he finds lacking in the program of the college today (Long, page 95). The relation of the social studies curriculum in the secondary school to that in the elementary and junior high school on the one hand and the college on the other is not discussed in any detail in these papers, no doubt because the scholar-authors recognize that such matters are really outside their own special competence. But it is perhaps reasonable to think that the secondary school curriculum in this field is critical, and that one can usefully work out of it in both directions.

Conclusion

To conclude, then, we can hope that a number of questions central to this enterprise can be answered in the affirmative: Is there a gap between the present secondary school curriculum in the social studies and the available scholarly knowledge? Is there room in the secondary school for more and/or better material in these fields? Are the students capable of managing the newly proposed material in economics or the behavioral sciences? Can the controversial aspects involved in social and personal values be handled? Can coherent organization and sequence of the material be achieved in the face of differences among the several disciplines represented? In short, a new social studies curriculum, i.e., new curricula, in the secondary schools should now be developed.

That this judgment is not restricted to the interested scholars is indicated by Mr. Todd's paper presenting the viewpoint of someone much closer to the high school classroom. He sets forth the need and the goal, as they have constantly been appreciated by the secondary school people themselves, and underlines the urgency of doing something now. His own suggestions deserve careful consideration, but whether those specific ideas or others are finally implemented, here is a clear case of agreement on objectives and general course of action between the university specialists in subject matter on the one hand and a spokesman for the social studies in the secondary schools on the other. That in itself is a signal event, and it is cause for hope that something will indeed be done.

As a guide we might take the first and last sentences of Petrovich's paper: "There has been a notorious lag between new advances in scholarship and their appearance in our elementary and secondary schools. . . . A 'crash program' is not enough." The former implies that we should start, the latter that we should take thought and take care, for such "revolutions" last a long time. Indeed, the NEA report of 1916 is still with us today. That is another reason, as I tried to suggest earlier, for building the social studies solidly on a foundation of scholarly and scientific knowledge in these fields, and not upon utilitarian purposes narrowly conceived. In a changing world, basic knowledge and fundamental skills last longer than any other kind.

Such a development would mean a great deal to all concerned and, quite properly, it would demand a great deal as well:

> *The disciplinary scholars in higher education* would have to co-operate in the redevelopment of the social studies curriculum: to become sympathetically knowledgeable about the problems of the secondary school as they affect that curriculum, to put aside disciplinary objectives as such, to collaborate in restating the basic knowledge of their field into materials appropriate for high school students. In return, they will not only have contributed to the greater good in general, but in addition the students reaching them in higher education will be both better trained and more numerous.*
>
> *The teachers of the teachers* would have to review and redo their own training programs in order to prepare the next generations of social studies teachers. This would mean a shift in the major subject emphasis now taken by such teachers, i.e., away from the history major that characterizes perhaps three-fourths of the social studies teachers now. It would mean the

* Simply from the standpoint of self-interest, the scholar in the colleges and universities should recognize that here too is an important difference between this field and the physical and biological sciences. The latter, with a full program of studies in the schools, has a much better opportunity for recruitment of talented students by that fact alone. A fuller and richer program in the social studies will provide students the opportunity to consider the social sciences as career possibilities, thus more nearly equalizing the situation with regard to recruitment (as McKeachie, for example, notes in his final paragraph). As it is now, for example, some parts of the social studies, such as the behavioral sciences, are not effectively presented to high school students as intellectual enterprises warranting their serious consideration.

preparation of new teaching materials based on the revised programs of study and the collaborative offering of a range of refresher courses for present teachers of the subject. Since this group is in higher education yet in close touch with the schools, there is a great opportunity for them to exercise considerable leadership in bringing about this whole development.

The teachers of the social studies in the schools must not only participate fully and equally with the other two groups in the reshaping of the curriculum, but they must, in the nature of the case, carry the real load. They are the ones who must, most directly, *do* it. The scholars can advise, the teachers of the teachers can train, but, in the end, it will be the teacher in the classroom who will determine the success or failure of the effort. The burden will be great, but so will the reward of achieving the first major revision of this curriculum in fifty years just when it is greatly needed by the society.

And as if all of that were not enough, these three groups, for the first time in decades, must learn to work together effectively. No one of the three can do the job alone, so they must collaborate to the common end. And they must continue to collaborate in order to keep the classroom teacher up to date on scholarly developments, so that the lag referred to will not emerge a few years hence. It is no use blinking at the fact that there are several obstacles in the way, not least the prevailing perceptions of one another. But the experience of such collaboration in other fields suggests that despite the "League of Nations problem," effective working relations are possible here as well.

The students in the secondary schools will receive a much better education in the social studies—and in such fields as economics and the behavorial sciences, most of them will receive an education for about the first time. The demand on the students is to demonstrate their capability of handling such material in a responsible way.

The society will get generations of young people better educated for the great problems that lie ahead. It will need to show patience and understanding about the handling of the inevitably controversial matters that will come up in any worthwhile social studies program; and it will need to protect the schools against the several minorities who will seek to use the program to advance their own causes. A professional, objective analysis in the classroom is the best answer, and a mature community will see, appreciate, and allow that.

These papers, then, are only a short start on the road toward the reforming of the social studies curriculum: to improve the old, to include the new. They will serve their purpose if they do indeed start the journey.

What is needed now is deliberation and experimentation: in programs, in their organization, in teacher education, in materials. The next step seems clear—and in the light of educational history in this country, it can be a giant one.

History

Joseph R. Strayer / Princeton University

EDUCATION IS THE training of the individual to take his place in society. All societies have some sort of educational process, but in many of them education is informal and unspecialized. The individual learns by taking part in the activities and rituals of his group or by serving an apprenticeship with men who have special skills and knowledge. Formal education is a device for speeding up and broadening the educational process. By generalizing and condensing past experience, by organizing and arranging scattered observations in meaningful patterns, more ground can be covered and a greater variety of skills, information, and attitudes can be inculcated. In a complex society this specialized educational process is absolutely necessary. Such societies offer such a wide range of experiences and require such a wide range of skills and information that no individual can play even a minor role in them without some degree of formal training. But while formal education is necessary, it always runs the danger of becoming divorced from reality. The degree of abstraction and generalization that is required even at very elementary levels is sometimes bewildering to students; they memorize phrases and formulae without understanding their significance or being able to apply them. At this point learning ceases and boredom begins.

The social studies are not exempt from this danger, even though we like to think that they deal with concrete facts and real-life situations. We often fail to realize how abstract some apparently simple and frequently used phrases are. Words like *revolution, empire, middle class, budget,* have no meaning unless they have been illustrated by many specific examples. And these are the easy words; there are others at a much higher level of abstraction. How many diverse events, how many conflicting interpretations, are summed up in the one word "Renaissance"! This is what creates the great dilemma of the social studies. The more new terms are introduced to describe social phenomena, the more detailed facts should be studied in order to explain the terms. But if a wide variety of social phenomena is studied, the number of supporting facts that could be introduced is almost limitless. Thus the social studies must either generalize without giving sufficient knowledge of detail, or else present so much detail that the generalizations fail to stand out clearly. Frequently they are impaled on both horns of the dilemma; they present too many inadequately explained generalizations and too many facts whose relationship to the generalizations is not made clear. There is always a temptation to try to do too much, and thus to do nothing very well.

The social studies are tempted to do too much because too much is expected of them. Other disciplines are allowed to specialize and to pursue their content rigorously. A teacher of French, for example, has a fairly limited objective—that of enabling a student to learn a specific language. He may also be able to give the student some general ideas about the way in which a new language is acquired and some notions about the nature of French culture, but these broader aspects of the subject are subordinated to the specific task of acquiring a certain skill. In the same way a teacher of physics has a fairly clearly defined body of material to present. Like the teacher of French, he may also have broader aims, such as giving some idea of scientific method, but there is fairly general agreement on the topics that should form the core of the course in physics. In contrast, the teacher of social studies is supposed to draw on all human experience in order to acquaint his pupils with all aspects of human behavior and all forms of social organization. He is expected to give information about every corner of the world so that his students will have a basis for understanding all current world problems. Every human activity is carried on in society. Every type of human behavior has possible relevance for the individual who is learning to take his place in society. As a result, it is very difficult to keep courses in the social studies from being overloaded.

Social studies in the schools are expected to do three things. First, they are supposed to teach the student about human behavior, and especially about human behavior in social organizations. The student is to learn about widely varying systems of belief and patterns of organization; his own narrow experience is to be broadened and deepened. He is to see how beliefs and institutions interact to form civilizations of different types. He is supposed to get some idea of the complexity of human society and the widely divergent responses to similar social problems.

In short, the social studies are supposed to give the student some understanding of social processes and the ability to recognize familiar elements in changing situations. This, if achieved, would be of tremendous value, for the completely unfamiliar is always bewildering and often terrifying. Intelligent reactions to new problems depend on finding some guidelines in past experience. The broader the vicarious experience gained through social studies, the better prepared the student will be to make intelligent decisions later in life.

The second aim of the social studies is to give the student essential information about the cultural history of mankind, the traditions of his own society, and the present world situation. The student should be able to understand what is meant by a reference to Plato or Hegel, to Mohammed or Buddha, to Phidias or Michelangelo, to Newton or Pasteur, if he is to make the most of his cultural heritage or comprehend discussions by the leading thinkers of his time. He should also know about the development of the American democratic tradition and the documents in which this tradition is expressed so that he can understand the values and aims of his own society. He should gain some understanding of the background of contemporary political and social issues; for example, how Communism acquired its present position, why Africa is in turmoil, or what factors are disturbing Latin American society. In its most ambitious—and unrealizable—form, the goal is to give the student all the information that he will need to make intelligent decisions as a voter.

In the third place, the social studies are supposed to inculcate certain attitudes and skills. The desired attitudes include respect for evidence even when it goes against prejudices and preconceptions, tolerance for differing points of view, appreciation of human dignity, a sense of civic responsibility and devotion to the welfare of the country. The skills are those associated with the analysis and solution of social problems: ability to discover relevant facts, to organize the facts into a meaningful pattern, to weigh conflicting evidence and discount biased statements, and to choose among various interpretations and policies.

Obviously all the social sciences have something to contribute in all these categories. In our schools, however, history has traditionally been the core of the social studies curriculum and has been asked to carry a large part of the burden of providing students with the necessary understanding, information, attitudes, and skills. There are good reasons for this policy. The narrative tone of history sustains student interest better than the analytical approach of other social sciences, especially in the lower grades. In fact, it is hardly possible to begin the analysis of social behavior until a certain number of historical facts have been absorbed. Much of the desired material appears most naturally in a historical context; for example, facts about earlier civilizations or about the origins and development of American democracy. Many social phenomena can be most easily understood as they develop throughout a historical period; for example, the transformation of an agricultural into an industrial society. And some of the concepts of the other social sciences are a little too abstract to be grasped by precollege students unless they are presented as a specific historical problem. Theories of money and banking, for example, are difficult to explain to high school students, but a good many basic ideas about money and banking appear in studying the economic aspects of American history.

Finally, the historical context is closer to the real situations that students will face later in life. In the actual world, political or economic problems are not isolated from other influences; they do not appear as neat equations that can be solved by knowing the proper formulae. They are always affected by special interests, traditions, and prejudices. There is seldom one single right answer to these problems; instead, there are various answers each of which has something in its favor. This is precisely the way in which important problems appear in the study of history, and history, rightly taught, can warn the student about the complexities of any social action.

Granting that history should be the core of the social studies curriculum, two things should be said at once. First, history has a duty to include all the types of material that will illustrate and lay a foundation for the work of the other social sciences. It should not be exclusively political history—which was a failing in the past; nor should it be exclusively economic history or cultural history—which is a failing of some present courses. Second, while history can do much, it cannot do everything. Some courses that draw more heavily on the methods of the other social sciences are necessary to acquaint students with new points of view and new ways of organizing the materials. Such courses are especially valuable in the upper grades, and a wide range of experimentation in them is desirable.

Even with assistance from other disciplines, it is a difficult task to achieve, or even to make a beginning at achieving the objectives of the social studies within the limits of three or four history courses. The problem is especially acute at the informational level. The other objectives can be attained by judicious sampling. A thorough study of two or three historical periods will demonstrate the variety of human behavior better than sweeping surveys that never get below the level of vast generalizations. The history of almost any period or country will serve this purpose, if the teacher is adequately prepared and if suitable educational materials are available. In the same way, the study of almost any kind of history will afford opportunities for inculcating the necessary skills and attitudes. Problems of evidence and interpretation occur everywhere; study of remote countries or past civilizations is a good way of acquiring tolerance for other points of view; the value of civic responsibility and patriotism can be illustrated in Greek and Roman history as well as in our own. But information is another matter. Sampling is less satisfactory here; there are so many facts that are or might be useful. If a goal of education is to prepare well-informed citizens, is there anything that can be left out? If a revolution in Laos can stir the world, should not the student have some knowledge of the history and institutions of every country?

It is reasoning of this sort that has led to the overloading of history courses, and especially courses in world history, with vast amounts of factual data. It is easier to state the problem than to find an acceptable solution. For it is true that the citizen of the next generation will need more information than his predecessors did. He will live in a very complex society in which generalizations based on inadequate knowledge will be dangerous. He will live in a world in which events in Asia, Africa, and South America will have a profound impact on his life. Knowledge of his own history and his own society will not be enough; he must have some understanding of other traditions and other ways of life. One of the great problems with which he will have to deal will be the competition and the interactions among many different cultures. But how can all this be done in the limited time that is available for the study of history in the schools?

One answer, of course, is that learning can continue even after formal education ceases. The schools can never teach everything; what they can do is to create interests and attitudes that make continuing self-education possible. And certainly the best way to create continuing interest in the study of human society is to make history courses interesting. They will not be interesting if they are weighed down with a mass of factual data that has no immediate meaning to the student, and which, not being meaningful, will soon be forgotten. They will be interesting if they keep the story in history, if they deal with a limited number of concrete problems, and if they give the student a feeling that understanding these problems is not impossibly difficult. If the student has become interested in a social problem in history and has learned how to deal with it, there is no reason why he cannot do the same thing with other social problems later in life. He will have acquired a taste for this kind of thinking, skill in collecting and weighing evidence, and some understanding of the complexities of social relationships. Such training is worth more than a collection of scattered and unrelated facts.

It is also true that even if the schools could devote twice

as much time to social studies as they now do, they could still not teach all the facts that might some day be useful to the student. Some choice has to be made; the main problem is to make an intelligent choice instead of yielding to old traditions or current pressures. One basic rule is clear enough; the student should have more information about his own country and his own age than about remote areas and times. This is simply because he has more chance of using this kind of information immediately and of fitting it into other aspects of his experience. Only facts that are assimilated and used are really part of one's education. Thus the student should know more about the United States than China and more about the nineteenth and twentieth centuries than the thirteenth. For most of history and much of the world the best that can be done is to give the student a few guidelines so that he will be able to acquire information by his own efforts if he ever needs it. Thus, without covering Chinese history in detail, the student can get the idea that China is an important country, with its own traditions and problems. He can also discover that the peculiarities of Chinese names are not an impossible barrier to learning something about China and that there are fairly readable books that he can use when he wants to learn more. In the same way, if a student realizes that the human race accomplished some rather remarkable things before 1800 he does not need a complete survey of ancient and medieval history. What he does need are a few landmarks, points of reference, which he can use when and if he requires more information. It is the utterly unfamiliar that seems utterly incomprehensible. It is better to whet the appetite than to satiate it, and a few brief allusions to the achievements of early civilizations are often more stimulating than long discussions about Greek literature or medieval parliaments.

The present program of social studies in the schools would at least enable us to make a start at achieving the aims stated above if all students took the entire sequence of courses. Unfortunately, a good many students miss one or more years of social studies. The only thing that is certain is that all students will take American history—several times over. European or world-history courses, especially at the senior high school level, are often omitted. This means that the American-history courses have to carry most of the load of giving the students essential ideas about the nature of human society, and the skills and attitudes needed to deal with social problems.

This limitation is annoying, but it does not create an absolutely hopeless situation. American-history courses in the schools have been improving steadily; the best ones now come very close to achieving most of the objectives of the social studies. The span of American history is short enough so that it can be studied in some detail, at the level of concrete problems rather than that of broad generalizations. At the same time, American history goes back far enough so that it illustrates many, though not all, varieties of human behavior. Finally, it offers good opportunities for introducing concepts and methods borrowed from the other social sciences. A brief discussion of the desirable content of American-history courses will illustrate these points. It will also suggest a few places where opportunities are being missed.

American history divides fairly easily into four periods marked by significant differences in political, social, and economic development. These four periods are the colonial, the early national (to 1861), the period of industrialization (to 1914), and the period of the emergence of the United States as a world power. A good deal can be done with the first two periods in elementary school and junior high school; the last two can be treated fully only in senior high school. This is not to say that nothing should be done with the twentieth century in the lower grades, or that a certain amount of repetition is undesirable. In fact, repeated coverage of a period with the introduction of new ideas and new materials is the only way in which a historical period can ever be fully understood. Nevertheless, the earlier periods should be emphasized in the lower grades and the later periods in senior high school.

The first and most obvious topic for the first two periods is the discovery and exploration of the North American continent. This is interesting in itself; it also furnishes a good occasion for teaching important facts about geography and its significance. Then there should be considerable emphasis on how people lived and the gradual growth of sectional differences in ways of living. This theme is important for all our later history, but it also has a value that goes beyond the limits of United States history. Early American society was largely agricultural, and an understanding of its interests and limitations helps to understand the general characteristics of other agricultural societies. And the transformation and splintering of this society under the impact of early industrialization has some value in explaining similar transformations and divisions that have taken place elsewhere or are taking place today.

Purely political topics are not very important for the colonial period, but the combined politico-economic topic of imperial policy deserves fairly full treatment. Not only does it help explain the growing estrangement between England and the colonies, it is also an example of the problems of imperialism. In the same way, the American Revolution should be carefully studied, not only because it created our nation, but also because it was the first of the great revolutions that have stirred the modern world. The ways in which it resembled and differed from other revolutions are worth careful exploration.

At about this point in the colonial section, and at similar points near the end of the other sections, the student should be asked to consider the questions: What is an American? How did these people view themselves? What did they believe were their greatest accomplishments—and greatest failures? In what ways did they feel that they differed from other peoples? A great deal of social and intellectual history can be introduced in seeking answers to these questions. And even if he comes up with only tentative answers, the student will have begun to learn something about the traditions and nature of his society.

The story of the framing, adoption, and implementation of the Constitution is the obvious place to discuss the nature of our government and the general problems of political organization in a free society. But care should be taken to avoid giving the impression that the Constitution contained all the answers to our political problems. It is a remarkable document, but even more remarkable is the fact that the American people have succeeded in adapting it to newly emerging needs over a period of almost two centuries. No other nation has succeeded in such an enterprise and the study of this process of adaptation tells more about the American political process than a theoretical analysis of the Constitution itself.

Many of the political issues that still confront us arose during the early national period, particularly the problem of growing sectional differences. These issues were usually intertwined with economic problems, and the early national period is a good place in which to introduce some basic topics of economic history. The farm problem, problems of international trade and tariffs, the questions of the proper relationship between government and business, of governmental responsibility for economic stability and economic welfare all come up at this time. Such topics are less complicated in this early period than they are after the Civil War and so it is easier to introduce some elementary ideas about economics at this stage of courses in American history.

The origins and the course of the Civil War should be taught in some detail, not only because the Civil War is becoming the great legend of our history, but also because it determined many of the developments of the next half century. It is one of the clearest examples of the impact that a war can have on the structure of a society. It was during the Civil War that the North made the transition to a fully industrialized society, and the victory of the North imposed this pattern on the rest of the country.

The period after the Civil War is perhaps the most difficult to teach. The transformation of our economy and our society should be the dominant theme, but there are few picturesque or striking episodes with which to illustrate this transformation. Perhaps the thread that can be most easily grasped by school-age students is the history of technological change. Of course, some elements of the history of technology will have been introduced earlier, but the really massive changes in transportation, communications, and industrial processes came after the Civil War. The contrast between the old and the new way of life and a sense of the accelerated rate of change in the modern world are ideas that can be grasped by almost every student. With this as a basis, the problems caused by rapid technological change can then be introduced—such topics as urbanization, immigration, government regulation of business, labor relations, and so on. Reactions to these problems can then be studied—reform movements, progressivism, farmer and labor organizations, and the like. This is probably the best place in which to bring in large blocks of material from the fields of economics and sociology, though they should always be tied to concrete historical examples as far as possible.

Both in the early national and post-Civil War periods there is a danger that developments in economic and social history will be treated as separate, almost isolated, episodes. When this happens students are apt to lose interest and the material becomes almost unteachable because it seems to lack significance. The economic history of the United States must be taught as part of a continuing process, the process of industrialization and modernization of the country. We were one of the first nations to go through this process, and our experience has some relevance to problems that other parts of the world are now facing. In fact, the story of the economic development of the United States is most interesting if it is compared to similar developments elsewhere. The comparative method is a powerful tool in awakening interest in and understanding of history, and the post-Civil War period is a good place in which to use it.

The post-Civil War period also gives an opportunity to take up a topic that is somewhat neglected even in our college courses—the emergence and growing importance of the scientific point of view. This should be more than a listing of significant scientific discoveries and theories, more even than a discussion of the impact of science on our way of life. What should be done, difficult though it may be, is to give some feeling for the scientist's way of looking at the world, some idea of the scientist's presuppositions and expectations. Thus, perhaps a start could be made in bridging the gap between the scientific and humanistic cultures about which C. P. Snow has written so eloquently.

While detailed examination of the role of the United States in world affairs should be reserved for the final period of American history, some preliminary material should be introduced when the period between 1890 and 1914 is studied. The basic pattern of the world situation in the early twentieth century should be given as a background for the first American attempts at playing a role as a great power. American overseas expansion and the problems of government and of conscience that it created should be briefly covered.

The most recent period of United States history is especially complicated, and it is hard to give it adequate treatment in a one-year course. States such as New Jersey that require in senior high school two years of United States history, or one year of history and one year of problems of democracy, are in a better position to do justice to this period. But even with a two-year sequence it is impossible to cover everything that might conceivably be useful to the embryo citizen. The chief themes can be fully stated and given adequate illustration, but some details will have to be omitted. For example, the main outlines of the farm problem can be made clear, but no high school class should be expected to learn about every act dealing with agriculture between 1923 and the present.

The two chief themes for this period should be the two that have already been introduced: problems of an industrial society and problems of the United States as a world power. Under the first would come such topics as the boom of the twenties, the Great Depression, New Deal efforts at recovery and reform, and recent attempts to guide and regulate the economy. The impact of these developments on our society, and the unsolved social problems that have resulted, should be studied in some detail. It should be made apparent to the student that he is living in an exceedingly complicated society, that actions in one field often have surprisingly far-reaching repercussions in other areas, and that there are no simple, one-shot solutions.

As for the role of the United States as a world power, the task is complicated by the fact that many students will not be very familiar with recent events in European or world history. It is difficult to discuss foreign policy intelligently with students who know nothing about foreigners. Some background material on the world situation in the interwar period and in the period since 1945 certainly should be included in the senior high school course on American history. Something will also have to be said about the history of the two world wars. Military operations can be quickly summarized, but more time should be given to the effects of the wars on European civilization and on the world balance of power. Something must also be said about the rise of the Communist powers and the worldwide trends against colonialism and toward modernization. It is only against such a background that the history of United States foreign policy makes any sense. With this background, the reasons for intervention and isolation, the aims of United States policy, and the problems of the post-1945 period can be discussed fairly quickly and clearly.

Finally, study of United States history should end with a discussion of the same sort of questions that should be raised at the beginning of our national history. What is an American? What do we think we stand for? What sort of a society and a world do we want? How do we think we are going to get it? How has our past conditioned our present? How can we make our present serve as a basis for the future we desire?

Even though every opportunity is taken to show connections with earlier periods of history and other parts of the world, the American-history courses can never be made broad enough to achieve all the aims of the social studies in the schools. American history is geographically Western, culturally European, and chronologically modern. Thus it ignores most of the world, most civilizations, and most history. It cannot treat certain types of human behavior and certain forms of social organization. It offers little opportunity to discuss the achievements of early civilizations, or the characteristics of non-European societies. It necessarily omits essential information about the origins and nature of the present world situation. Therefore the American-history courses should be supplemented by courses in the history of other parts of the world.

Here we run into serious difficulties. No conceivable reorganization of high school curricula would allow enough time to teach European or world history as thoroughly as historians would like to have it taught. The most that can be expected is one course at the junior high school level and another course in senior high school. Many students will not take the second year of non-American history; fortunately they are most likely to be those in the college preparatory program who will have later opportunities to study the subject. But even assuming that most students have two years for European or world history, there are so many possible topics to cover that the temptation to overload becomes almost irresistible. There is general agreement among historians that most school courses in world history are far less successful than those in American history.

They go too fast and they try to teach too much. At the same time, because they introduce so many new topics, the student seldom has an opportunity for developing real understanding of the historical process. He memorizes generalizations on the one hand, and names and dates on the other, without ever seeing a connection between them.

As for the courses in ancient, medieval, and modern history that are still taught in some schools, they avoid the danger of overloading by accepting the danger of overspecialization. They are ordinarily much better courses than those that attempt to cover all history, and they do give the student opportunities either to learn something about early civilizations or to acquire information about the background of the present world situation. But they cannot do both, and both are desirable. Study of civilizations that are remote in space and time increases the understanding of human behavior and promotes the desired attitudes of tolerance and respect for human achievement of any kind. Knowledge of recent history is almost essential for anyone who is going to take his duties as a citizen seriously. Both these aims can be more easily achieved in a world-history course than in one that deals with one period or country.

We come back, then, to the problem of content in courses that must cover many centuries and civilizations in a limited period of time. Much more must be omitted from these courses than can be taught. Two basic rules should be followed in selecting topics. In the first place, there should be diversity in both time and space. The student should learn something about at least one early civilization and about at least one non-European civilization. In the second place, there should be a fairly detailed study of the nineteenth and twentieth centuries in order to give the student the background that he needs for understanding the modern world.

Within the limits set by these general rules there are certain themes that should be stressed. The nature of preindustrial societies should be made clear, and the change from agricultural to industrial society, first in Europe and then throughout the world, should be explained. The importance of new ideas, in science and technology, in politics and economics, should be demonstrated. At the same time the significance of tradition in shaping responses to new situations should be discussed. The great revolutions that have shaped the modern world should be examined in some detail. Finally, the increasing interconnectedness of all peoples and all countries should be emphasized.

There are many ways of bringing these themes into a course, and material to illustrate them can be drawn from the history of many countries and periods. One of the problems that is often discussed is that of continuity: Is it necessary to proceed with an unbroken narrative from a beginning to a terminal date, or is it better to study one period in some detail and then jump to another era or area that also can be studied in depth? A sense of continuity is certainly one of the desirable products of the study of history, but real continuity is difficult to achieve in a survey course. Given the limited time available, some regions and periods have to be passed over so quickly that they leave little impression on the student. On the other hand, a certain amount of continuity can be provided by remarks by the teacher, even if there are breaks in the reading. The method of studying a few periods in depth gives greater opportunity for suggesting the comparisons and contrasts that are so useful in stimulating interest in and understanding of history. But as long as a real effort is made to introduce these comparisons and contrasts it probably does not matter greatly how it is done. The decision as to which method to adopt should be based on the interests and training of the teacher and on the materials that are available for instruction. And whatever method is used, the teacher should remember that it is impossible to cover the whole course of human history in a single year.

If continuity is desired, the teacher could begin about 1450 with a quick sketch of the European medieval background. The predominantly agrarian nature of medieval society, the role of the Church, the intellectual and artistic interests of the fifteenth century, and the characteristics of the chief European governments could be briefly treated. Then the two main themes of the early modern period could be introduced: the rise of the sovereign state and the transformation of Europe into the world center of trade and manufacturing. Under the first heading could be brought such diverse topics as the Reformation, the growth of bureaucracy and absolutism, and the economic policies of European states. Under the second would come the great explorations, the beginnings of colonialism, the nature of intercontinental trade, and the development of the technology that gave Europeans the opportunity to extend their influence throughout the world. At the same time, brief accounts could be given of the state of other civilizations at the time of first contact with Europeans.

The next main theme would be the intellectual revolutions of the eighteenth and early nineteenth centuries. The Enlightenment in its narrowest sense could be treated fairly briefly, though some emphasis should be given to the rise of new political and economic theories. On the other hand, a great deal of attention should be paid to the origins and development of modern science. Here, even more than in the American-history course, is an opportunity to consider the interests and attitudes of scientists, the nature of the scientific culture and its relationship to the traditional culture.

Next should come a study of what Palmer has called the Age of the Democratic Revolution[1]: a brief description of the English Revolution of the seventeenth century, a quick reminder of the nature and significance of the American Revolution, and a fairly detailed study of the French Revolution and its effects on other European countries. Emphasis should be placed on revolution as a social phenomenon: What causes revolutions? How do they develop? What impact do they have on society?

Then should come the study of the industrialization of Europe. It should be treated in some detail, for this was the first example and in many ways the model for what happened later all over the world. Here again is an opportunity to introduce some of the basic concepts of economics and sociology, as the student considers problems of economic growth, urbanization, labor relations, and the like. Internal political developments can be tied to the story of industrialization: the rise of the *bourgeoisie*, the demand for constitutions and a wider suffrage, and the beginnings of socialist theories and parties. Special attention should be given to Russian developments in order to lay a foundation for the Russian Revolution.

The development of the European state system in the nineteenth and early twentieth centuries should receive a certain amount of attention. The unification of Italy and the partitioning of the Turkish Empire can be passed over fairly briefly, but more time should be given to the unification of Germany in order to explain the peculiar behavior of Germany in the twentieth century. Then there should be a discussion of the international rivalries that led up to World War I and, after a brief treatment of the war itself, an analysis of the peace settlement and the effects that it had on the traditional European political system.

The diplomatic history of the interwar period can be passed over fairly quickly, but internal developments need more extended treatment. The economic problems of Europe that culminated in the Great Depression should be discussed. The rise of fascism and, even more, the coming to power of the Nazis, should be explained in relation to the political and economic stresses of the period. At the same time, the growth of the Soviet political and economic systems should be covered in some detail. Finally, the origins and course of World War II should be briefly treated.

The interwar period would also be a good point at which to introduce the topic of the impact of the West on the rest of the world through colonialism and modernization. Some account should be given of the state of the traditional cultures of India, China, and Japan in the early nineteenth century. Then the interaction between these traditional cultures and new ideas, the rise of nationalism in the colonial world, and the aspirations of backward peoples for economic development should all be discussed. In this way some background can be given for understanding current problems in the underdeveloped countries.

The final group of topics should deal with the present world situation: the state of Western civilization, the challenge posed by the Communist bloc, and the impact of both Western and Communist forces on the uncommitted countries. It would probably not be necessary to go into great detail on these topics if the proper foundation had been laid in the last weeks of the course. But some connection between current problems and the history of the twentieth century should be made.

An alternative way of achieving the same objectives—familiarity with diverse civilizations and knowledge of the background of current problems—would be to pay less attention to historical continuity and to study two or three early civilizations in some detail. The course could begin with a survey of Graeco-Roman civilization at its height, followed by treatments of early India (to the end of the Gupta dynasty) or early China (through the Tang dynasty). Something should probably then be done with medieval Europe in order to get some ideas about important elements in our civilization, especially Christianity and the Church. There could then be a jump to the eighteenth century and the intellectual, political, and economic changes of that period. The remainder of the course would follow the same pattern as the one already outlined, giving about half the time to the nineteenth and twentieth centuries.

The topics that have been listed above for American and European history are not meant to be complete or rigid course outlines. They are simply illustrations of the sort of material that should be taught in the schools. Topics such as these would demonstrate both the variety of human behavior and the ways in which human behavior can be studied. They would show the interaction of political and economic developments with new ideas and new techniques. In doing this, they would permit the introduction of many of the basic concepts of the other social sciences and give the student some idea of the way in which the political scientist, the economist, the sociologist, and the anthropologist analyze and explain human behavior. The basic unity of the social sciences, and the aid that each of the social sciences can give to the others, would be demonstrated.

Finally, and most important, topics selected according to the principles suggested in the earlier part of this essay would prepare the student both for further study in college and for life as a citizen. The student who went on to college would have some familiarity with historical techniques, with the content of American history, and with some aspects of world history. When school courses are properly taught, survey courses in college become unnecessary. This is already true of American history; it could be true of world history. By omitting surveys, more students could go on to advanced work in history and study periods and regions that had been passed over rather lightly in school. At the same time, they would have some foundation for their work in the other social sciences. Survey courses would still be necessary in subjects such as economics, but they could begin at a higher level and cover more ground. Thus students would have a better opportunity to get fairly solid training in the social sciences, one of the most important parts of their education.

For the student who does not go to college, content of the sort suggested would be a reasonably adequate preparation for his responsibilities as a citizen. He would know something about the history and traditions of his own country; he would have some idea of what it means to be an American. He would have much of the information needed to take an interest in and make sensible decisions about current problems. He would have gained some skill in weighing evidence, analyzing complex social problems, and reaching conclusions based on his own judgment. And if his courses were well taught he would have acquired a taste for history and a continuing interest in the problems of society.

This continuing interest is, of course, the final goal of all education in the social studies. If it is achieved, omissions of certain information in school courses do no harm, for the gaps will be filled in later life. If it is not achieved, the most carefully planned selection of facts will be futile because the facts will soon be forgotten. This is why overloading must be avoided, why a narrative tone should be preserved, why comparisons should be made whenever possible, why connections between past and present should always be pointed out. It is why we should avoid introducing too much unfamiliar material too quickly, why there has to be a certain emphasis in both American and world history on the nineteenth and twentieth centuries. If we can create interest in history, if we can make our students want to read history on their own, we will have done much to make them good and useful citizens. There is no other academic subject in which it is easier to maintain an interest; history has no highly technical vocabulary and its basic methods can be understood early and remembered long. A body of citizens that reads serious books and thinks about the problems of society would be highly desirable during the difficult years that lie ahead. There is a good chance that history, properly taught, might aid greatly in creating such a body of citizens.

1. Robert R. Palmer, *The Age of the Democratic Revolution*, Princeton University Press, 1959.

Geography

Preston E. James / *Syracuse University*

ALL EDUCATION, we may assume, is aimed at the transmission of the values of our culture and the development of socially acceptable attitudes toward problems and conflicts. But sometimes we overlook the fact that all education starts in the home. The earliest transmission of values, and the first impressions concerning how conflicts are to be met, take place in the family—if there is a family. By age six, the child is already formed, with values and attitudes built in. Formal education in the schools can polish what is already there, or it must undertake radical remedial programs to overcome the results of a bad start.

Among all the objectives toward which formal education might be aimed, three stand out as of major importance in our kind of society. One is to preserve and develop the spirit of curiosity. Human beings are naturally curious, but in the process of growing up the child quickly learns to conceal curiosity behind a mask of sophistication. The family is happier this way, and when formal schooling begins, the inborn curiosity has been brought under control. All too often the schools complete what has been started in the home; and if the schools do not do it, the first year in college does. If intelligent curiosity is a needed quality, as the writer believes, the school must rescue the child by providing success experiences in the satisfaction of curiosity.

The second major objective of formal education must also be cultivated by providing success experiences. This is the predisposition to accept the rules of evidence and logical thought. When a cause-and-effect question has been asked and a reasonable answer has been formulated, the next step is to confront the reasonable answer with observed facts. The scholar has learned that when observed facts fail to agree with a hypothesis, the latter must be modified or abandoned. Any one who reads detective fiction knows how facts can destroy a hypothesis. Experience in what may be called the scholarly method must be repeated throughout formal schooling at higher and higher levels of sophistication.

And perhaps the third objective of formal education is the most important of all. This is to polish and enrich the techniques of communication, to develop an appreciation of the beauty of the English sentence, to gain a reverence for the precise meaning of words. This may require more than just success experiences with language. Command of the techniques of communication takes drill—repeated, dull, hard drill.

The social studies ought to meet these three objectives within the fields of specialization of the social sciences. But people concerned with the schools are beginning to suspect what the pupils have known for a long time: that the lack of a coherent and unified body of knowledge in the social studies makes it difficult sometimes to know what to be curious about. As a result of the critical reappraisal of our educational methods, a certain sense of dissatisfaction has been expressed concerning this part of the curriculum.

No small part of this dissatisfaction stems from the diversity of purpose inherent in the idea of social studies. "The social sciences," writes Pendleton Herring, "are not a single, ordered body of fact and theory, operating through an internally consistent and generally accepted uniform methodology.[1] Insofar as the social studies are derived from the social sciences, it has been most difficult to identify a coherent and unified core of concepts and factual content.

The statement of purpose most often presented as the goal of social studies has been "to provide insight into the mainsprings and directions of human behavior, and the resulting interactions among people." The behavioral disciplines among the social sciences are those that are chiefly concerned with why people act the way they do. But as Joseph R. Strayer suggests in another chapter of this volume, some of the concepts regarding human behavior developed by these disciplines are found to be "too abstract to be grasped by precollege students unless they are presented as a specific historical problem."[2] History has traditionally provided the framework for the organization of the social studies, and an attempt was made to fit the concepts of human behavior into this framework. However, the concepts of the behavioral sciences could not be permitted any very full development because the social studies are also expected to provide a view of the main currents of Western history, and especially of the steps in the growth of American democracy.

But the social studies are also expected to contribute to another purpose. It is expected that they will provide perspective regarding the diverse conditions of the modern world. The lay public was shocked when it appeared that pupils were not adequately informed concerning American history; but the lay public was also shocked to find that graduates of our secondary schools were incredibly ignorant of even the most elementary facts of geography. In spite of our current concern with Laos, Iran, and Berlin, in spite of the great issues of public policy with which America is faced in dealing with these places, a recent poll of undergraduates in an American college showed that less than thirty per cent could locate these places on a map closely enough to permit any study of the significance of position as a factor in the policy decision. There is a growing demand that the schools should provide a more effective treatment of world affairs, and a better understanding of the significance of the arrangement of people, resources, and political organization in the modern world. This purpose is not well served by using the behavioral concepts in a historical framework. The processes of rapid and revolutionary change now sweeping over the earth must be examined not only as the contemporary results of historical trends, but also as forces working on the varied habitats of the earth to create contrasts from place to place that are an essential part of world understanding. This is the unique contribution of geography to the social studies.

What Geography Is and Is Not

Geography is that field of learning in which the characteristics of particular places on the earth's surface are examined. It is concerned with the arrangement of things and with the associations of things that distinguish one area from another. It is concerned with the connections and movements between areas. The face of the earth is made up of many different kinds of features, each the momentary result of an ongoing process. There are physical and chemical processes developing the forms of the land, the shapes of the ocean basins, the differing characteristics of water, soil, and climate. There are biotic processes by which the plants and animals spread over the earth in complex areal relation to the physical features and to each other. And there are the economic, social, and political processes by which mankind occupies the world's lands.

As a result of all these processes the face of the earth is marked off into distinctive areas; geography seeks to describe and interpret the significance of likenesses and differences among places in terms of causes and consequences. Geography makes use of the concepts developed by the behavioral sciences, but it examines these concepts not as they work in isolation, where "other things are equal," but as they work in the context of particular places on the earth. Geography makes use of the perspective of history, but it does so by re-creating past geographies and tracing geographic changes through time—which is not history. Geography must make a selection of features and processes to use in building up a knowledge of area that is relevant to the basic purposes of formal education—promoting curiosity, predisposing the pupil to accept the rules of evidence and logical thought, and providing training in the techniques of communication. One of the special and distinctive techniques of communication provided by geography is through the language of the map.

Geography is not restricted to the study of the relation of man to his physical and biotic environment. This idea developed in nineteenth-century Germany at a time when the physical sciences were developing rapidly but when the sciences dealing with man were still rudimentary. Friedrich Ratzel attempted to bring the treatment of man into line with the treatment of physical features. In the first volume of his *Anthropogeographie* (1882 and 1899) he organized his material in terms of the natural conditions of the earth, in relation to which he examined the cultural features. In the second volume (1891 and 1912) he did the opposite, organizing his material in terms of the human culture, in relation to which he examined the physical features of the earth.[3] Although Ratzel did formulate certain concepts regarding the relation of man to his habitat (physical and biotic environment), he was thoroughly in sympathy with the tradition of Alexander von Humboldt and Carl Ritter. He never lost sight of the need for direct observation of all relevant elements of a situation. Thus, in his classic volume on *Deutschland* he pointed out that two physically similar areas, the Black Forest and the Vosges Mountains, had developed in quite different ways because of the differences in economy and historical tradition.

Some of Ratzel's disciples were not so careful to observe all the relevant interrelated phenomena. Especially those who were trained chiefly in physical geography insisted that a geographic analysis must show a relationship that crossed the border between physical and human phenomena, thus leading to neglect of the relationships on the same side of the border—for example, the relation of language to economic system, or economic system to law. Few geographers ever subscribed to such extreme forms of environmental determinism as suggested by the historian H. T. Buckle and others; but many went forth deliberately to find examples of environmental influence on human activities, and many remained blind to contrary evidence. As a result geography was divided into physical geography (a well-developed field of science) and human geography (a relatively superficial treatment of man's relation to the physical earth). The adjective *geographic* came to refer to the physical character of an area. Thus a "geographic factor" was some condition of the physical environment to which human activities were to be related as "responses" or "adjustments."

Geography as the "science of man-land relationships" persisted longer in the English-speaking world than elsewhere. It found few adherents in Germany, where Alfred Hettner was developing the ideas associated with the main stream of geographic thought. It was effectively attacked by the French master, Paul Vidal de la Blache and by those who followed him. But it was given persuasive support in Great Britain and the United States. The American scholars who developed this theme included William Morris Davis, Ellen Churchill Semple, Wallace W. Atwood, Ellsworth Huntington, Robert DeC. Ward, R. H. Whitbeck, and others. One of the critical problems to be faced in promoting the use of modern geographic concepts in the schools is that so many of the teachers have derived their geographic learning either directly or indirectly from these American exponents of environmentalism. In spite of the vigorous efforts of professional geographers over the past thirty-five years or so to disclaim this deviation from the traditional direction of geographic thought, there are still many teachers and many scholars in other social science fields for whom the adjective *geographic* refers to the physical environment exclusively.

Let us be clear about this. Modern geography does not neglect the treatment of the spatial distribution of the physical and biotic features of the earth as the home of man. In fact, geographers insist on the essential importance of considering human activities in their areal association with the features of the habitat—the resource base. But modern geographers insist on the principle that the significance to man of the physical and biotic features of the earth is a function of the attitudes, objectives, technical skills, and other aspects of the culture of man himself. In other words, the physical environment has different meaning for different groups of people, or for the same group at different stages of development. They insist, also, that geography examines the relationships not only between man and his habitat, but also between man and the various cultural features resulting from economic, social, or political processes. With each change in the culture of a people the meaning of the habitat must be re-evaluated. Geography cannot be divided into physical geography and human geography for separate treatment; and a geographic factor is any phenomenon that—being irregularly distributed over the earth—contributes to the differentiation of the earth's surface.

The Concept of Areal Association[4]

It is important to understand what a geographer means by the concept of areal association because this concept makes up the core around which geographic theory is built. Areal association does not refer to an inventory of whatever things happen to be present within a given piece of terrestrial space. John K. Wright once referred to such an inventory as "the trash-can approach." To list the contents of a trash can, or to list all the features that happen to occur together within the confines of a place, is not a rewarding intellectual endeavor. But to identify those physical, biotic, and cultural features that are tied together causally, and which therefore give distinctive character to an area on the earth's surface, does provide the kind of educational experience that was presented as one of the three objectives of education in the opening part of this chapter.

Let us suppose, for purposes of simplifying this concept, that we are concerned with the areal association of people and rainfall. An inspection of a map of rainfall and a map of people suggests the hypothesis that the density of population is less where rainfall is either too little or too much. The areal association can be identified from the inspection of maps if the two maps are on the same scale and degree of generalization. But modern geography can describe the association more precisely. The statistical procedure known as regression analysis can be used by taking random readings from the two maps at the same points and plotting the pairs on a graph. If population and rainfall are causally related, the points on the graph will tend to fall along or close to a line. The equation that best fits the pattern of points can be calculated and thus it becomes possible to represent in mathematical form the degree of areal association. It is also possible to have a precise measure of the amount of variation of population density that is areally associated with variation of rainfall, and also the amount of variation of the one that is not associated with the other. The places can be identified where there is a greater density of population than would be expected from the amount of rainfall. By using the method of multiple regression analysis it is possible to determine what other phenomena—physical, biotic, or cultural—are also areally related to population and rainfall, such as accessibility to a market, quality of soil, proportion of the population of different religious faiths, or any other measurable factors. Statistical procedures make possible the analysis of variance, the analysis of covariance, and a number of other procedures for finding the answers to questions concerning areal associations.

Geographers also study the flow of goods, or people, or ideas, or any other measurable phenomena that tie one area to another. These movements are also areally associated. The statistical procedure known as linear programming permits one to find the minimum-cost flow of goods over a transportation system, or the maximum profits to be derived from retail stores at different locations. Procedures for giving a precise measurement to differences of accessibility can be used, based on the hypothesis that a concentration of population exerts an influence that varies directly with the size of the population and inversely with the distance from it.

A major challenge faces the professional geographers and the specialists in social studies. The more sophisticated aspects of these statistical procedures are clearly not applicable to the secondary schools. But the same basic method of study can be used in simplified form. Regression analysis can be used at an early age by plotting two or more phenomena on graph paper. The requirements of the method are fundamental: 1. that a meaningful question be asked concerning the areal associations of two or more features; 2. that a hypothesis be formulated that might account for an apparent association; 3. that the hypothesis be tested by proper method; and 4. that the meaning of the result be communicated.

The Regional Concept[5]

The effective use of these procedures requires an understanding of the nature of the face of the earth. And since the face of the earth has been, and continues to be, shaped by physical, biotic, and cultural processes, geography cannot restrict itself to any one of the familiar divisions of the curriculum. The field has long suffered from the efforts of nongeographers to fit it into the conventional categories of the academic world. Geography, by looking at things from the perspective of areal association and spatial distribution, makes a contribution to an understanding of the modern world not derived from other fields of study. But to do this successfully the teacher must have a sound understanding of the underlying regional theory.

The regional concept holds that the face of the earth can be marked off into areas of distinctive character that are homogeneous in terms of specific criteria. Since no two points on the face of the earth are identical, no area, even a small one, can be entirely uniform and homogeneous. Even a field of corn includes much surface on which there is no corn, and there may be more ragweed plants than corn plants in the field if it is poorly tended. Yet the field is described as homogeneous in terms of a specific criterion—a cultivated crop. The region is a geographic generalization, an intellectual concept. There is no such thing as a "true region," or one that might not be further subdivided if subdivision were desirable. Regions are defined for specific purposes, and for each purpose a different regional system may be needed. Regions are judged good or bad by the degree to which they illuminate a problem: regions that have the effect of obscuring area relationships are bad regions.

There are many kinds of regions. Some are homogeneous in terms of the phenomena or associations of phenomena that occupy them; others are homogeneous in terms of the performance of a specific function—such as the trade area of a town. Some are simple because they are defined on the basis of a single phenomenon or function; others are complex because they embrace areas within which two or more phenomena, or two or more functions, are causally associated—such as a steel industry and its market area.

Scholars curious about what makes one place different from another on the earth have been drawing regions since man became conscious of his surroundings. Primitive man must have been deeply concerned about "what it was like" beyond the horizon. This natural, inborn curiosity about the nature of strange places has not been entirely transferred to the moon. It was reflected in the writings of Homer, and achieved the status of science at the time of Thales of Miletus (650–546 B.C.). Some of the earliest regional systems developed by the Greek geographers were brilliant generalizations concerning the known world; but like all generalizations, with the advance of knowledge it is necessary to make revisions or modifications. Two examples of regional concepts that have a long history, and that are relevant to the school curricula in social studies, will serve to illustrate the application of basic theory.

THE CONCEPT OF THE CONTINENTS

One of the traditional ways of organizing the elementary and secondary curricula in geography, and to a certain extent also in history, is in terms of the continents. There are units of study devoted to Europe, Asia, Africa, North America, South America, and Australia. Because there are no people on Antarctica this ice-covered area receives scant attention. The continents are treated as regions and it is assumed that useful generalizations can be formulated regarding the interconnections of cultural, physical, and biotic features within these areas. But are they useful regions? Is the pattern of man and of man's activities on the earth made clearer by generalizing about conditions in Europe as a whole, or in Asia as a whole?

Are statistical data more or less revealing of the significant differences from place to place on the earth when they are summed up separately for Europe, for Asia, or for Africa? Or is some other regional system for the world more illuminating? Clearly to divide the Soviet Union into European and Asian parts obscures the unity of that country, and to include statistical data for the part of the Soviet Union that lies west of the Ural Mountains with the rest of Europe only has the effect of blurring the contrasts between the heartland of Eurasia and its periphery. Similarly, to omit Egypt from a study of Southwest Asia is pure nonsense. Asia is a vast area, including diverse peoples and products—so vast that generalizations about Asia as a whole tend to obscure important generalizations that might be made concerning parts of Asia. How did it happen that it has become traditional to separate Europe and Asia? To answer questions of this sort we must look at the historical record.

To find the origins of the concept of the separateness of Europe and Asia we must go back to the ancient Greeks. Before the days of the gnomon (sun dial) and the compass it was not easy to identify directions. The Greek sailors named directions for the winds and for the distinctive weather types that came with winds from certain directions. But they also easily identified two directions—toward the rising sun and toward the setting sun. The direction toward the rising sun they called Asia (derived from an Assyrian word); the direction toward the setting sun they called Europe. The two sides of the Aegean Sea became known as Europe and Asia. But so far the words referred to directions, not regions.

As Greek geographic horizons were enlarged the whole of the Mediterranean became known, and as a result of the marches of Alexander, Greek geographic knowledge was extended eastward even to the Indus River. It became desirable to identify regions in order to clarify the major significant differences within the Greek world. The Greek geographers defined three major regions: on the northern side of the Mediterranean was Europe, with a comfortable climate, with many small rivers and delta plains suitable for the intensive agriculture of the Greeks, and this region was the home of Greek civilization; to the east was Asia, with a climate that was much drier than that of Europe, with certain notable rivers (Tigris-Euphrates, Indus, Nile) that supported ancient civilizations based on irrigation, and the civilizations themselves stood in notable contrast to that of Greece; and to the south was Libya (later Africa), very dry, very hot, thinly peopled by Negroes who lived so close to the sun that they had burned black. This threefold regional division of the Greek world illuminated in a clear-cut manner the major areal associations of land, climate, and culture that existed within the range of Greek knowledge.

But as the whole world became known, and as modern systems of communication and transportation have brought all peoples closer in contact, this threefold division of the Eastern Hemisphere no longer illuminates the important contrasts within that part of the world. Long ago the organization of world geography or world history into units dealing separately with Europe, Asia, and Africa ceased to be effective, and only contributes today to continued obscurity.

A similar difficulty arises from the division between North America and South America. It has been customary to include in North America the whole of the Isthmus of Panama, and all of the islands of the Antilles. Yet generalizations concerning a North America, so defined, obscure the important contrasts; and the failure to include the southern part of North America with South America blurs the major regional differences within the hemisphere. The persistence of this use of poorly defined regions in our school curricula, as well as in the curricula of other countries, is nothing short of distressing.

THE CONCEPT OF THE CLIMATES

Another example of the persistence of error, and the continued failure to illuminate the important facts of areal differentiation on the earth, is offered by the concept of climates. For the origins of this concept, also, we must go back to the Greeks.

The Greek scholars after the time of Pythagoras (born 582 B.C.) had no doubts about the roundness of the earth. They knew how ships at sea disappeared below the horizon; they knew that when the earth threw its shadow across the moon, the edge of the shadow was rounded; they knew that by traveling north the pole star would be higher above the horizon; and they knew about the seasonal differences in the position of the sun. Parmenides, about 500 B.C., was the first of the Greek scholars to divide the surface of the earth into "slopes," which he called *klima*. The round surface sloped away from the sun, and each zone of latitude (as we would say today) could be identified by measuring the altitude of the sun at noon, or by measuring the altitude of the pole star. These *klima* were essentially astronomical zones. It was Aristotle (384–323 B.C.) who turned these zones into climatic regions. He gave mathematical definition to the zone near the equator and 23½° on either side of it, within which the sun was overhead twice each year. He defined the polar regions within which the sun failed to rise at the solstice each year. These were the Tropics of Cancer and Capricorn, and the Arctic and Antarctic Circles. Aristotle went farther—life, he wrote, was impossible in the equatorial regions because of the intense heat, and in the polar regions because of the intense cold. He defined the Torrid Zone as the very hot area under the vertical sun, and the Frigid Zone as the very cold area where the sun was never very high above the horizon. In between was the Temperate Zone, neither too hot nor too cold. But he recognized that the most habitable part of the earth was the middle of the Temperate

Zone, where Greece was located, and that life became more and more difficult toward the margins of the Temperate Zone.

Actually, in light of what the Greeks knew, this regional generalization concerning climate and habitability was a good one. Lacking central-heating systems, they knew that only barbarians could live in Europe north of the Alps where men had to spend so much energy just keeping warm. Farther north, clearly, life would be impossible. Just south of the Mediterranean is the great Sahara, the world's largest area of very high temperatures. In fact the highest air temperature ever observed at an official weather station is located only twenty-five miles south of Tripoli in Libya (136.4° F.). Modern knowledge makes it possible to outline an area within which temperatures over 110° F. occur at least once each year—the belt extends from near the west coast of Africa eastward across the Red Sea and Arabia to the Persian Gulf. There is a separate area farther to the east in the Indus and Ganges valleys of Pakistan and India. The northern limit of this belt of high temperatures is along the southern shore of the Mediterranean and around the northern side of the Tigris-Euphrates Valley. The southern limit extends east and west across Africa a little to the south of Lake Chad. In India the belt of high temperatures does not quite extend as far south as Bombay. Nowhere along the equator have such temperatures been observed. In the Amazon Region there have never been temperatures observed as high as 100° F. The hottest part of the Western Hemisphere is in southern California east of the mountains, and a belt of heat where temperatures of 110° F. are observed at least once each year extends from northern Mexico almost to the border of Canada through the Great Plains. No similar area of high temperature exists all the way from northern Mexico to northern Argentina.

In other words, Aristotle was wrong. No Greeks had ever been south of Syene on the Nile (about on the Tropic of Cancer), and neither Greeks nor Romans penetrated far into the

Sahara. Aristotle reasoned that if temperatures were so high at 32° north of the equator within the southern part of the Temperate Zone, they must be much higher directly under the sun in the Torrid Zone. This zone near the equator must be uninhabitable. But Aristotle arrived at this conclusion by logical thought, not by direct observation. He taught his pupils, especially Alexander, to "go and see." Just before his death, Alexander was planning to send an expedition southward along the eastern side of Africa to see whether his teacher was right. But the expedition never started. For centuries the world believed that the Torrid Zone was uninhabitable, or unbearably hot. Some social studies teachers in America in 1962 teach that near the equator there are "steaming jungles," in which work is difficult because of the heat.

There can be no doubt that the division of the world into Temperate, Torrid, and Frigid Zones obscures the facts of climate. That the Torrid Zone is not so torrid as the Temperate Zone was established as a fact in the fourteenth century by the Arab geographer Ibn-Batuta, who traveled along the east coast of Africa across the equator. That the Torrid Zone was uninhabitable was doubted by such European scholars as Pope Pius II, Cardinal Pierre d'Ailly, Roger Bacon, and others. Was Aristotle right? This was a major problem at the Geographical Institute at Sagres established by Prince Henry the Navigator early in the fifteenth century. Slowly the Portuguese explorers sent out from Sagres pushed southward along the west coast of Africa, always fearful that around the next promontory they would find the boiling water that Aristotle had promised. Not until 1475 did a Portuguese ship cross the equator, and the sailors on board did not turn black. In 1482 a ship went all the way to the southern end of Africa. It had taken more than half a century to overcome the effect of Aristotle's vivid but erroneous portrayal of the world's climates.

To teach the world's climates in 1962 in terms of Temperate, Torrid, and Frigid Zones cannot be excused. If a social studies teacher wishes to refer to a general position in latitude in the world, it is possible to use the terms Low Latitudes, Middle Latitudes, and High Latitudes—but without any connotation regarding the supposed effect of climate on man's activities. As a first step toward the better treatment of geography, it is necessary to eliminate the outdated theories and generalizations. And perhaps the best way to do this is to review the story of how man found out what the earth is like; how, step by step, he has pushed back the geographic horizons, how he has formulated hypotheses to explain his observations, and how the hypotheses of one generation must be revised or even dropped as new knowledge becomes available. The process still goes on.

The Teaching of Maps

In the process of finding out what the earth is like, geographers have had to face the problem of how to communicate knowledge about the earth. There is one great difference between the writing of history and the writing of geography. Words are organized in sentences, paragraphs, chapters—always to be read in sequence. The sequence of events in history is reproduced in words that follow one another through the same time dimension. But geography deals with things that are located beside each other, at the same moment of time. Word descriptions that must be read in sequence provide a poor vehicle for reproducing areal relations. The language of the map, on the other hand, is ideal for such a purpose. Over the thousands of years since the Greek geographers prepared the first true map the technique of presenting geography in this way has been perfected.

To be more than a diagram or a picture, a map must permit the measurement of distance, and must show direction with reference to the lines of latitude and longitude. Certainly by the end of the twelveth grade pupils should know how to identify the scale of a map—by reference to a graphic scale or to a representative fraction.[6] And the pupil ought to be able to identify the directions. The uncritical habit of referring to north as "up" and south as "down" is a form of map illiteracy that is very common—and sometimes has ludicrous results as when a college student is unable properly to identify the "upper Nile," and even argues that a river "cannot flow up." The use of up and down results from hanging continent maps on the classroom walls with north at the top. But the only true position for a map would be lying on the floor, with north on the map agreeing with north on the ground. This is called "orienting" a map, because in medieval times maps were made with east at the top, and they were oriented by pointing them toward the east.

The common use of continent maps on classroom walls has left a deeply ingrained impression on generations of Americans that the Atlantic Ocean lies between them and Europe, and the Pacific Ocean between them and Asia. One of America's most eminent military leaders once described the Pacific Ocean as a moat separating North America from Asia. But even a glance at a globe shows that the east coast of Asia and the west coast of North America form one straight line. The ocean that separates North America from both Europe and Asia is the Arctic Ocean.

The common use of the Mercator projection to show the whole world has also left a seriously blurred image of the world in the minds of Americans. Geographers since the times of Hipparchus (born about 160 B.C.) have faced the question of how best to represent the curved face of the earth on a flat surface.[7] It is impossible to make a curved surface lie flat. For this reason the only precise reproduction of the earth is the globe. All flat maps are in one way or another distorted. They may be stretched so that distances are only correct along a base line and areas are not comparable but directions are true (as on the Mercator map); or they may be twisted out of shape so that the continental outlines are distorted but areas are true; or—as is most common—the errors of both distance and direction are spread over the map to effect a workable compromise. The Mercator map, on which the lines of latitude and longitude cross each other at right angles, shows true directions by straight lines, but to do this the distances are distorted. Area becomes more and more exaggerated as one moves away from the equator. To compare the size of the Soviet Union and the United States on a Mercator map is impossible. Furthermore, if one starts out from New York to fly to Paris, one does not follow the same compass bearing all the way. Navigators know about great circle routes—the shortest distances on a sphere. To reach Paris one starts from New York toward the north over New England. But you would not be able to read this easily from a Mercator map. Yet until recently no less a newspaper than the New York *Times* used a Mercator map to show the position of trouble spots in its weekly news summary, and many TV news commentators have a Mercator map as a backdrop for the discussion of world affairs. Clearly these mass media, as well as the individuals they serve, are geographically illiterate.

People do not read maps naturally, any more than they could read words without training. The features commonly shown on maps that adults take for granted are usually meaningless for children, and even adults may fail to get the full meaning from maps. Consider, for example, the problem of showing what the surface of the land is like. The traditional classroom maps are colored to show altitude above sea level. These maps may seem simple, but are, in fact, almost impossible to read precisely. On such maps the green color is often used for areas less than 500 feet above sea level; yet the green is commonly read, even by adults, to mean plains. Where mountains border the oceans, as on the coast of California, and where the mountains rise directly from the water with steep slopes, the green band close to the coast does not mean that the land there is a plain—it is only the lower 500 feet of mountain slopes. Take the case of Denver—a city that is located 5,280 feet above sea level. On many maps colored to show altitude the brown color indicates land more than 5,000 feet above the sea. On such a map Denver is in the brown; and most people when asked to tell whether Denver is in the mountains or on the plains will insist that it is in the mountains. Actually Denver is on the plains, some 20 miles east of the Rocky Mountain front. New kinds of maps that avoid these problems are often rejected by social studies teachers because they seem unfamiliar. The teaching of map skills ought to begin in the earliest elementary grades, and proceed systematically grade by grade through the secondary school. The sequence of map concepts suitable for each grade is presented elsewhere.[8]

The Earth as the Habitat of Man

Reading maps is a necessary skill if geographic ideas are to be effectively presented and if pupils are to be taught how to "think geographically"—that is in terms of the significance of differences from place to place on the earth. But what kinds of differences need to be examined for their significance? One kind of subject matter essential to geographic analysis has to do with the physical and biotic features that combine to form the habitat of man.

The study of the earth as the habitat of man involves the use of concepts and content that run across the man-made border between the natural sciences and the social sciences. Under the heading of natural science one usually finds a laboratory treatment of the processes of physics, chemistry, and biology. The processes are isolated from the total environments of particular places on the earth. This is an important part of the educational program, but it does not provide a substitute for the geographic treatment of the earth. We need to know how these processes operate out of doors, and how they interact when they are not isolated. It is indeed unfortunate that the science teachers have been so busy in their laboratories that they have no time left for physical geography and biogeography, and that the social studies teachers, with few exceptions, consider any meaningful treatment of the earth to be outside of their field of interest. Geographers would like to select certain processes that have been studied in isolation by the separate disciplines and put them back together again to see how they are areally associated on the earth.

SURFACE FEATURES, CLIMATES, AND VEGETATION

There are certain elementary facts concerning the world's surface features, its climates, and its cover of vegetation that every one should know something about by the end of the twelfth grade. Most of the major categories of surface features are described by simple English words—plains, plateaus, hills, low mountains, high mountains, and ice caps are the chief kinds of features found in humid climates.[9] In the arid lands, however, there are three somewhat less familiar kinds of surface features, two of which are described by Arabic words because they do not occur in English—*hamada, erg,* and basin range (or mountain bolson).[10] Each of the continents has its own peculiar arrangement of surface features; it should be possible to distinguish one continent from another, even without the familiar continental outline as a guide.

The world's climates, unlike the surface features, are symmetrically arranged on the earth. To understand this symmetry it is necessary to go back to some of the basic controls of climate—latitude, the distribution of land and water, major wind systems and storm belts, the pattern of high mountains. The traditional description of the wind zones is no longer considered adequate, but new ways of describing them that accord with modern knowledge have been made available.[11] Once the interaction of these basic conditions of the atmosphere is understood, the arrangement of temperature and rainfall on the earth becomes clear. If one knows the latitude and altitude of a place and whether it is located on the western side, the eastern side, or the interior of a continent, it is possible to say what the climate is likely to be. But this involves saying something more important about the climate than simply that it is temperate, or healthful, or enervating.

The pattern of climates is reflected in a general way by the pattern of vegetation. Of course man has made fundamental changes in the vegetation, especially during the past century or so. Nevertheless, certain broad categories that existed when European man first came to the various parts of the earth can be used as indicators of the nature of the habitat.[12]

NATURAL RESOURCES

Even in the elementary grades pupils ought to be stimulated to ask questions about what the habitat means to its human inhabitants. And because the meaning of the habitat changes with each change in the culture of the people, it follows that, for geographical purposes, the habitat and the use of the habitat cannot effectively be separated. At no point is this principle more clearly demonstrated than in the discussion of so-called natural resources.

What is a natural resource? Is coal a natural resource? Most people would say yes. But an examination of what coal has meant to different people and at different times shows the need for careful consideration of this problem. In Europe coal was not a resource in Roman times. In North America, where a large part of the world's coal is concentrated, the Indians paid no attention to it. Coal was not a natural resource when the United States became independent.

The beginning of the use of coal in Great Britain came in the thirteenth century. The forests had been so extensively cut away for firewood that King Henry III gave his consent to the mining of coal at Newcastle. The people of London protested against this new fuel on the grounds that it fouled the air and endangered health. By 1650 there were still only two sailing vessels regularly employed in carrying coal from Newcastle to London, but by this time English coal was being exported to Belgium and France. By 1700 there were six hundred sailing vessels carrying coal to London. Coal mining began in France in 1715. In 1709 the first use of coal in the smelting of iron was made at Coalbrookdale. But after the development of the steam engine in 1769 the demand for coal began to increase rapidly. Yet it was not until 1859 that the development of the new beehive method of converting bituminous coal to coke, and of using coke in the large-scale steel industry, resulted in making coal a major natural resource. It is only for the past hundred years that the presence of bituminous coal underground has been associated with the concentration of cities and manufacturing industries above ground. During the whole history of mankind, this kind of geographic association had never before appeared.

What about soil? Is soil a natural resource? Most people would say yes. But consider the case of the black prairie soils of the United States, which are generally rated among the world's most productive soils for grain and meat. A century ago it was difficult to raise both grain and meat on these lands, and they were rated poorly.

The transformation of the prairies of North America from lands of low potential productivity to highly productive lands took place as a result of a series of mechanical inventions. The railroads had been extended to the margins of the prairies by the middle of the century, for the first time making it possible to ship bulky products to distant markets. But in the absence of forests it was impossible to fence the prairies. For the first time in 1873, when barbed wire was invented in De Kalb, Illinois, the fields could be fenced cheaply, and animals and crops could be produced on the same farm. The fencing created new problems. Cattle had formerly gone to the nearby streams for water, but on fenced pastures water had to be supplied. Well-drilling machinery had to be made available to replace a man with a shovel. Then an efficient windmill had to be invented to bring water to the surface. Furthermore, drilling machines and windmills had to be manufactured in large quantities and sold at prices the farmers could pay. To turn the prairie sod, the steel plow had to replace the old ironshod plow. And to harvest crops from large acreages where the yield per acre was low, new harvesting machines had to be built. All these mechanical innovations appeared during the mid-part of the nineteenth century, and as a result all over the world the great areas of humid grasslands (prairies) became the chief sources of food. For the first time the black prairie soil could be listed among the natural resources of the United States.

The development of technology may also remove a natural resource from the list. Bog iron ore, in the bottoms of the New England lakes, was the natural resource on which New England's early iron industry was based. But no one would think of listing bog iron ore as a resource today.

The general concept that accounts for these changes in the meaning of natural resources has already been presented: that the significance to man of the natural features of the earth is a function of the attitudes, objectives, and technical skills of man himself. Resources become resources by virtue of man's technology, and changes in technology may cause them to cease being resources. Yet at any one stage of technology, the pattern of resources is an essential part of the analysis of the strength of nations, or of the economic development of communities. This is not environmental determinism, for it recognizes that no nation can be condemned to poverty for lack of resources. Nature is neither friendly nor unfriendly, except as man has always personified the natural forces about him and given them human attributes. The limitations that impede man's progress toward the goals he sets for himself are to be found in his traditional ways of doing things, in the skills and attitudes that are passed on from generation to generation. Inherent, also, in man's way of living are the energy and ability to overcome obstacles or to compensate for lack of resources.

Man himself is a major agent of change on the face of the earth. The natural processes—those that operate without human plan or purpose—have produced the varied character of the earth's habitats; but planned human action produces many changes in the habitat. Man is often a destroyer of what nature has built,[13] as he is when his fires rage out of control, or when his sheep and goats eliminate the last vestiges of a once-thriving woodland, or when his plows on steep hillsides result in the ugly scars of erosion, or when his voracious appetite for minerals lays waste the land. On the other hand, man's technology has, in some instances, built rather than destroyed the capacity of the land to support people. The great cities of the modern world are places where almost all traces of the natural features of the surface of the earth have been transformed.[14]

The Geography of Population

An essential element of both elementary and secondary curricula in the social studies is the geography of the world's population. Where and in what density are people spread over the earth? What is the areal relation between the pattern of people and the earth's varied habitats? Before the end of the twelfth grade pupils should be able to name, locate, and discuss the origin of the world's chief concentrations of urban and rural people, and to identify the larger areas that still remain empty of human inhabitants. There are two aspects to the study of population that might be included in the elementary and secondary programs. These are the study of the distribution of people, and the interpretation of the significance of differences in density of people from place to place. Other aspects of population geography, such as the demographic characteristics of populations in different places, should probably be treated at college level.

THE DISTRIBUTION OF PEOPLE

The facts of population distribution and density over the earth are not so easy to find as one might expect. Scholars who deal with the problem of mapping population realize that there are reliable data for very few parts of the world. Census data for different countries are gathered by such diverse methods that in many cases they are not comparable; and even where there are censuses at more or less regular intervals the changes in areas of enumeration and in categories of enumeration are such that any precise comparison is very difficult. For a large part of the earth's population the only available population figures are estimates. Yet it would seem that one of the central concerns of the social studies ought to be the map of the distribution of people.

The construction of maps of population at different scales is an excellent way to arouse curiosity. Why is it that the census counts people where they sleep, not where they work? This is the standard procedure all over the world where there are censuses. In rural areas where people sleep close to where they work, this was a good way to be sure that the same person was not counted twice. But in our modern urban society, where people may travel many miles between sleeping places and working places, the pattern of sleeping people is not at all the same as that of working people.

Then there is the problem of enumeration area. Census data are summed up within arbitrary areas or districts that are usually unrelated to the problems geographers want to study. City populations, for example, are usually given for the political city rather than the metropolitan area. When data for one city are compared with those for another it is necessary to know how much of the whole geographical city is included in the enumeration area. Take the case of Boston: the 1960 census gives Boston a population of 697,197; but the whole of the Boston metropolitan area, which is geographically (if not politically) one city, included 76 separate municipalities, with a total population of 1,303,000. Is Tokyo the world's largest city, as some data suggest? Tokyo's population was estimated in 1959 to be 9,021,000: New York City in 1960 had a population of 7,782,000, and London had 3,254,000. But these figures are strictly not comparable, as a simple geographical comparison of the cities can show. Taking the whole urban complex of greater New York the population is about 12,000,000; the whole of greater London is about 8,250,000; and Tokyo's figure includes the whole of the urban complex. Clearly the only way that city populations can be compared is after a careful study of the enumeration areas, and after the whole of each urban complex is counted.

Reports on the 1960 census in the United States underlined the assertion that cities were declining in population. The only city of over a million people that increased in 1960 over 1950 was Los Angeles. Again a geographical study reveals that this assertion is quite unwarranted. Not only are all big cities gaining in population, but the largest one, New York, is gaining faster than any of the others. What the census data proved was that fewer people were sleeping in New York City in 1960 than in 1950—which is quite a different matter.

A similar geographical error is committed when the densities of population of two large countries are compared. For example, Canada had a density of population in 1956 of 4.2 people per square mile; the United States in 1955 had a density of 54.4 people per square mile. But before it is possible to make any intelligible statement about the density of population it is necessary to distinguish between the total national territory, and the effective national territory (defined as that part of the total territory from which the citizens of the country derive a living). There are vast areas of Canada that are empty, and from which the citizens of Canada do not derive a living. On the other hand, only a small part of the United States lies outside of the effective national territory. Empty areas should be subtracted from total area before the ratio of population to area becomes comparable.[15] In any case the use of geographic method in the study of population raises many questions that can only be answered by looking at maps.

THE SIGNIFICANCE OF DIFFERENCES OF DENSITY

The next step is to look for the significance of differences in density of population. Having established figures, and maps, that are comparable, the questions then arise. Why are these people arranged in this way? Why are people concentrated in certain areas, and why do some areas remain empty? Why is it, for example, that although the mid-latitude mixed forest regions occupy only seven per cent of the land area of the earth, they are occupied by thirty-nine per cent of the world's population?[16] Or, looking at the earth and its inhabitants more closely, why is it that in strictly similar climatic regions in eastern China and in southeastern United States, the population in the former is concentrated on the river floodplains, leaving the hilly lands very thinly populated, whereas in the latter the floodplains remain almost empty and the population concentrated on the higher ground?

Posing such questions and seeking answers to them bring out several important principles. One is the familiar one that the significance to man of the physical features of the earth is a function of the attitudes, objectives, and technical skills of man himself. Thus, in very similar habitats, the Chinese rice farmers concentrate on river floodplains whereas the Negro sharecroppers prefer the hills. Furthermore, in southeastern United States, the replacement of the cotton farmer and his mule, with modern large-scale farms equipped with machinery, has resulted in a change in the kind of land that is selected for cotton. Now the cotton is concentrating on the flat places rather than the hills. For the first time the map of flat places is significant.

Another principle is that the search for simple answers to world-wide regional generalizations is not rewarding, and may even lead to false conclusions. The mid-latitude mixed forest lands are found in many widely separated parts of the world, including parts of East Asia, parts of Western Europe, and parts of eastern Anglo-America. The causes of population concentration in these areas are not simple: they differ in different parts of the world, and they differ in the same part of the world at different periods. The concentration of people in these regions in East Asia is related to the advantages they have for growing rice and wheat. The concentration of people in these regions in Western Europe is related to the growth of modern industrial cities in relation to raw materials and markets. The concentration of people in the eastern part of Anglo-America was related at one time to agricultural advantage, but more recently to the pattern of manufacturing industry.

And why are industries to be found in some areas and not in others? Why is it that some people in the same habitat cleared the forests and planted crops, others used the crop land to pasture dairy cattle, and still others let the cleared lands grow up again in forest while they crowded into cities in the valleys? The answers to these questions involve an analysis of the relation of areas of dense population to the varied background of the habitat: but they also involve an explanation of the differing attitudes and objectives of different human groups, and an analysis of man's changing technology. This is what social scientists call "culture."

The Use of the Culture Concept in Geography

Culture, as the term is used in this chapter, refers to the "aggregate of the thoughts and deeds of a people," to their ways of living.[17] It summarizes their attitudes, objectives, and technical skills, their languages and religions, their patterns of thought and action.

It is important to point out that in the popular vocabulary

the word culture refers to one aspect of the way of living—it refers to the cultivation or refinement of taste in the appreciation of art, music, or literature. Unless this popular meaning of the word is made clear, its use in a special anthropological sense may be confusing.

The anthropologists are able to view the whole span of human history with broad perspective. They point out that during the 50,000 years of the presence of *Homo sapiens* on the earth there have been three periods of revolutionary culture change, and that between these periods of change life remained relatively stable with respect to basic attitudes and skills. The first period of change, starting about 8,000 B.C., was the agricultural revolution, when man first learned how to plant crops and domesticate animals.[18] The second, starting about 4,000 B.C., was marked by the rise of the Early Civilizations.[19] The third, just getting under way during the past two centuries, is made up of two kinds of culture change—the Industrial Revolution and the Democratic Revolution.

THE EARLY REVOLUTIONS

Each of these early revolutions changed the meaning of the habitat with reference to man. The cultivation of crops and the domestication of animals made the presence of fish or wild game less important, and raised the importance of a soil favorable for a particular kind of crop, or a type of vegetation suitable for pasturage. In places that were well endowed by nature with those characteristics that had been made significant by culture change, the population increased, and so also did military strength.

The culture revolution that produced the Early Civilizations began with the development of the arts of government. Rulers appeared who were able to extend their control by force over separate agricultural communities, thus putting an end to intervillage warfare and general insecurity. As a result a part of the population was relieved from the necessity of working on the crops. The remaining farmers could raise more food and fibers than were needed in the villages, and a class of people appeared who made a living from buying and selling things and transporting them. Another nonfarming group was made up of government officials and people employed in the armed forces. And still another group, the priesthood, could devote itself to the study of the stars, the sun, and the moon, and to the first steps in finding out about the earth. There were six Early Civilizations, each of which occupied a distinctive habitat. They included: 1. the civilization of Mesopotamia in the valley of the Tigris-Euphrates; 2. the Egyptian civilization in the valley of the Nile; 3. the Indus civilization, in the valley of the Indus; 4. the Chinese civilization in the valley of the lower Yellow River and its tributary the Wei Ho; 5. the Maya civilization in Yucatán and what is now Guatemala; and 6. the Andean civilization in what is now Peru and Bolivia.

These Early Civilizations are more than historical curiosities, and if they are to be given fuller meaning as a background for the understanding of the contemporary world, the historical approach needs to be supported by the anthropological concept of cultural revolution, and by the geographic concept of the region. The place where each of these revolutions developed was distinctive, and its distinctive character resulted from a complex of interconnected features of both cultural and natural origin. Each developed connections with a particular kind of habitat, endowed with its own particular kinds of resources. Each developed in a particular kind of culture setting. The places where a new culture is forged are known as "culture hearths." Yet, in spite of the unique character of each culture hearth, there are certain generalizations of a regional nature that can be drawn from a comparative study. One conclusion of wide and continuing significance is that culture change and culture revolution do not take place in isolation, but rather are stimulated in those positions on the earth where the currents of human movement come to a focus and where ideas from a variety of sources come together. For the weak and the fearful, to live in an era or in an area of revolution is not at all comfortable. From each culture hearth the new way of living was carried outward—by conquest, by trade, by migration, and by many other ways that the anthropologist can describe. Along the advancing front, conflict and reaction is developed; and as the front sweeps into new habitats, the original revolutionary culture becomes further diversified. This kind of study, in which past geographies are re-created and geographic changes through time are traced, is called "historical geography."[20]

After the development of the six Early Civilizations, and after the ideas they generated had spread over the earth, there followed thousands of years during which no fundamental changes in culture took place. This is not to say that there were no wars, conquests, and human suffering, for these things are inherent in the way of living developed by these Early Civilizations. Empires grew, reached the stage when they extended over vast areas, and then collapsed. In the economic life, power was produced by human or animal muscles, by wind or falling water. Transportation was costly and limited to goods of high value. No community was secure from the impact of natural disasters, and the strongest state was the one that was most nearly self-sufficient—that is, could be supplied with its needs from the resources of its own territory. The strongest states, also, were protected by "natural barriers" that could be easily defended against invaders, such as water bodies, high mountains, or densely forested hilly uplands. France, in such a habitat, became one of the strongest of the pre-nineteenth-century states. But the basic conditions of life had not changed for thousands of years.

THE CONTEMPORARY REVOLUTIONS

We are in the midst of the third of the great revolutions that have changed the relation of *Homo sapiens* to the earth and of groups of men to each other. Being so close to it and so much involved, the processes of change in the modern world can be made clearer if we identify two separate, but contemporary, revolutions. One we call the Industrial Revolution, the other the Democratic Revolution.

The Industrial Revolution began as a change in technology, but it soon became much more than this. The revolution in technology took place when controlled inanimate power replaced the traditional sources of power—human and animal muscles, wind or falling water. In 1769 James Watt patented his first successful steam engine in Scotland, and soon thereafter became a member of the firm of Boulton and Watt at Birmingham, England, to manufacture and operate the new engines. Other inventors improved the machine and applied it to transportation by water and by land. Used in the manufacturing process it resulted in an enormous increase in the volume of goods, and shattered the economic institutions that had been geared to an economy of scarcity. After the steam engine came the electric motor, then the internal combustion motor, then the motor run by nuclear power. This basic change in the availability of energy was followed by a whole series of transformations of the preindustrial world. These changes may be outlined as follows:

Man ceases to be "a lifter and mover," and becomes a puller of levers, a pusher of buttons, a repairer of complex machinery.

Man enjoys an unprecedented change in material comfort of living, in the volume and variety of foods and other goods he uses, and in security from the impact of natural disasters.

New facilities permit the bulk shipment of low-value goods over great distances.

The new industries that are so productive create an unprecedented need not only for vast volumes of earth resources, but also for a long list of earth materials never before considered resources; to provide these raw materials at low enough cost, mining tends to concentrate on the very few major occurrences of ores in the world.

Great cities appear because many industrial and commercial activities are better performed where people are concentrated, and because the new transportation facilities for the first time make possible vast concentrations of people who do not produce their own foods.

Population becomes progressively more urban and less rural: areas of concentrated population become more concentrated, and thinly peopled areas become more thinly peopled.

There is a decrease in the proportion of the working force employed in agriculture, and an increase of employment in industry and in a variety of service occupations; a vast increase in the variety of kinds of employment takes place.

Prestige is given to the owners of capital rather than to the owners of land. There is a great decrease in the proportion of illiterate people.

Enormous advances are made in medicine and hygiene, with a resulting spectacular drop in the death rate and an increase of life expectancy—all of which produces fundamental change in the demographic structure of society.

The population explosion appears, a result of decreasing death rates and of birth rates that remain high.

There is an incredible change in the speed of communications, making isolation of any human groups impossible.

"Research and development" is given highest priority in both economic development and military preparedness.

Science replaces supernaturalism, and control of the natural features of the habitat rather than adjustment to them becomes an objective.

The Industrial Revolution started in the eighteenth century in Great Britain. Why in Great Britain? Why not in France, or the Netherlands? Why not in China? Certain prerequisites had to be present in a preindustrial society to make this kind of revolutionary development possible. In the first place there had to be a core of people for whom the scientific habit of thought had been accepted—which eliminates China and most other parts of the eighteenth-century world. But there were scientists on the Continent, as well as on the island of Great Britain. There also had to be a widely held attitude that permitted innovators to try new things without being persecuted. Such a spirit did not exist among the politically and economically powerful people of France at this time, but it did exist in Britain and in the Netherlands. The new technology created new demands on earth resources never before made. There had to be iron ore, and raw materials required in the smelting of iron. As long as the chief use of iron was in making anchors, chains, bells, or nails, a simple forge with charcoal as the fuel would suffice. But the steam engine created an entirely new volume of demand for iron, and the use of the steam engine on railroads created a new demand for steel. On the island of Great Britain there were easily accessible bodies of raw materials; in fact there was one shaft from which it was possible to extract iron ore, limestone, and coal in one operation. Britain's supplies of iron ore and coal are small, on a world scale, but these supplies were critical in the eighteenth century. The Netherlands had no such easily accessible raw materials. The contrast in the habitat, at this stage of economic development, was a fundamental factor in explaining the significance of differences from place to place on the earth.

The spread of the Industrial Revolution over the earth since the early nineteenth century has produced fundamental changes in the economic life of peoples all over the world. Although certain stages of economic development can be identified,[21] nevertheless the impact of the new technology and of the new attitudes that are associated with new technology upon the preindustrial societies has created new areal associations and new diversity on the face of the earth. First it is possible to define the attitudes and economic conditions that must exist in a preindustrial or underdeveloped country before economic development can take place. The initial phase of the Industrial Revolution, which Rostow describes as the "take-off," requires that from five to ten per cent of the gross national product of a country must be removed from immediate consumption and plowed back into new capital formation each year. After a few decades the process of economic growth becomes self-sustaining, and the drive to maturity begins. During the drive to maturity, from ten to fifteen per cent of the gross national product must be devoted to new capital formation each year. After some fifty years, a mature economy is achieved—an economy marked by diversified industries, and by a completion of most of the changes listed above. Upon reaching maturity, according to Rostow's thesis, a country has a choice: to enter a period of high mass consumption in which the great majority of the people are able to make use of a great variety of goods and services; to organize a welfare state in which consumption is restricted in favor of security; or to embark on a program of conquest in the manner traditional for powerful states since the rise of the Early Civilizations. For a people suddenly, and without much preparation, involved in so profound a change in the technology of living as the Industrial Revolution, it is much easier to follow the traditional ways that have been followed for thousands of years than to think through to new solutions that have no sanctity in human experience.

All these changes in the economic life have both a history and a geography. The geographers insist that knowledge about where events take place, and in what cultural and national context, is as important as knowledge about when, and in what historical sequence, they take place. These twin perspectives are both needed in order to derive fuller meaning from the contemporary scene.

The Industrial Revolution began in Great Britain, and after a time spread to the countries grouped around the North

Sea. Britain reached a mature stage in its economic growth about 1850, and thereafter for more than half a century Britain enjoyed the benefits of having the only mature economy in the world. By 1900 the United States reached maturity, and thereafter edged into a condition of high mass consumption. In 1910 both France and Germany reached maturity, and Germany elected to enlarge its *lebensraum* at the expense of neighbors and to increase its command of resources.

The Industrial Revolution is still in process of spreading from its area of origin around the North Sea. The new way of living, with its basic requirement that the principle of international interdependence must replace the idea of national self-sufficiency, met resistance in Europe but was moved forward rapidly in Anglo-America, where the combination of culture background and habitat was extraordinarily favorable to this kind of development. The Industrial Revolution is today sweeping rapidly over Latin America; and it is being eagerly promoted in the Soviet Union, where, by government decree, more than twenty-five per cent of the gross national product is being used for new capital formation. But in many of the preindustrial countries of the world, either the preconditions for take-off are not present, or there is a lack of basic raw materials, or both. The geographic appraisal of the major regional contrasts of the world with regard to the status and prospects of economic development is of major importance.

The other aspect of this revolutionary period in which we live is the Democratic Revolution. This also needs to be carefully defined. It includes:

The demand for equal treatment before the law

The demand for protection for the individual from the arbitrary acts of those in authority, and for the protection of minorities from the tyranny of the majority

The demand for the right to select a form of government without outside pressure or dominance

The demand for the right to be represented where the government makes laws or levies taxes
The demand for majority rule and secret ballot
The demand for free access to knowledge, and for the free public discussion of issues of policy

These were the ideas that made up the Democratic Revolution in its area of origin in Western Europe.[22] It was in Great Britain that the ideas of equality before the law and of protection for the individual against arbitrary acts of the authorities originated. The idea of government by the consent of the governed originated in Great Britain and the Netherlands; one of the earliest written statements of this principle was the Mayflower Compact of 1620, written by men from Great Britain who had been living in the Netherlands. But in Great Britain ideas of popular sovereignty were slow in appearing, even universal male suffrage did not come to Britain until the 1880's. Popular sovereignty was a French contribution to the Democratic Revolution. The various ingredients were combined around the shores of the North Sea, and burst into revolutionary flames during the second half of the eighteenth century.

From its center of origin the Democratic Revolution has been spreading. It spread rapidly in the relative freedom of Anglo-America, and in Australia-New Zealand. But in other parts of the world the various predemocratic societies put up different degrees and kinds of resistance. The reaction against democratic ideas took the form of fascism in some places, and the strongest current reaction is put up by the communists. There are many parts of the world where the individual has never had rights and has never aspired to gain rights: here the Democratic Revolution takes the form of a vigorous demand for an end to colonialism, and for national independence for every self-conscious group however small. This sets off a political fragmentation that is one of the facts of the modern world. The face of the earth is now differentiated, not only in terms of economic development, but also in terms of the reaction to the inflammatory ideas of the Democratic Revolution.

The World's Major Culture Regions

The world seems to have been thrown into chaos as a result of the impact of these two great contemporary revolutions in human living. But on closer examination it is possible to discern a pattern, and this pattern can be used to provide a framework for the portrayal of the modern world. We need to find uniformities of areal association, within which useful generalizations can be made regarding the problems of economic development, the problems of national independence, the problems of population and resources, and the problems of conflict among states and groups of states. We need to experiment with different kinds of regional systems,[23] as, indeed, geographers have been doing.[24]

We suggest here the definition of culture regions in terms of the impact of the two great revolutions on pre-existing cultures in particular habitats. Because of the importance of the state in the contemporary world we propose to define these regions in terms of politically organized areas. Each region must show some degree of homogeneity with respect to the processes of economic development, and with respect to the redefinition of the status of the individual. Technological change is, of course, desired everywhere, but the methods of achieving it are quite varied; democratic ideals are understood and accepted in some regions, but in parts of the world where ideas of individual equality are totally foreign, the Democratic Revolution takes other forms. The characteristics that distinguish any one culture region will be most clearly revealed in the core of each region, and there must necessarily be wide zones of transition in which the characteristics of neighboring regions are mingled. The regions that are suggested as a framework for the presentation of a coherent picture of the contemporary world are as follows:

European
  Western, Southern, and Northern Europe
Soviet
  The Soviet Union and Eastern Europe
Anglo-American
  Canada and the United States
Latin American
  Mexico, Central America, South America, the Antilles, and the Bahamas
North African—Southwest Asian
  The Moslem countries from Morocco to Afghanistan and Israel
South Asian
  India, Pakistan, Ceylon, and border countries
Southeast Asian
  The "shatter belt" between India and China
East Asian
  China, Japan, and bordering countries
African
  The countries south of the Sahara
Australian-New Zealand
  The countries of British origin in Australasia
Pacific
  The islands of Melanesia, Micronesia, and Polynesia

The Concept of the Viability of States

Within the culture regions, the basic units of action and reaction are the politically organized areas—the states. Each state has within its national territory a particular arrangement of natural features and resources, and this resource base must be appraised in relation to the attitudes, objectives, and technical skills of the people. In relation to the habitat there is a pattern of population—of areas of concentrated settlement with central cities, of areas thinly populated, or areas that lie outside the effective national territory. Also, in relation to habitat and population is the pattern of the economy: the agriculture, the mines, the manufacturing industries, the transportation facilities. And finally, all these elements enter into the analysis of the viability of the state.

Viability refers to the effectiveness with which the state can be operated to fulfill its purposes. A state exists for the purpose of preserving the traditions and objectives of the people who are its citizens. The particular body of traditions and objectives that the people have in mind is known as the *state-idea.* This is the reason for the existence of the state, the reason people give their support to the state, the reason the state continues to exist.

There is a difference between the nation and a state. A nation is a body of people with common traditions, conscious of belonging together. Often a nation is tied together by the use of a common language and by the literary traditions inscribed in that language; but there are states that have overcome the handicap of using different languages, and have nevertheless achieved unity and coherence. A state, on the other hand, is any politically organized territory. A nation-state exists when the people of one nation are organized in one state; but there are examples of nations that are divided among several states, and of states that include more than one nation. The interplay of state and nation is an important element in world tensions, and in the analysis of viability.

In any state there are integrating and disintegrating forces. Those that tend to hold a state together are integrating forces; but these are always competing with forces of disintegration that tend to break the state into separate parts. A strongly held state-idea is an integrating force; but where a national territory is divided into two parts, in each of which people adhere to a different state-idea, there is great danger of civil war. If a state is divided into more than two parts there is less danger;

and if strongly supported differences of opinion regarding the state-idea are intermingled throughout the state, the danger of disintegration is very much less. States that lack a strong state-idea may have to be held together by the power of a central authority, forming a police state in which differences of opinion are not permitted expression. All these and many other alternatives must be weighed in any analysis of the viability of a state.

The Concept of the Land Hemisphere

In discussing the relative importance of states, or groups of states, in the international world, it is necessary to make use of a relatively new geographic concept—the concept of the *Land Hemisphere.*[25] If we pick up a globe and turn it around freely (without regard to its axis), we find that there is one position we can hold it in that permits us to see within the half of the globe visible from one point, the largest proportion of the world's inhabited lands. We find that the center of the Land Hemisphere is at Nantes, in France. Within the hemisphere centered on Nantes, there is ninety per cent of the land area outside of Antarctica. On these lands there are ninety-four per cent of the population of the world, and ninety-eight per cent of the world's economic production. The other half of the world is mostly water, and the countries that occupy the other half are relatively remote from the central part of the inhabited world. Events that take place in or near the central area inevitably affect more people than do events that take place in the more remote locations.

Location near the center of the Land Hemisphere became a significant geographic fact only in the second half of the twentieth century. It became significant only when the technology of transportation and warfare made it possible to move from place to place by the most direct route, disregarding such barriers as mountains, ice, or storms. As World War I approached, H. J. Mackinder described the conflict in terms of sea power against land power.[26] His analysis led him to conclude that Western Europe had attained its great power position as a result of the supremacy of sea power, but that with the improvement of land transportation the states occupying the great heartland of Eurasia, access to which could be denied to sea power, might be in a position to control first the peoples around the continental margins, then the peoples of all of Eurasia and Africa, and later the whole world. But the changed technology of transport and warfare after World War II now render Mackinder's analysis obsolete. For the heartland is no longer defined in terms of access by sea or land but rather by air. For the first time it becomes important that more people are close to Western Europe than to any other one part of the world. For the first time the center of the Land Hemisphere itself may be described as the heartland. The significance of this is of vital importance in an understanding of world strategy.

The Perspective of Geography

The perspective that comes from seeing and understanding all the many faces of the modern world throws additional light on the position of the United States, and on its responsibilities and opportunities. By inserting the framework of geographic concepts into the social studies, much needed unity and coherence are provided, and the inborn curiosity about places beyond the horizon, which most children learn to hide under a mask of sophistication, may be recaptured. Instead of fear of the unknown, graduates of our schools may substitute organized knowledge about places and countries and about the processes of change now sweeping over the world. That we are the custodians of some of the most revolutionary new ideas the world has seen for twenty-two centuries endows America with a responsibility and a purpose to which our young people quickly respond. The perspective of geography, added to that of history and to the concepts of human behavior, can bring the changing world into focus and illuminate the road ahead.

1. Pendleton Herring, "Toward an Understanding of Man," in *New Viewpoints in the Social Sciences* ed. by Roy A. Price, Twenty-Eighth Yearbook, National Council for the Social Studies, 1958, p. 1.
2. Joseph R. Strayer, p. 24.
3. Johannes Steinmetzler, *Die Anthropogeographie Friedrich Ratzels und ihre ideengeschichtlichen Wurlzeln,* Bonn, 1956.
4. Richard Hartshorne, *The Nature of Geography,* Association of American Geographers, 1939.
   Preston E. James, "Toward a Further Understanding of the Regional Concept," *Annals of the Association of American Geographers,* Vol. 42, 1952, pp. 195–222.
   Edward A. Ackerman, *Geography as a Fundamental Research Discipline,* University of Chicago, Department of Geography Research Paper, 1956.
   Preston E. James and Clarence F. Jones, eds., *American Geography, Inventory and Prospect,* Association of American Geographers, 1954.
   Richard Hartshorne, *Perspective on the Nature of Geography,* Association of German Geographers, 1959.
   Preston E. James, ed., *New Viewpoints in Geography,* Yearbook, National Council for the Social Studies, 1959.
5. Derwent Whittlesey, "The Regional Concept and the Regional Method," in *American Geography, Inventory and Prospect, op. cit.,* pp. 19–68.
6. Preston E. James, *A Geography of Man,* 2nd ed., Ginn and Co., 1959, pp. 489–520.
7. Wellman Chamberlain, "The Round Earth on Flat Paper," National Geographic Society, 1947.
8. Edward B. Espenshade, Jr., "Cartographic Developments and New Maps," in *New Viewpoints in Geography, op. cit.,* pp. 93–111.

Gertrude Whipple, "Geography in the Elementary Social Studies Program: Concepts, Generalizations and Skills to be Developed," *op. cit.*, pp. 112–43.
Clarence B. Odell, "The Use of Maps, Globes, and Pictures in the Classroom," *op. cit.*, pp. 200–10.

9. *A Geography of Man, op. cit.*, pp. 101–02.
10. *Ibid.*, pp. 48–51.
11. Clyde P. Patton, "Professional Contributions to Physical Geography," *New Viewpoints in Geography, op. cit.*, pp. 19–33.
12. *A Geography of Man, op. cit.*, pp. 35–37.
13. William L. Thomas, ed., *Man's Role in Changing the Face of the Earth,* University of Chicago Press, 1956.
14. Lewis Mumford, *The City in History,* Harcourt, Brace and World, 1961.
15. L. E. Klimm, "The Empty Areas of the Northeastern United States," *Geographical Review,* Vol. 44, 1954, pp. 325–345.
16. *A Geography of Man, op. cit.*, p. 585.
17. Melville J. Herskovits, *Man and His Works: The Science of Cultural Anthropology,* Alfred A. Knopf, 1948, p. 239.
18. R. J. Braidwood, "The Agricultural Revolution," *Scientific American,* Vol. 203, 1960, pp. 130–48.
19. R. M. Adams, "The Origin of Cities," *Scientific American,* Vol. 203, 1960, pp. 153–68.
20. Andrew H. Clark, "Historical Geography," *American Geography, Inventory and Prospect, op. cit.*, pp. 70–105.
Phillip Bacon, "An Approach to Social Studies Through Historical Geography," *New Viewpoints in Geography, op. cit.*, pp. 144–61.
21. W. W. Rostow, *The Stages of Economic Growth,* Cambridge University Press, 1960.
Norton Ginsburg, ed., *Geography and Economic Development,* University of Chicago, Department of Geography Research Paper, 1960.
22. R. R. Palmer, *The Age of the Democratic Revolution,* Princeton University Press, 1959.
23. Preston E. James, "The Use of Culture Areas as a Frame of

Organization for the Social Studies," *New Viewpoints in Geography, op. cit.,* pp. 162–76.
Preston E. James and Nelda Davis, *The Wide World,* Macmillan, 1959.

24. Richard J. Russell, Fred B. Kniffen, and Evelyn L. Pruitt, *Culture Worlds,* Brief Edition, Macmillan, 1961.
Rhodes Murphey, *An Introduction to Geography,* Rand McNally & Co., 1961.
Jesse H. Wheeler Jr., J. Trenton Kostbade, and Richard S. Thoman, *Regional Geography of the World,* Holt, 1955.
Preston E. James, *One World Divided,* Ginn and Co., to be published 1963.

25. S. W. Boggs, "This Hemisphere," *Department of State Bulletin,* Vol. 12, 1945, No. 306, May 6.

26. H. J. Mackinder, "The Geographical Pivot of History," *Geographical Journal,* Vol. 23, 1904, pp. 421–37; *ibid., Democratic Ideals and Reality,* Holt, 1919, 1942.

Political Science

Norton E. Long / Northwestern University

THE SOCIAL STUDIES broadly conceived are concerned with the observation, measurement, conceptualization, and description of the patterns of human interaction in society. Their objectives are the development, ordering, testing, and increase of the particular bodies of knowledge that comprise their several domains.

The object of education in the social studies is first in so far as practicable to acquaint the student with the broad outlines of the existing state of knowledge in the disciplines. This knowledge consists both of factual content and of the theoretical ordering and description of this content that is presently considered most consistent with the data. Secondly, education in the social studies is concerned with imparting to the student an understanding of the methods by which knowledge in the several fields is pursued and verified. Both the content and the methods of the social sciences are a part of the educational objective. Thirdly, and here the social studies differ from the natural sciences, they have in part become responsible for transmitting and critically evaluating certain aspects of the culture that form the heritage of values of American and Western civilization.

The social studies are thus concerned with imparting a body of factual knowledge, a theoretical apparatus for giving order and significance to this knowledge, a methodology of inquiry and verification, and, in addition, a philosophical appreciation of a range of values embodied in the subject matter of the disciplines. The social studies accordingly are a mixed enterprise on the one hand concerned with the value of neutral objective pursuit of scientific knowledge and on the other concerned with the humanistic and philosophical task of entering the student into an informed and critically intelligent appreciation of his cultural inheritance and even of the broader milieu in which the educated and responsible citizen of today must function.

The concern with the humanistic and philosophical aspect of the social studies is closely related to the problem of citizenship education. In a sense, citizenship education combines applied science with the philosophical study of responsible choice. The area of citizenship education is perhaps one of the most critical areas, if not the most critical area, of controversy in the field of education in the social studies. It presents all the problems on the one hand of indoctrination and propaganda and on the other of the dangers of a scientific neutrality with respect to the main values of the culture.

From the point of view of political science, one might, as in the natural sciences, mathematics, the languages, or indeed any of the collegiate disciplines, wish for that kind of precollege grounding that would provide the most valuable foundation for the most rapid and full achievement of the student's educational potential in college in the particular discipline. Selfishly, one could design a program of study for the schools that would make possible a college introductory course at a considerably more advanced level of sophistication and content than is now possible. Certainly it would be a great gain for college teaching of political science to be able to take for granted the general possession by students of certain types of information and familiarity with a range of concepts and their analytical use. If we could afford it there would be much to be said for political science in the schools designed to meet the different needs of the future student of the subject as well as the educational needs of the general run of students. This dilemma has been posed acutely in the natural sciences and in varying degrees is presented by all the disciplines. The difference between the layman's need for a cultural understanding of science and mathematics and the future specialist's need for an exact grounding is a well-known and perplexing problem, especially given our limited educational resources.

The solution at the collegiate level of the problem of science for the layman has often been a cultural course in the sciences avoiding the more forbidding stumbling blocks of laboratory and mathematics. This kind of approach resembles that of art or music appreciation. The objective of such courses is to meet the need of the educated man for some critical appreciation of the key elements of the culture. This might be considered a kind of consumer education, an education of the audience in the sympathetic understanding of what it can not itself produce. In the case of the sciences, some conception of their methods and limitations seems essential if the non-scientist is not to bow down in worship before the prestigious magic of a cult rather than accord a free man's assent to a rationally warranted position. Beyond this there is, of course, the sheer importance of opening the student's eyes to a range of human achievements to which he can only be blind at the cost of an acutely impoverished vision of his world.

The case of political science in particular and the social sciences in general approaches that of the natural sciences but differs from them in important respects. There is, of course, a sense in which every man must be his own scientist at least to the extent of settling with himself why he is willing to credit the "scientific views" that he builds into his own world view. But there is certainly much greater possibility of divorcing the layman from natural science than from political science—at least so one might think in a democracy. Newman's remark about theology in his *Idea of a University,* that it was either the highest form of knowledge or pernicious nonsense, might well apply to political science in a democracy. If the case for science for the citizen may seem somewhat doubtful in view of the abstruseness of modern natural science, the case for political science for the citizen must seem in some fashion compelling.

Here we are confronted not only with the need, a very important one be it said, for the educated man to come to terms with key elements of his culture if he is to be philosophically whole and humanistically and aesthetically alive, but with the basic social need for a saving remmant of the citizens of a democracy to understand the theory and practice of politics. Political science is in the uncomfortable position of being, as a discipline, in a position to make a significant contribution to the applied science of politics in our society. This entanglement of the discipline with the world of action is fraught with challenge and cost. Involvement in the issues of practice meant a bitter debate between theology and the natural sciences that is too recent to be forgotten. The social sciences are even less equipped than the natural to stand up under the temptations and pressures of the forum. But it is probably unrealistic to imagine that they have any option but to be involved. With an important subject matter bearing on the issues of controversy, they can scarce avoid being brought in even though as unwilling witnesses.

What is probably of greatest moment is to define the position to be adopted on a firm basis of critically and consciously held values. The political scientist knows that education is a central part of the political process. He can have few illusions that education in political science can be neutral to that process. And if he attends to the world about him, he can have few illusions as to the exposed position of the high school teacher and that teacher's competence to deal with a subject that must be controversial among pressures that are intense and often menacing. One might well be tempted, given the relative immaturity of political science and its lack of prestige as compared with the natural sciences, to avoid the schools and leave the difficult task to the historian. Such a course, however expedient, is in all probability impossible in practice and ultimately unwise.

No society worthy of survival will fail to fight to defend its values. The political values of our society are in need of defense, not only from attack from without and within, but from the far more deadly enemy of neglect and lack of understanding on the part of those who nominally adhere to them. Walter Lippmann has eloquently deplored the erosion of the *Public Philosophy*. An age of the mass society has witnessed the increasing decay of the great tradition of Anglo-American constitutionalism. This decay is exhibited in the excesses of McCarthyism and the prevalence of trial by newspaper and legislative committee—activities directed at the exploitation of mass emotion and aimed at eroding the constitutionally protected areas of individual freedom, especially the freedom of dissent from orthodoxy. The failure of aristocratic elements of the bar or elsewhere to appreciate the basic conservative interest in the protection of minorities is both disturbing evidence of our political health and an indictment of our political education. We may well wonder whether our educational institutions are doing a passable job of passing on a decent understanding and critical appreciation of the Anglo-American political heritage. Too often it is assumed that the social capital, the product of centuries, tied up in our political institutions and values, is passed along as readily as a biological inheritance.

To a large extent we have relied on history and literature as the appropriate disciplines to acquaint students with the culture into which they are being socialized. The role of these disciplines is certainly critical. A wide knowledge of the history of Western and other civilizations is of the first importance for the social sciences. The student needs something to think about as well as the ability to think. An informed and critical appreciation of his own culture requires both a familiarity with its history and the perspective of other cultures and their development. In an age like ours we can ill afford to be provincial in time or space.

The dimension that political science can add to history or perhaps disentangle from it is a critical understanding of the development of political institutions and the values with which they are related. Political philosophy and a broadly conceived constitutional history can unite in an attempt to provide the student with an appreciation in depth of the genesis of our institutions, the struggles through which they were forged, the conflicts of values out of which they emerged, and the immense amount of social effort that went into their construction. The background of history and comparative government against which the student may more clearly appreciate the salient features of his own political culture should also enhance his sense of its precariousness and its constant need for renewal. While one would certainly wish to avoid a Burkean obscurantism with respect to the Anglo-American inheritance, some degree of reverence before the achievement might not be amiss.

It may be conceded that a critical, informed, and intelligent appreciation of our political institutions is a desirable objective for political science in the schools. Possibly one could carry along the reader in the view that the best means for attaining this objective would be through the study of the development of our institutions and the value conflicts that were involved with as much attention to the study of contrasting political cultures as the available educational resources would allow. Study of the institutions over time would permit a critical approach to institutions that in their flat contemporaneity must be given fulsome and uncritical admiration at peril of attack. Understanding in depth of the history of institutions gives the student the criteria for making his own evaluation of contemporary departures from the main stream of our tradition, however sanctioned. Thus the student who has a real acquaintance with the historic reasons for the protection against self-incrimination will be better able to evaluate the reasons for and the importance of the Fifth Amendment.

The lack, especially among the middle class, of an intimate acquaintance with the law as a dangerous instrumentality gives them only a thin and vicarious appreciation of due process and the constitutional safeguards. What were near things to the framers of the constitution are ghost stories, if that, to the youth of today, this despite what should be the compellingly vivid experience of current history abroad. One can but assume that the lessons of history current or past are far from self-evident. Some exemption mechanism of great power is at work similar to that which denies the reality of the gas chambers. Forceful teaching is needed to bring home relevant truths that deny America's immunity to the unpleasant.

History properly taught gives the student something to think about. It is the business of political science to teach him how to think about it. This involves dealing with two orders of propositions, propositions of value and propositions of fact. The problem of responsible choice is central to the action of a citizen in a constitutional democracy. The study of both American and English political thought in an institutional context should bring the student to grips with values in a real world of historic action. The problematic aspects of choice can be explicated and the emergence of a matrix of related values and institutions can be examined. The student needs to know how he and his society got here. He needs to be given the materials with which to arrive at a critically self-conscious political philosophy that he can employ in making his decisions and evaluations as a citizen.

The citizen needs not only to appreciate the values of his own political culture, he needs a tolerant and informed understanding of other and competing values that vie in today's world for the allegiance of men. In appreciating the genesis of his own political values and that of others, he will be less inclined to see the world in sharp contrasts, or to believe in the easy possibility of the wholesale adoption of his own views by others with a radically different history and circumstances.

If politics is the art of the possible, one of the prime tasks of political science is to provide the student with some idea of the limits in the range of realistic choice in the particular situation. Many problems that confront responsible American statesmanship stem from a Quixotic utopianism in the electorate that renders it an easy mark for demagoguery. In its concern with propositions of fact, political science should provide the student with some critical appreciation of the folk wisdom's limitations. Much of folk political science rises no higher than the good guys and the bad guys of the comic strips, and newspaper analysis frequently provides a not much more sophisticated variant of this homely moralism.

There is at present no adequately developed empirical body of theory that can be taught the student independently of the study of particular institutions. Comparative government is more a name for an aspiration than for an achieved reality. Yet clearly the best way to understand and to evaluate is to compare. The empirical weakness of political science beyond the description of the institutions of particular countries creates a problem for the teacher in the schools, who is in this respect as much on the frontier as his colleague in the university, and more exposed to boot. At least the fortunately less differentiated state of the social sciences in the schools will permit him the fruitful comparison of history—one that is unfortunately all too seldom exploited by his university colleagues.

The various attempts to provide a theoretical model to explain international relations suffer from the same theoretical immaturity as the rest of political science. Here again we are probably best off by relying on the history of the policies of the powers and the description of the institutions of international relations. This does not mean that instruction should not seek some theoretical ordering of a jungle that otherwise might merely overwhelm the student. The work of Haas and Whiting provides a useful approximation of what can be done to provide the student with some means to organize the materials for responsible thought.

The student in the schools is not only a future student in college and a potentially appreciative member of his culture, he is also a potential actor in the political life of his country. As a voter, as a critic, as an elected or appointed official in the numerous governments in which he may serve, there are complex and important roles that he may be called upon to play—roles on whose performance by at least a saving remnant of active citizens the whole enterprise of constitutional democracy depends.

We cannot assume the automatic possession of a sufficient fund of political competence by enough of our citizens to insure anything like an adequate pool of personnel from which to man the civic table of organization. It is true that our folk culture socializes a far higher level of competence to run a constitutional democracy than do many others. But we can make no safe assumption that Americans possess any peculiar inborn genius for running democratic institutions or even an adequate motivation to do so. The easy Jeffersonian faith in the political competence of our older agrarian society was founded on peculiar conditions of his time. This faith, if ever justified, no longer rests on the conditions he assumed. The natural aristocracy required to provide an adequate leadership for our mass democracy is no assured product of our present institutions.

What should be the role of the schools in providing the youth with a fund of competence for the performance of the necessary roles that must be filled in the operation of our political system? First, one should be clear that this is a question that cannot be avoided. One does not need to be a follower of Plato's to recognize the critical importance of the schools in transmitting the culture and molding attitudes toward its components. Education, by its neglect, fear of, and downgrading of the political, powerfully conditions the attitudes of the young toward the public life. To the extent that this reinforces family apolitical norms, two of the most powerful institutions of our society are engaged in sabotaging the development of democratic leadership. Many studies attest the effectiveness of this learning process in generating a widespread belief that politics is a dirty business that is well to leave alone. One suspects that the implicit political theory of much of our education accepts this view and provides only a utopian answer to how the job of government in our democracy is to be done under the circumstances.

We can scarcely expect to motivate the young to any lasting and strong desire to effectively participate in the community's politics with the milk-and-water moralism of the average civics text, nor is the bland emptiness of a junior chamber of commerce get-out-the-vote campaign such that it inspires a ritual of even ceremonial significance. Political competence can stem from a hard material purpose that schools itself to a realistic study of the facts. The upward mobile and the hungry who find in politics a relatively open avenue to their goals have reason enough to master the tricks of the trade. While the contributions of these earthy drives to manning the ranks of politics are essential, it seems foolhardy to rely on them as the well-nigh exclusive source of democratic leadership. An education that provides no adequate political philosophy to enlist the imagination of a significant portion of the youth in the challenge of governing fails the cause of constitutional democracy.

Constitutional democracy is a highly aristocratic form of government depending for its success on the self-selection of a natural aristocracy to provide a leaven to the civic lump. In a society that dishonors its public life and attaches a negative prestige to the profession of politics, the recruitment of a competent and materially disinterested democratic elite is increasingly difficult. The stored-up social capital of the British aristocratic tradition and of the Jeffersonian natural aristocracy of the gentry, even the middle-class *noblesse oblige* of the Mills, has largely run out. The spiritual void deplored by Walter Lippmann in his *Public Philosophy* is a matter of gravest concern for the equality of American life. No number of well-packaged slogans can convince the world or ourselves that the values of our tradition still compel men's imaginations and inform our public life.

Can a democratic mass education be expected to educate and motivate a governing class? At first blush it might seem that there is some contradiction between education for democracy and the production of an aristocracy. However, Jefferson himself was a strong believer in a natural aristocracy and saw in education a major means for its development. The humanist Irving Babbitt entitled a major work *Democracy and Leadership,* and eloquently argued the profound import of the quality of leadership for the very survival of democracy. One needs be no elitist to agree. An open society is not incompatible with leadership. In fact, as a relatively rare product of human history, it acutely depends upon it.

What is especially needed in the schools is the development of a sense for a great tradition to which the youth can adhere not in a spirit of uncritical acceptance but as a matter of free and intelligent allegiance. One of the more effective ways of developing is to choose a sound model and imitate it imaginatively and creatively. Plutarch played a useful role in our education when Tully's *On Offices* was standard fare. Hero worship has an aura of Carlylean bombast and Nietzschean connotations, but a generous admiration for some embodiment of nobility in human action would seem a sheer necessity if other than grossly material motivations are to dominate the political scene. The public life is an artifact of the society, and standards for its critical appraisal are derived from models of its practice. If students are to be given some sense for the challenge and reward of active citizenship, they need to have the barren abstractions of theory given the warmth of the flesh-and-blood reality of historical practice. Not only the "American Tradition and the Men Who Made It" but an elevated view of Western civilization and civilization itself needs to be imparted as an endless adventure and enterprise. A combination of political theory, the critical study of the development and functioning of institutions, and an appreciation of the lives of significant actors would provide an educational means through which some sense of the political tradition could be attained. The political theory must escape the tendency to be a lifeless history of ideas. Rather, the ideas must furnish criteria for the criticism, adaptation, and reshaping of institutions. As Coleman Woodbury has well said, one of the key questions for research in our explosively expanding urban areas is whether we are dealing with communities at all.

The nature of our local institutions for self-government is a problem for American political theory. What we wish to make politically of our emerging metropolitan areas is a major challenge to the creativity of our political imagination. The potential of these new forms of settlement is at once a heady challenge and an ominous threat. The problem of the political involvement and commitment of a heavily migratory population is another critical challenge to our capacity to create a territorially mobile but significant citizenship. A political philosophy that is to instruct the youth in more than a quiz-kid knowledge must grapple with the immediate problems that confront the achievement of active citizenship. The gap between rhetorical exhortations to be a good citizen, to vote, to participate, and the significant translation of these maxims into meaningful personal practice must be bridged if the futile piety of the civics course is to give way to action-oriented knowledge.

There is both economy and reinforcement in the study of the genesis of contemporary institutions. Trial by jury takes on a more vivid meaning when it is studied in the course of its development. The bewildering and sometimes meaningless complexities of Congress and the state legislatures sort themselves out and acquire meaning when seen against the main lines of parliamentary development. Local government, which is frequently a neglected stepchild, gains vitality through understanding of the problems with which it has grappled. Concepts, such as legitimacy, that may seem farfetched when applied to party conventions or close elections take form in the student's mind as he gains a feeling for them in the monarchical past.

The approach here suggested would require the development of course work that would combine American and British history with analysis and description of institutions and the political process. A similar approach to courses in Western civilization or indeed to courses in world civilization would be desirable. In fact, the use of history as a common body of knowledge for the other social sciences has much to recommend it both from the point of view of economizing on time and bringing the abstractions of analysis to bear on a historic reality that is rich in vicarious experience. Again the loss in depth and dynamics that is frequently deplored in contemporary social science would receive a useful correction by an initial grounding in history in the schools.

Given the scarce teaching resources of the schools and the probable impracticability of having each of the social sciences represented by a specialist, there is a real challenge and opportunity for the development of a social science generalist with an interdisciplinary competence. A major part of the job of getting political science taught adequately in the schools rests with political science faculties doing an adequate job of teaching political science to the students of the schools of education. Beyond this there is a need for continuing relation with and support of teachers in the schools by their university social science colleagues. Teachers in the schools are exposed and isolated, and need whatever backing they can get from the universities both against the pressures to bowdlerize their subject and to overcome their separation from the main stream of scholarly work.

Training Teachers

In a sense, what we can get taught of political science in the schools will depend pretty much on the co-operative relationship between political science departments and schools of education in the training of social science teachers. It would be most helpful if joint planning could be undertaken so that teachers of the social studies have adequate backgrounds in history, sociology, economics, and political science. Given the heavy requirements in education, there is a real danger that secondary school teachers will have no more than a smattering of these subjects.

Quite clearly we can not have better instruction in political science in the schools than one can reasonably expect from teachers with a rather minimal undergraduate preparation in the field. The social studies in most secondary schools take a considerably inferior position to that of the so-called hard subjects, the natural sciences and mathematics. In the social sciences history is queen, and this tends to be a history taught with little if any critical appreciation for the social science generalizations embedded in its common-sense narrative. Those few teachers with a political science background are all too likely to have a romantic orientation toward peace and international relations or toward area studies—if very bold, Russia or the Orient. In general, while much lip service is given to citizenship education, this subject is treated in a formal, shallow, and sentimental manner that frequently amounts to little more than manipulated supportive behavior on the part of student leaderships to attain the ends of school authorities.

Ideally, one would like to have teachers responsible for political science in the schools know something about the history of political thought and institutions, comparative government, international relations, constitutional law, and American government. This is probably a good deal more than one can expect in the undergraduate education of the average teacher of social studies who will be responsible for some of the political science offerings in the schools. It is probably not too much to expect that in the better-staffed secondary schools at least one member of the faculty should be at least this well equipped. If such a person with such training could be placed in the social studies faculty with sufficient status to command respect for the discipline he represents, the appropriate political science objectives could be fitted into the school curriculum.

What is needed is not so much a proliferation of courses to represent the specialized social sciences as the peculiar analytical capabilities and perspectives of the social sciences as applied to the common field of social action. History taught by social scientists could make a manifold contribution to the student's education. The danger of history as presently taught is that the plausible common sense of the historian's narrative is accepted as valid social science generalization and becomes an uncriticized part of the student's folk political science, folk economics, or folk sociology. This danger exists, of course, wherever the student is exposed to ex cathedra remarks of putative authorities. Even geography texts have banal imbecilities on the causes of graft and slums in cities. A major objective of the social sciences is to expose this folk wisdom of common sense to the light of logical analysis and empirical inquiry.

It has been the contention of this paper that political science could make its best contribution in the schools by applying its perspective and methods to the interpretation of history. All the social sciences would profit immensely by being able to take for granted a first-class grounding in political, economic, social, and intellectual history. This grounding, however, should be given by teachers of social studies who are themselves keenly aware of the relevance of the various social sciences to the interpretation of history. History should not be allowed to remain at the level of plausible common-sense narrative with a literary criterion of truth. The problems approach so successfully used in many of the colleges might with profit be extended to the secondary schools.

It is too much to expect a superior education in the secondary schools to that presently provided in college. Yet if one asks what one would wish political science to accomplish, for example, in the high schools, it would be difficult not to set goals for achievement that are not presently being attained in college. High school graduates are potentially and in varying degrees actually going to become political actors in American democracy. Their roles as voters, critics, elected and appointed officials, and the like should benefit from a knowledge of political science. One way of looking at the appropriate presentation of political science in the secondary schools is to ask how it can be made to have maximum value in improving the student's effectiveness in his future adult political roles.

Politics is often regarded as an amateur sport at which anyone can play, learning the game as he goes along. The professional in politics is usually regarded as a sordid mercenary whose contributions are in the main negative. This view of professionalism contrasts sharply with our valuation of it in the life activities that we take seriously. In general, few men would consider an academic preparation for public life as functional and fitting. The present incumbent of the White House is one of the rare exceptions who seems to have read the political-science literature on his job. If this is true for the presidency, it is not surprising that such a state of affairs should apply to the lesser roles of American public life.

A political science that grappled meaningfully with the various public roles of the citizen would have much to say that could be said effectively in the schools. Many of the students will find themselves confronted with the job of acting in an executive or legislative capacity; most, as voters, need some ability to keep score on the performance of public officials and parties. There is elementary know-how about the functions of the executive and the structure and functioning of organizations that would save a brutal breaking-in period for the innocents who think swimming a natural gift. Much the same holds with respect to legislative activity. But of all the roles the most general and pervasive is that of voter, the consumer, and critic of politics. How does one acquire the information and develop the standards to appraise political performance? No subject is more important than this for discussion in the schools. No performance, if we may judge by our studies of voting behavior, is more cause for concern.

As we leave behind the familiar subjects of village government, the credentials of a local democracy for self-government become less and less impressive. The salvation of mass democracy depends increasingly on its capacity to develop, support, and choose among responsible elites for leadership in a bewildering number of increasingly complex fields. The contribution of the schools in this respect is their capacity to develop in their students the ability to apply critical and reflective judgment, armed with a perspective of history, to the competing claims of the contending elites. By teaching the habit of analysis, the demand for evidence, the need for tolerance, and the capacity to develop critically held standards of judgment, the schools will make their greatest contribution to the future public life of their students. The objective is the application of philosophical and scientific analysis to the process of politics with a firm grasp of the cultural background of our society.

*Economics**

Ben W. Lewis / *Oberlin College*

I HAVE BEEN INVITED to prepare a statement on the content objectives of social studies in the schools from the point of view of economics. Invitations of this kind are heady, and I am susceptible. Even so, I cannot presume to represent my response as *the* view of economics or of economists; it is the view of one confessed economist. It carries the belief, however, and the hope, that quite a number of other economists see these things much as I see them.

To come quickly to the point: from where I sit, the content objective of economics in the schools is the economic understanding demanded by responsible citizenship—*really re-*

* In the preparation of this paper, I have been helped by comments and suggestions from James W. Bell, Clark Bloom, Edgar Edwards, Kenyon Knopf, Laurence Leamer, Lewis Wagner, and E. T. Weiler. I am grateful and, of course, absolve each and all from any responsibility for the result.

sponsible citizenship. Further, I am aware of no considerations that dictate content objectives for the other social studies in the schools different from the objective of responsible citizenship, as I understand that objective.

Economics is a social study. In the schools, as in the colleges, its role is to contribute to an understanding of society's economic problem and of the economizing processes of the total society in which all of us live as human beings, and in which we participate as producers and consumers and as citizens. Economic understanding serves many purposes, both functional and cultural; its development and spread are important for many reasons. In a democratic political society such as ours, concerned increasingly with issues of political economy, broad economic understanding may well become crucial. I suggest that the clear case for the teaching (and the improvement of teaching) of economics in the schools that derives from the demands of our democratic political economy also fixes the overriding objective of economics in the schools—responsible citizenship. I suggest, further, that to enlist the teaching of economics explicitly in the service of citizenship is in no sense to debase economics or to pervert economics as a science. Good citizenship needs good economics and straight economics, not cut and not seasoned to taste—just as good and as straight as scientific purpose and standards and drive can make it. Nor does economics for citizenship minimize the importance of other interests or objectives that economic understanding may serve, or prejudice in any way the influence that they may appropriately exercise upon the direction or pattern of teaching. It is a happy fact that the economic understanding that will genuinely serve the demands of responsible citizenship will also serve, and serve well, all other interests to which a basic understanding of economics can contribute. The schools will blanket the target—they will miss nothing that needs to be reached—if in teaching for economic understanding they set their sights surely and steadily on citizenship.

Economizing, Political Economies and Economics. Economics as a social science—a social study—

> is concerned with the ways in which, as a people, we manage our productive human and natural resources and the goods and services which result from the employment and use of these resources. Economics starts from the simple, undeniable proposition that, over all, mankind does not have and never will have enough human, natural and produced resources to enable all men to have all they want (and will come to want) of goods and services. Mankind's desires for goods in the aggregate are so vast that no purpose is served by regarding them as other than *unlimited:* the resources available to society for the production of goods in the aggregate are clearly *limited.* In relation to our total desires, our resources are scarce. We cannot visualize a time when all men will have more of everything in the way of private goods and public goods than they want. Certainly no such affluence is known today, anywhere.[1]

Aggregate wants in excess of our aggregate capacity to satisfy our wants require us to be concerned about and to manage well—to economize—the resources that bound our capacity. Let me spell out the concern of economics—economizing—taking pains at the outset to guard against any confusion over the key concept of "scarcity" that may arise from focusing attention upon great accumulations of wealth in the hands of a fortunate few, or even upon the quite comfortable circumstances enjoyed by many more in our own rich country. Within a stone's throw of all of us are scores of thousands whose unsatisfied *basic* wants are vast; and this says nothing of the reaches of unsatisfied wants, still in our own economy, for *public* goods and for intended leisure, or of the teeming millions in underdeveloped areas abroad whose unsatisfied wants, to attain a state even of human decency, are staggering. These unsatisfied wants are real, even desperate, and they testify to the haunting presence of economic scarcity on a scale so great as almost to defy comprehension. Nor may we be led by gluts in particular markets, or by the appearance of inadequate over all-market demand in our kind of economy to believe that we have outdistanced the specter of scarcity—that we now have the capacity to produce more than we can consume. These phenomena attest not to the spectacular levels of our capacity to produce; they stand rather as evidence (sometimes shocking evidence) of our glaring capacity for economic mismanagement—of our failure adequately to "economize."

> The fact of scarce resources poses the over-all *economic problem** that faces all societies and dominates all economic situations and issues. It also poses the task of the science or discipline of economics. Since our limited means, even at their very best and most productive, will not permit all of us to have all the goods we want, we are forced to be concerned about how our means are used—how fully they are used, how efficiently they are used, what goods they are used to produce and in what quantities, and in what proportions the goods are distributed among us all—and, of course, what goods must be forgone. The degree and manner and direction of resource use and the disposition of the produce of resource use have, of sheer necessity, been of primary moment to all societies through the ages. And all societies have established and maintained (or acquiesced in) economic systems or economies—man-made and man-remade arrangements to turn out and effect the decisions that society wants to give to the multitude of questions [what, how much, and to whom?] generated continuously by the basic economic problem.
>
> The discipline of economics is the study of the economic problem in all its parts and manifestations, and of the arrangements, institutions and processes which men have devised to grind out the answers to the manifold questions which it raises.

* The nature of what, in common with other economists, I refer to here and later as *the economic problem* might, perhaps, be made clearer to the non-professional reader if it were termed *the economic task*. The over-all *economic problem* of resource use has confronted society from its very beginning, and has involved society constantly and continuously

Economics in a Democratic Society. In abstract terms, this is what economics is about—economizing and economies. In terms of sweat and blood and tears and tranquilizers, what these concerns mean to us as participating, working members of the far-flung, complex, throbbing social organization we know as the economic system is borne in upon us virtually throughout our adult lives. In fact, in large measure, economics *is* our life. Most of us are never completely free from the pressure of gaining money incomes and transmuting them into want-satisfying goods and services within the system. None of us who has the power to think is ever free from the pressure of the myriads of public economic issues generated by our need consciously and collectively to make the economic system in which we live more responsive to the requirements of our life together. I shall comment later upon the absorbing subject of winning and consuming (fortified) bread, and its bearing upon economics in the schools. It is the *public* economic issues, however, that urgently demand the presence of economics—economics effectively taught—within the school curriculum, and which should point its direction and set its tone and content.

To list these public economic issues seems a work of supererogation; they are familiar to all of us. They are omnipresent; we dodge or duck or rise above one only to be slapped by others. The sheer fact is that, as individuals, we are overwhelmed by them, and our collective capacity to deal with them is not yet proven. Here are a few, the first dozen (a

---

in the *task* of economizing. It is not, of course, coordinate with such economic problems (or issues) as "the farm problem" or "the labor-management problem" or "the public debt problem," which are manifestations of *the economic problem* (task) in particular areas and instances and times. *The economic problem* involves all of society, always, in a task which has rolled in upon us from the dim shadows of the past and which stretches endlessly into the future. There is no "solution" for *the economic problem;* there can be no relief from the everlasting task of economizing which it imposes.[2]

baker's dozen) to come to mind, and not necessarily first either in importance or urgency: inflation, taxation, foreign aid, growth rate, public health, full employment, labor-management relations, trade restraints, support for agriculture, public power, balance of payments, deficit financing, federal support for education. These really are not samples of public economic issues, but of categories of public economic issues (much bigger than bite-size chunks) with which our consciousness is ceaselessly bombarded by our highly efficient media of mass communication (which reminds me that mass communication, too, has its public economic aspects). They are not concoctions of, or a phantasmagoria dreamed up by, columnists and telecasters; they flow quite naturally, but nonetheless relentlessly and frighteningly, from the fact of economic scarcity. They call for public, political choices, with far-reaching economic consequences, on the uses of resources so scarce that all uses cannot be accommodated. Our lives are affected by these choices: either directly, or indirectly through the interweaving of economic forces and processes, every one of us stands to gain or lose in material satisfactions depending upon whether, in particular instances, the choice is yes or no, or the vote is yea or nay. Sometimes, all of us may gain or lose together, at least over time; sometimes, inevitably, some of us will gain at the expense of others.*

* "Depression brings unemployment and personal disaster to millions. What should be done? Give unemployment relief? Decrease taxes and create a government deficit so as to increase private purchasing power? Reduce wages and other costs? Just wait?

"Needs for more and better schools mount. Can we afford them? If so, who should pay for them? Should we borrow to pay the cost or enact new taxes? What would be the effects of new income, sales, or property taxes on private spending by consumers and businesses?

"Foreign competition threatens the markets of American firms. Should American tariffs be raised? Is the answer lower American costs through increased efficiency and restraint on wage increases? Broadly, are international trade and lending good or bad for America?

"Electronic computers and scientific advances bring automation that

This is *public* economizing; the processes through which it is carried out are governmental processes. *This means us!* We, collectively, *are* the government. This is *our* political economy. Our choices will not be made and should not be made on the basis of economic considerations and consequences alone, but they will be made at our personal and collective peril if they reflect ignorance of, or indifference to, economic processes and effects—if they are made without economic understanding, or with misunderstanding.

I have spoken of far-reaching economic consequences that flow from public economizing—government economizing. The government I am talking about, and in which all of us have a substantial stake, is government by the governed—representative democracy, or even more elliptically, democracy. Government by the governed in today's world, and even more in the world of tomorrow, requires the governed to deal—"professionally" if you please, or at least "semiprofessionally"—with public economic issues. This is what democracy means: every last one of the scores of millions of us is privileged and required to express himself, either actively and overtly or by withdrawal and silence, not only on matters of his personal economy (where, incidentally, he exercises his modicum of control over the total economy), but ceaselessly and without stint on public economic issues that go to the very heart of our common life together. Our ability to perform in this capacity—how well we do the job—plays a large part in determining whether our economic world is a happy one; its effect on whether we can long continue to enjoy the luxury of government by the governed will be decisive.

---

eliminates both unskilled and skilled jobs. Who gains and who loses from such changes? Should labor unions oppose them, insist on slow introduction to minimize transitional unemployment . . . or welcome them? What is the interest of consumers and others in the economy?

"Such questions could be multiplied indefinitely. The issues fill our daily papers and our daily lives." *Summary of the Report of the National Task Force on Economic Education*, September 1961, p. 6.

In the kind of economy that is developing in the United States, the public—all of us—plays an important part, even outside both the market and the framework of formal government, in decision making on public issues affecting wide areas and millions of people. Public opinion, however manifested, weighs heavily upon and conditions major decisions made by persons in key positions in the private sectors of the economy. Examples are many; notably, decisions on wage levels and on price policies in oligopolistic industries: consider, for instance, wages and prices in steel. These matters have come by the force of circumstances to be public issues; the decision makers recognize them as such, and seek assiduously to gain the amorphous support of "public opinion" for their policy decisions. Without commenting upon the desirability of this condition, and without attempting a prediction as to how long it will persist as a characteristic of our economy, I must not fail to note that, just as in the area of formal, collective governmental decision making, none of us can shun his privilege or avoid his responsibility to be counted in the summing up of a total public opinion that may be decisive. For better or worse, this is the way we operate—in part—in the third quarter of the twentieth century. *Opinions count!* I venture to suggest that we will operate more effectively and happily if our opinions, as well as our ballots, reflect economic awareness and understanding.

Individually, most of us enter upon our formal and informal roles in our democratic political economy under substantial disabilities: we are not born with a working understanding of economizing and the economy, and osmosis is at best a weak and unreliable process for supplying the deficiency. Further, public economic issues are charged for each of us with a personal interest (economic gain or loss) that raises our blood pressures, and pours heavy emotion on top of our considerable ignorance as we undertake our economizing duties. Finally, most of us are unaware of our infirmities and, hence, are inclined to stride heavily and even to prance where, if we were just a little wiser, we might be reluctant to venture more than a cautious step. We are inclined to believe that wisdom in matters of economic public policy consists largely in what we like to call old-fashioned horse sense (with which each of us is convinced he is generously endowed). We overlook the fact that while horse sense may have helped many a horse on many stormy nights in the past to find his way home to his cozy stable, there are very few horses around today to tell and relish the story. It becomes increasingly evident that the great and complex political economic issues of our time will not yield to intuition alone, whether of horses or of men, and that widespread economic illiteracy hopped up by emotion and made brazen by its very shortcomings will be hurtful rather than helpful to us in the times that lie ahead.

Frankly, if we think of ourselves, the governed, as its operatives, our political economy is not too impressively staffed and equipped. Its future in our hands may not yet appear so insecure that we should race for the panic button. But, storm warnings are called for: urgency is too close for comfort. Thus far, we have not done badly; in fact we have done rather well. Physical environment has been generous to our political economy, and our heritage and experience have served it faithfully and with good effect. But, our economy is fat; it has not yet been put to a telling test. As we grow in numbers, and as technology knits us ever more tightly together, problems calling for collective political-economic decisions also grow in volume and complexity. The great problems of employment, growth, inflation, taxation, welfare, international economic relations, big business, big agriculture, big labor, and the like do not wear their solutions on their sleeves. Momentarily in our history we can contain them; we can deal with them by herding them onto their respective reservations. But the reservations, even now, are beginning to show the strain; their boundaries are bursting. We "got by" in the thirties. It is not evident that the seventies will be so kind. Without preparation by all of us for the task, it is not certain that our kind of political economy can measure up—that our democracy can survive the pressures generated by the prosecution of great tasks by small talents.

To put it mildly—and I am determined not to be dramatic about all of this—the operating personnel of our democratic political economy, the governed who govern, could presently use and soon will be in desperate need of a substantial charge of *economic understanding*. This will come, if it comes in time, through our schools and only through our schools. I do not forecast the end of democracy if each child is not presented at birth with a copy of Samuelson's *Economics* and is not required to pass an examination on money flows and linear programming as a condition for entering the fifth grade. Nor do I contend that economic shoals are the only ones that lie ahead. I argue simply that the demonstrated capacity of our democratic political economy to perform, and hence its capacity to survive, will be substantially affected in the years ahead by the extent to which our people become equipped to face up to public economic issues with an understanding of "what it's all about" and how to get on with the job.

I shall elaborate in a moment on my notion of "economic understanding"; let me equate it here with a good working sense of the nature of economizing, and of the economy as an economizing apparatus, and a rational as distinct from an emotional approach to the disposition of economic problems. We will live better and more satisfyingly if economic understanding is widespread. I believe we will not live democratically *unless* it is widespread—unless in the years ahead it comes to be extended virtually as widely as our school-graduating population. Economic understanding on the part of public leaders is called for, of course, but this is not enough unless we are willing to accept as democracy something far removed from government by the governed. If we cherish democracy, the very least for which we dare to settle is economic understanding by our people sufficient to ensure the identification and choice of understanding leaders, and strong support for their leadership.

Economic understanding of a quality and on a scale required for the successful exercise of government by the governed in a world crowded with public economic issues will not just happen. It can be had only if the task of providing it is set explicitly for, and accepted wholeheartedly and carried out vigorously by, the schools. The colleges will reach a fraction, and of these some will be touched quite deeply; but only the schools can provide for the mass of our people the chance to gain a measure of economic understanding through formal, systematic study. And we know something now that most of us did not know a decade ago: the schools *can* do the job.

Let me pause, briefly, over the problem of indoctrination. I have linked the schools, economics, economic understanding, and responsible citizenship with the effective operation and performance and, so, the very preservation of our democracy and our democratic political economy. Let me make it crystal clear that I am not urging a "responsible citizenship" orientation for economics in the schools either as a form of, or as a front for, indoctrination. Personally, I happen to be very, very high on democracy as I understand it, on every ground that strikes me as significant. I happen also to believe that in my capacity as a teacher it is neither my duty nor my privilege to try to sell my personal ideological views to my students, or to urge other teachers to do so. This does not mean, however, that as a teacher I may not urge an approach to the economic issues common to all economies and all peoples that stresses insight and rationality; in fact, unless my approach and influence lie precisely in this direction, I should, in my judgment, turn in my badge. Let me put it this way: insight and rationality are the hallmarks of objective scientific scholarship—the very antithesis of indoctrination in the classroom. It is also the case that no responsible citizen, as a citizen, should be without these qualities. It is fortunate, but it is nonetheless true, that insight and rationality are also the very stuff of economic understanding, and that economic understanding is the bulwark of government by the governed in this age of economic issues. I may not "sell" democracy to my students, but, fortunately for my peace of mind, it is my duty as a scholar and teacher to press for an approach that offers democracy its one big chance to "sell" itself.

The Nature of Economic Understanding. By "economic understanding" I mean, essentially, an understanding of economizing and of our total (market and government) economizing apparatus, and a feel for—a way of thinking about—economic considerations and issues as these grow out of, reflect and bear upon, the central problem of all economies and of economics. I suggest that

> to have economic understanding is to have a genuine sense of "what" it's all about as far as the economic phases of our lives together are concerned—a "feel" for economic issues—a rather clear impression of "having been here before" in the presence of economic situations calling for policy judgments, and hence a sense of direction and a workmanlike touch.[3]

A word, first, about the workmanlike touch: the most important step toward understanding in economics (as in other areas of knowledge), if, indeed, it is not the culmination of economic sophistication, is, as the National Task Force has put it, "the replacement of emotional, unreasoned judgments by objective rational analysis," in reaching conclusions on matters that by their very nature invite us to think with our hearts and stomachs rather than with our heads. The Task Force goes on:

> The essence of economics is the necessity to choose among alternatives, since there are never enough resources to satisfy all human wants. Reasoned choice on economic problems thus involves, in each problem or situation: (1) defining the prob-

> lem which faces us; (2) identifying our goals or objectives and giving them some rough order of priority; (3) laying out the principal alternative ways of obtaining these objectives, given the limited resources available to us; and (4) analyzing the consequences of each possible line of action and choosing that course which seems likely to contribute most to the desired goals. These are nothing more than the stages in a sound businessman's thinking as he makes an important decision, the steps that a good scientist or physician follows in his work, and the process that a wise government goes through when it determines economic policies. Economics is a rational way of thinking about economic problems, not a party line or a set of "answers."[4]

Note that the rational approach and workmanlike touch do not involve the exclusion in economic decision making either of value judgments or of self-interest. Far from it. The selection of goals, particularly since we must choose between desirable goals that conflict with each other and that, therefore, cannot all be fully achieved (complete "freedom" means less than complete "equity"; "progress" is bound to upset "security"), is clearly a matter of values. Economics does not dictate value judgments, but its processes would be sterile without them. It is the part of economics to clarify ethical issues, not to solve them. Increased economic understanding would almost certainly increase the debate over values and goals, but it would dispel confusion and set the issues in sharper relief; it would add meaning and quality to the debate. As for self-interest, we not only recognize it and accept it as a normal force in economic matters, we virtually enshrine it as an essential part of the economizing mechanism in any free market economy. A scientific approach in economics requires not that we shall deny or exclude value judgments and self-interest, but that we shall employ them with understanding, and never be unaware of their presence or of the weight that we accord them in our calculations.

The *substance* of economic understanding? In my view, to have economic understanding is to grasp the meaning and the significance of the central core of economics, the economic problem, together with its operating and institutional manifestations—economizing and the economy (economic system). The economic problem—how shall we use our limited resources in light of our unlimited desires?—is the most important concept in economics. It lies at the heart of economic understanding. The data, the materials, the concepts, the "principles" and "laws" with which economics is concerned, and the issues to which it attends all stem from and bear on this central problem. All other economic problems and issues are simply outcroppings of the central problem in particular quarters and under particular conditions; and they can be dealt with meaningfully only in the context of the central problem.

Consider, for instance, the tariff, a problem of adjustment that has been with us since the beginning of our national life, and which is destined to occupy a particularly prominent place in public debate during the next few months. The outcome of the debate will affect the economic fortunes of many people. The efficiency (and, hence, the amount) and direction and composition of production will be at stake, as will the pattern of income distribution. We shall be making choices involving the issues of security versus change, and the spreading of social costs. But, these issues and alternatives are old hat to us; they are the very essence of the economic problem, the old, old concerns of economizing—what, how much, to whom? And so it is with the farm problem, the wage problem, the "fair trade" problem, and the problems of public health, public education, inflation, antitrust, and all the others. To identify each of these as a manifestation of the economic problem is not, of course, to solve it; but it does place it squarely on the target, in clear focus and with its essential elements plainly exposed.

The central economic problem should be the starting point of our economic teaching, and its destination. Between the take-off and the happy landing students should become familiar—easily and confidently familiar—with the nature of the economizing process and its techniques, and with the nature of the economic system—*any* economic system—as a man-made set of arrangements instituted, maintained, and modified by society to guide, induce, and compel the economic behavior of individuals and the ordering of resources in patterns that reflect society's desires. They should gain a working knowledge of the significant features of our own economy, with its ever-changing combinations of, and interactions between, free market and collective governmental economic processes and activities. They should understand its purposes and rationale, its dynamic concerns, and how it has come to be what it now is and how it contrasts with earlier and other economizing ways and arrangements. Students need to know something of the structure and operations of our major economic institutions and of the forces that affect and determine the size, make-up, and division among us of our national output of goods and services. They should experience the centering of issues, and the marshaling and weighing of facts and considerations involved in the rational disposition of typical controversial public economic issues. But, let me emphasize that all of this—processes, systems, institutions, mechanics, issues—all of this should be tied constantly to the core of economics, the economic problem, and to the purposes for which men build economic systems.

A student—a citizen—who comes to possess economic understanding will move in his consideration of public economic issues with confidence and purpose from the central core, the starting point, home base. He will know his way around and his way home. He will have a working sense of the interrelationship of economic phenomena, the "oneness" of the economy, and the tie-in between each sector of the economy and the whole, and between the economy and himself.

He will face such choices as those between alternative satisfactions, between present and future goods, between alternative methods of production, between production and leisure, between stability and security and innovation and progress, and between economizing by the market and economizing by government, under whatever conditions and guises these choices may appear, with awareness and a balanced sense of consequences.

He will know that products come from production and will have an appreciation of the contribution made by diverse groups to the totality of production.

Familiarity with the mechanics of economics will not blind him to the reality that the operating forces in any political economy are human. He will know that economic life involves, essentially, the rational living together of human beings—a constant adjustment and readjustment in economic matters comparable to, indeed a part of, the constant adjustment and readjustment that characterize the total business of living together. He will realize that these adjustments frequently bring discomfort, even pain, to those established (vested) interests which are required to adjust, but that failure of one group to adjust may mean privation for other groups and stagnation for the economy as a whole. And he will relate this to situations in which his own interest lies in resistance to change (tariff, price supports, "fair trade," "featherbedding") as well as to those in which his own interest would be served by the adjustment of others.

He will distinguish between areas where "scientific" economic answers are possible, areas where such answers are impossible because necessary information or data are absent, and areas where only value judgments are called for and possible. He will realize that it is not the function of economics to provide answers to ethical or value problems but, rather, to help to define and identify such problems and to place them in sharper focus.

Finally, his realization that, in the very nature of the case, economic problems permit of very few "right" answers will be one measure of the depth of his economic understanding—and the realization will fill him with a sense not of futility but of purpose. It will point up for him his personal role in the political economy in which he lives.

This is what economic understanding can mean. This is what we would like to have for all of our people as members of a free, democratic society. We will never have all of it for everyone, but we cannot afford to seek and work for less in the schools.[5]

The Content of Economics in the Schools. If we want students to gain economic understanding, to what substantive content should they be exposed during their years in school? Except for a brief comment, I shall sidestep questions of the stages at which economics should be introduced into the curriculum, of courses in which it may be possible and salutary to introduce it—courses in "straight" economics, American history, civics, social studies, problems of democracy, business, consumer problems—and of methods of presentation. My reluctance to deal with these matters stems from a realization of my professional incompetence in this area, not from any notion that the area is unimportant. Indeed, I should like to reaffirm my conviction that in the development of economic understanding in the schools, the teaching process, in the hands of qualified teachers, is of pre-eminent importance. I am under no illusions on this score; I do not believe that the job of imparting understanding to the school population has been done —indeed, that it has been more than nicely started—by any formulation by professional economists of the content of economic understanding. The task of organizing and structuring and phasing and setting forth the essential content so that by the time the student has left the school—whether for a place in the productive economy or for further study—the content has become a working part of his understanding is as great as it is imperative. It calls for imagination, great skill, hard work —and, if you will permit me, economic understanding exhibited by the teacher, both substantively and in approach. Let me add one further thought: if economic understanding is to be derived as a valuable by-product from courses other than those in straight economics, the economics must be identified, and integrated explicitly, imaginatively, and with great care into the total body of material. Economic understanding lurks in these courses, but it is not likely to be captured by inadvertence.

Turning, then, to content, I can serve the subject no better than to set forth the findings of the National Task Force on Economic Education, findings which I helped to draw, and with which I am almost completely in agreement. If I had any misgivings at this point, they would be quieted by the fact that the findings are in line with all of the statements by economists on the content of economics in the schools that have come to my attention, and these statements, in turn, are in substantial agreement with each other. There is variety in trimmings, of course, but virtual unanimity on matters that count.[6] I shall be surprised if the recommendations of the Task Force do not find wide acceptance within the economics fraternity.

AN OVERVIEW OF THE ECONOMIC SYSTEM

> We urge that students be given a good overview of the way in which our economic system solves the big, basic economic problems:
>
> (1) *What* shall we produce with our productive resources;
>
> (2) *How much* can we produce in total and how fast shall the economy grow;
>
> (3) *Who* shall get the goods and services produced?
>
> These are the big questions faced by every economic system, be it capitalist, communist, or any other. What? How much? For whom?

What will be produced
How much will be produced?
How will it be produced
How shall it be distributed

It is important for students to realize that different economic systems solve these problems differently; that most economic systems are "mixed" in the way they set their goals and manage their resources, neither purely private enterprise nor purely socialist; and that most economic systems are constantly changing.

For our largely private enterprise economy, students need to understand (leaving government aside for the moment) that consumers' money demands largely determine what is produced. They should see that businessmen, in striving to make profits, try to produce those goods and services which consumers want; and try to do so at the lowest possible cost, in some cases also seeking to influence consumer demands through advertising and other selling activities. They should understand that businesses, in trying to maximize profits, draw productive resources (such as labor, land, and machinery) into those occupations where they will contribute most to meeting consumer demands; and that businesses simultaneously pay out incomes to workers, land-owners, and other suppliers of productive services. These incomes, in turn, make it possible for consumers to buy the goods they want. Students should see, therefore, that markets, in which prices rise and fall in response to changing demands and supplies, provide the links which mesh together consumers and businesses, each seeking to make the best of his own position and abilities, into a working system. They should recognize that when individuals and businesses save part of their income and invest those savings in new productive facilities, this increases society's capacity to produce in future periods.

In understanding the operations of our economy, it is important for students to see that individual freedom of choice is central to our "private enterprise way." But they also need to understand that these individual freedoms, of the consumer and of the businessmen, are limited by laws and by social and moral pressures, for the protection of the individual and society. Thus, markets and prices, reflecting shifting demand and supply conditions, are the main regulator of the allocation of scarce resources into the production of the most desired goods and services; but governments set the rules under which competition takes place and sometimes participate actively in the processes of production and distribution.

In suggesting the areas of understanding that seem to us essential within this broad overview, we have organized them under four main heads in the full report. Here we merely suggest some of the main problems and concepts under these same four heads. Throughout, it is a few simple analytical concepts, a few major economic institutions, and the main economic relationships that students need to grasp—not an elaborate set of technical terms, abstract theory, or detailed masses of factual information.

WHAT DOES THE ECONOMY PRODUCE, AND HOW?

The main framework of the market system, through which consumer demands largely determine what is produced, was outlined above. Students need to understand the interaction of supply, demand, and prices in markets. They need to recognize the crucial role played by profits, both as an incentive to businessmen to produce most efficiently what consumers want and as a source of funds for business investment. They need to understand that the benefits from individual and business economic self-interest accrue to society as a whole only when reasonably active competition prevails. They need to understand something of the structure and financial arrangements of the modern corporation.

Governments directly control how we use a substantial portion of our productive resources—through collecting taxes and providing highways, schools, national defense, general government, and many other services. Governments also provide many of the "rules of the game" within which the private sector of the economy operates. Students need to think through how much they want government to do in both these capacities.

The international scene provides another big area of major importance. In the world of today, students should understand that the basic case for division of labor and exchange of the resulting products is the same internationally as within the nation—that with specialization and exchange a larger total quantity of wanted goods and services can be produced with any given supply of productive resources. They should understand something of the financial arrangements surrounding foreign trade—especially the balance of payments—and should consider some of the arguments for and against tariffs and other restrictive devices which attempt to obtain special trade advantages for individual countries.

ECONOMIC GROWTH AND STABILITY

Turning to the problem of economic growth and stability (*how much*), students should see that many of our greatest economic problems center around how to obtain stable economic growth, avoiding the excesses of inflationary booms and of depressions. Here, as in the analysis of the market system, they need to understand the big but relatively simple analytical concepts and relationships. The upper limit to an economy's real output at any time is set by its stock of productive resources and the technology for using those resources. But the level of total output depends also upon the amount of total spending (effective demand) in our profit-motivated system, and this total spending sometimes exceeds and sometimes falls short of the level needed for stable economic growth. When this occurs, the result is inflation or recession and unemployment. In understanding growth and fluctuations of the economy, they need to see that consumers, business firms, and governments comprise the three major groups of buyers in our economy, and to understand something of the motives and patterns of spending of each of these three major groups.

Here again it is important for students to examine the role of government—to recognize that government budget surpluses can decrease total (government plus private) spending, and that government budget deficits can increase total spending. Government taxes and expenditures thus provide one mechanism for influencing the level of income, employment and prices in the economy. The resulting fluctuations in the size of the national debt also need to be recognized and examined.

To understand changes in aggregate spending, it is necessary also to understand the role of money in our system. Our money supply depends importantly on the lending and investing operations of commercial banks, which are controlled in part by the Federal Reserve System. Here, as in other highly technical areas, it is unrealistic to expect high school students to delve deeply, but a broad understanding is feasible. It is essential that students understand roughly the process by which the money supply is controlled through private and governmental decisions in our society.

Lastly, the rate of economic growth (in output per capita) has become a vital economic issue—in the United States and especially in the underdeveloped economies which are striving to raise their living standards above the poverty level. Students need to understand the basic factors determining growth rates in such different types of economies.

THE DISTRIBUTION OF INCOME

On the third big economic question—who shall receive the goods and services the economy produces—it is important for students to see that the market mechanism largely gives the answer in our economy, modified significantly by government regulations and by government taxes and expenditures. People receive incomes mainly as payments for the productive services they render and for which employers are willing to pay them, given consumer demands for the final products. These incomes are paid both for personal services and for the use of accumulated (sometimes inherited) capital. Students should understand that high American wages rest fundamentally on the high productivity of American labor, and that this productivity arises both from the activities of workers themselves and from the accumulation of capital and technological and managerial advance. They should know something about the incomes different groups of people receive in our society, and should understand that struggles over income shares are one of the most vigorous and continuing of our economic problems.

In this connection, the history and actions of American labor unions in trying to improve the position of workers provide an excellent opportunity to study this issue of income distribution. The "farm problem," the "social security problem," and other current economic issues offer similar opportunities for the application of fundamental economic analysis to major social problems at an elementary level.

COMPARISON OF ECONOMIC SYSTEMS

Finally, we believe that every informed American should have a general impression of how other types of economic systems operate, especially communism. Fear of dealing with controversial subjects should not be permitted to exclude objective discussion of this topic from the classroom. The same broad questions—what, how much, and for whom—provide a framework for comparing alternative systems with ours.

IMPORTANCE OF ANALYTICAL CONCEPTS AND INSTITUTIONS

These paragraphs provide only the most sketchy outline of the economic understanding needed for effective citizenship. They are intended to rough in a broad picture, not to provide in any sense a precise statement of what students should know. As with any such rough outline, much is omitted. But the understanding we propose does not require complex, elaborate concepts and theories. On the contrary, what is needed is an understanding of a few essential concepts and a few major economic institutions (such as the market place, supply and demand, the corporation, labor unions, profits, wages, and the like), plus an understanding of how these fit together in the functioning of our economy.

THE IMPORTANCE OF STUDENT ANALYSIS

Lastly, we emphasize the importance of teaching that leads students to examine and think through major economic

> problems for themselves. We recognize that many high school students lack the maturity and full understanding required to do a good job of reaching their own conclusions on complex economic issues. But these are the young men and women who will soon be the citizens of tomorrow. Unless they are given the opportunity for this kind of economic analysis under objective and sympathetic guidance in the schools, we have little right to hope that they will be able to reach reasoned conclusions on their own as they vote and live in our free democratic society.[7]

This, I believe, is the content of economics that can and should be taught in the schools. I should like to make it abundantly clear that, in common with the other members of the Task Force, I look upon the Task Force Report as furnishing guidelines. It does not purport to be a textbook. It offers the content of economic understanding, but with the full realization that only under very favorable conditions will it be possible to achieve in the fullest sense all that is set forth. What is offered is the meat; its preparation and service—in whatever amount, in whatever form, and in whatever style—is for the schools (and the gods) to determine. Let me make one point crystal clear: economics in the schools must not be conceived of as a watered-down, thinned-out version of economics in the colleges. Economics for the schools is economics *for the schools!* It may properly be thinner than economics for the colleges only in the sense that it may be "leaner" (and "wirier"?), not thinner by dilution.*

In finding and charting their way through economics in the schools I should hope that students might gain a systematic overview—a sense of the total task of an economy—and that they would come to know and to use profitably a few essential

* Cf. R. A. Gordon, *Economists and Economic Education,* Joint Council on Economic Education, 1961: "A superficial reader's first impression may be that the Task Force has merely summarized what is in the standard sort of college textbook in elementary economics. I hope that a more careful reading will dispel this impression."

concepts and tools of economic analysis: markets, margins, opportunity cost, and the like. I should hope that they would experience the pain and the satisfaction of bringing their best intellectual equipment and ways of work to bear on controversial, emotion-rousing issues. I cherish for them an adventure conceived and conducted with such insight and skill and in such a spirit that they will be brought as fully as may be into the true fellowship of active, productive workers in our democratic political economy.

One final point on content, for clarification and caution. Economics is concerned with many things that concern businessmen and consumers, and the study of economics embraces many matters that also are treated in courses in business and consumer problems. An understanding of the economy and of economic forces clearly calls for an understanding of business institutions and behavior, and of the behavior of consumers. In some measure, at least, businessmen and consumers will operate more intelligently and rewardingly if their decisions are made within a framework of broad economic understanding. But, the activities of businessmen and consumers are only a part of the over-all economic scene. The boundaries of business and of consumption are not coterminous with the boundaries of economics, and the arts of business and of buying do not constitute the science of economics. There are, of course, areas where the rational functioning of the total economy and the rational ordering of his own personal economic affairs by each individual seeking his own greatest gain or satisfaction within the framework of the market tend, operationally, to coalesce, and where, hence, it is easy to picture economics as undertaking to uncover rules and to provide precepts for individuals to follow in business and consumer situations. The picture is an illusion. The discipline of economics, contrary to a rather widely spread impression, is not to be equated with the art of running a business or of behaving wisely in the market; and economic understanding is far different from knowledge about how to make and spend money. A man may be very shrewd in his personal dealings in these matters and still be sadly deficient in economic understanding.

Economics is a *social science,* its concerns are the concerns of society in the rational, intelligent functioning of society's economizing institutions and processes; and even in this context, of course, economics is not concerned to offer kits of "answers" to public problems, or rules, precepts, or advice on "correct" or "wise" behavior by individuals as citizens, or by governments. And, most certainly, rules and precepts and advice about the use of credit facilities, and installment buying, and insurance, and when to buy or rent, and when to get into or out of the market are not to be accepted as economics or in lieu of economics.

I hasten to acknowledge a working relationship, and to insist that courses in business and in consumer problems offer a splendid opportunity for the development of a measure of economic understanding, and that economics can be helpful indeed in accomplishing the objectives of these courses. Nonetheless, the school curriculum that offers work in consumer problems and business does not thereby satisfy the claims that arise from society's need for economic understanding. I must emphasize that I am not addressing myself here, even by inference, to the merits of courses in consumer problems and business, or to their place in school curricula. I have no quarrel with these except as they may be passed off or accepted as "economics." I am speaking solely about the *content of economics for economic understanding,* and my point is that its specifications are not met by the content of consumer problem and business courses.

Content Objectives Other Than Responsible Citizenship. This is the time to return briefly to tie up a package that I left prominently displayed but loosely wrapped at the beginning of this piece—the proposition that economics taught for responsible citizenship will serve fully all other important objectives that economics is suited to serve. A case certainly can be made for the study of economics, and hence for setting its objective and molding its content in the curriculum, to serve the purposes of culture and of intellectual facility and growth; and, as we have just reminded ourselves, economic understanding is not without its bearing upon the rewarding pursuit of business and consumer activities. The science of economics can easily find its justification and make its stand on cultural grounds—the sheer satisfaction that can come to the fully "educated man," who knows and understands, and who is intellectually at home in the midst of the crosscurrents and forces at work in the world in which he lives, whether his economic interests and reliance are mainly in the market or in the political-economic process—whether or not his inclinations are to adjust to, rather than to adjust, his world. It may be pushing the claims of economics too far to assert that for most people economics is fun, but it is entirely supportable that the world of economics can be exciting indeed to anyone interested in human cogs and wheels, and in what makes them go round—even though, at least at the outset, he has no idea of doing anything about any of it.

It seems clear, as well, that economic understanding is itself an instrument of intellectual growth. The processes by which economic understanding is gained make their own contribution to intellectual growth in the individual; and there is cross-fertilization, at levels both of process and content, between economics and other disciplines that are concerned with human behavior and which carry on their work in the scientific tradition. We might very well gear economics in the schools to culture and to intellectual growth.

I am convinced, however, that we encompass the objective of economics for culture and for intellectual growth when we build our economics offerings to meet the demands of responsible citizenship. The patterns are virtually identical, there is no conflict and there are no significant gaps in coverage. An economics designed to produce the economic understanding required for responsible citizenship will do nicely across the board. Economics for citizenship means economics for understanding—for awareness, insight, grasp, confident concern, and a rational approach. Economics for culture and for intellectual growth also means economics for understanding —the same kind of understanding.

Let me suggest a synthesis. My plea is for an economic understanding that will work to sustain and strengthen democracy, not only because of the better economic world that will result, but also (and principally) because in the very practice of government by the governed, the lives of all who participate will be made fuller and richer. I am not millennium-eyed about the material results; we will not reach political-economic perfection under any system—certainly not under democracy. But, we will do well; the material satisfactions we can enjoy under democracy are well worth human aspiration and effort. But more, much more, is to be had: *in the very process of working together for the attainment of the goals we seek, with understanding and with responsibility in all of us for the outcome, we will embrace the greatest good of all.* This is the way men of understanding *can* live. If I may be permitted a value judgment, this is the way men of understanding *should* live.

1. Ben W. Lewis, "Recent Developments in Economics," *Liberal Education,* May 1961, p. 255.
2. *Ibid.,* pp. 256–57.
3. Ben W. Lewis, "Economic Understanding: Why and What," *American Economic Review,* May 1957, pp. 653, 663.
4. *Summary of the Report of the National Task Force on Economic Education,* Sept. 1961, pp. 6–7.
5. Ben W. Lewis, "Economic Understanding: Why and What," *op. cit.,* pp. 668–69.

6. See, for example, Paul R. Olson, "This Is Economics in the Schools," *American Economic Review,* May 1961, p. 564; and Howard S. Ellis, "This Is Economics," *op. cit.,* p. 571.
7. *Summary of the Report of the National Task Force on Economic Education,* Sept. 1961, pp. 8–12. This summary statement is spelled out in greater detail in the full report of the Task Force, Chap. III.

Cultural Anthropology

Douglas Oliver / Harvard University

CULTURAL ANTHROPOLOGY (as distinguished from physical) is in one sense a residual category: as the subject is practiced and taught in this country it concerns many matters logically within the bounds of other disciplines—but largely ignored by them. It concerns, for example, the history of history-less peoples (including the prehistory of the more historical ones), the government of stateless communities, the economics of nonmarket economies, the social relations and languages of technologically simple societies, the aesthetics of "primitives." In my view the first step in devising a curriculum for the social studies in secondary schools would be to reassign these matters to their substantive contexts; for example, to treat nonpecuniary as well as pecuniary transactions when talking about economics, to discuss Eskimo legal norms as well as the English common law when treating social control.

Separating these topics from their logical disciplinary contexts and placing them all together under anthropology seems indefensible, on two grounds. First, there is implied in this separation a notion that written documents are the only legitimate kinds of evidence for reconstructing the past. And secondly, the separation promotes the attitude that the peoples studied by anthropologists are fundamentally different from those whose institutions are described in conventional economics and sociology and political science. This attitude is not only ethically pernicious but it tends to defeat efforts toward scientific generalizing.

Part One of this paper will consist of some suggestions concerning the kinds of anthropological data and concepts that could with profit be integrated into a social studies curriculum under the more conventional headings. The secondary school would seem to be the appropriate place for establishing these connections, for when the student reaches college he will be thrust into an institutional setting where the old arbitrary frontier lines are firmly set, save in a few general-education courses.

In addition to the above, there is another sense in which anthropology has a part to play in secondary education quite distinct from its role as a supplier of *pre*historical and *cross*-cultural data for the traditional social science disciplines; this will form the subject matter of Part Two of this paper.

Part One

HISTORY

1. At the outset of any presentation of history it would seem useful, in fact essential, to point out that human behaviors are continually changing—cyclically, contingently, and cumulatively. Individuals' habits change as they become older, although the way they change depends importantly upon their societies' different ways of conceptualizing those changes. Families and other kinds of groups have characteristic natural

history cycles—which of equrse vary from place to place. Whole societies undergo cyclical changes, including adjustments to such environmental changes as day and night or winter and summer, as well as to such arbitrary units as weeks and the like. Ethnographic literature is rich in examples of these kinds of cyclical changes, and might with profit be utilized in a social studies program to illustrate that history has its short-term regularities.)

Anthropology is also concerned with longer-range cycles, such as revitalization movements and almost rhythmic changes in fashion and art; some attention devoted to these phenomena would serve to emphasize similarities in ways of life every-

where.

But most of all, anthropologists have been preoccupied with very long-range cumulative change, as exemplified in such formulations as cultural evolution and diffusionism. Time devoted to these matters would have the advantage of broadening generalization beyond the scope ordinarily permitted by conventional courses in history. For example, an objective examination of the causes and sequences of cultural change would provide a context for contrasting and evaluating the various theories of history underlying so many competing political ideologies.

2. Inasmuch as most American children begin to learn about cave men and Aztecs and the like as early as kindergarten it would appear unnecessary to devote much time to straight description of such ways of life in a crowded high school social studies program. On the other hand, there are certain particularly crucial eras of prehistory that deserve fuller treatment, not only because of their intrinsic interest but because of their more general implications for the understand-

ing of human life.

One of these concerns the developments that comprised the transformation from *hominoid* to *hominid*, from an occasionally tool-using precursor of both man and apes to an

Study of Ojibwa Indians (see p. 100

in Crusial

habitual tool-making man-ape. I refer here to developments in South and East Africa involving the well-known australopithecines, some half to a quarter million years ago. I shall return to this subject in Part Two.

The second era of prehistory that deserves special treatment is that of the beginnings of food growing and animal domestication, now believed by archaeologists to have started first of all some 10,000 years ago in the highlands bordering the Fertile Crescent.

And finally, some consideration should be given to the peopling of the Western Hemisphere out of Asia, and to the development of cultivation in the New World. In addition to the intrinsic interest this may have for young Americans there is the lesson contained in the fact that New World civilization, including its technological bases, was almost wholly an independent development.

In addition to these matters of substantive history, I suggest that one of the most effective ways in which to fix the past in the student's memory is to provide him with some insight into the way anthropological historians—in this case, archaeologists and ethnologists—actually go about gathering and interpreting data (for example, the techniques of stratigraphic archaeology, of tree-ring and carbon-fourteen dating, of glottochronology, and of ethnological reconstruction).

SOCIOLOGY

Before any student is presented with data on human society I feel that he should be made aware of the fact that social life is not a peculiarity of humans, that there are few species of animals characteristically *a*social, that in fact there are societies even more "social" than those of humans—like those of termites, or starlings. A closer look into the social relations, say, of bees and of gibbons would provide a more general background for teaching about human social relations, and would at the same time encourage receptivity for a view of life less restricted by notions of discontinuities.

As a corollary to the above, I feel that the student should be made aware of the fact that language as a form of social communication is not limited to human interaction.[1]

3. Every high school student will of course know that his own community's social institutions are not universal—that different societies have different forms of families, religious congregations, etc. In my view, however, this more or less vague awareness of differences should be filled in with more detailed cross-cultural considerations of two or three institutions whose local forms will be familiar to all students. Such, for example, as the custom of marriage. Or possibly even more appropriate would be a survey of the wide differences among societies in the ways their members recognize, conceptualize, institutionalize, and ritualize an individual's life cycle, from social birth to social extinction—the former often does not correspond with physiological birth, and the latter may precede physiological death by a number of years, or it may even never take place.

4. Through a kind of tacit division of labor, sociologists have tended to leave to anthropologists and psychologists matters relating to an individual's socialization; but surely even a minimal treatment of social institutions should make some reference to this subject. And the anthropologist can only urge that if treated at all the subject ought to be presented in a broadly cross-cultural manner.

POLITICAL SCIENCE course:

students are taught → No community is anarchic; all have some form of government, comprising concerted action by all or most full-fledged citizens. Some such actions may be based entirely on customary procedures—as in the case of a governor's Thanksgiving Proclamation; but even in societies without governors there will always be found to be some situations requiring decision making by certain legitimatized role-holders. The scope and domain of government differs widely from society to society, as does the degree of centralization of governmental authority. All this being so, it would seem desirable for students to be made aware of these circumstances, both for a better understanding of society at large, and for a clearer perspective about their own form of government.

A similar point deserves to be made on the subject of law, to the effect that no human society lives under the so-called automatic sway of custom. Every society known to anthropologists possesses some rules that are backed up by *coercive* sanctions exercised by legitimate, by publicly acknowledged, officials. Societies differ widely with respect to the kinds of behavior subject to officially sanctioned laws; but some behavior will be found to be subject to such rules. Moreover, wherever they have looked, anthropologists have succeeded in identifying analogues, however informal, to our own judicial processes.

ECONOMICS

The economist preparing a curriculum for secondary schools will rightly insist upon a rigid definition of his subject matter, both in terms of the kind of transactions dealt with and the kinds of assumptions made about such behavior. But in addition the student should be made aware of two other facts:

- Many valued objects and services in our society circulate in ways quite different from those treated by economics.
- There are many societies throughout the world in which the institution of the price-fixing market simply does not exist, but in which, nevertheless, valued objects and services circulate widely and more or less efficiently.

Part Two

Now, to consider the respects in which anthropology may enrich the social-studies curriculum not merely as a purveyor of data and theory to the other disciplines but as a contributor of the special kinds of facts and points of view implicit in its label as the generalizing science about *all* varieties and *all* aspects of mankind. These data and points of view have to do with the following:

The structure and function of the behavior systems comprising human societies

The connections between biological make-up of human beings and their habitual behavior systems

These are large and fundamental matters. They are also all too arcane, partly because of the confusion that reigns concerning some of their most basic terms. Since some of these terms are also basic to all other social studies as well, it would seem highly desirable for curriculum makers to agree upon some common usages at the outset, in an effort to reduce the many disagreements, misunderstandings, and reifications that keep social studies from becoming social sciences. It is in this spirit that I propose the following attempt at clarification.

I propose to call the smallest unit in this set of terms a *habit*, i.e., an habitual (as contrasted with a random, nonrepetitive) behavior. Examples of such habits are: regularly holding the hand in front of the face while sneezing, addressing one's male parent as "Father," habitually putting fertilizer on a new garden, and so on. For certain purposes it may be useful to break down each of these behaviors into smaller units; for instance, dividing "father" into its constituent phonemes for linguistic analysis, or describing what kind of fertilizer and how it is applied; but such distinctions are not important for present purposes of illustration.

The writer differs from many anthropologists in choosing to use the word *habit* rather than the more specific *custom;* this usage avoids the pitfall of prejudging whether the behavior is in fact inherited or learned—a discovery that can only be reached in some instances after careful research. A habit, either inherited or learned, refers to the habitual behavior of a single individual or to the identical shared habitual behavior of any aggregate of individuals: groups (a family, a work team); biological categories (females, children); activity categories (priests, canoe builders); social categories (a class, a caste); a whole community, tribe, nation, set of nations; or, to all mankind.

Continuing, I find it essential to distinguish three kinds of habits: historical, suppositional, and normative. *Historical* habitual behaviors are those known to have actually taken place. *Suppositions* comprise the opinions, believed in but unproved, which people hold concerning the occurrence of habits—including myths, fantasies, etc. *Norms,* of course, refer to the ideas people have concerning what habits there ought (or ought not) to be, including desired goals or end states of action, and desirable ways of reaching such goals.

One can, for example, speak of an actual, *historically* observed ceremony; or a cosmological *supposition*—a belief about the origin of life; or an aesthetic *norm*—what color a basket ought to be. Suppositions and norms follow the same kind of distribution as historical habits; i.e., some may be held by a single person, some by particular classes or groups of persons, and some by practically the whole community—or by whole nations, or by all mankind, for that matter. Moreover, while some suppositions and norms may be overt, explicit—church creeds, popular myths, codified laws—others are covert, implicit, or even unconscious—requiring the keenest of analytic insights to discover and formulate.

So much for basic terms.*

* We believe this scheme of references has the analytical advantage of denotation and flexibility through its use of a single root term (habit) and a number of independent modifiers. It can also be applied up to a point to the behavior of *all* organisms, thereby permitting wider comparative usage and avoiding the kinds of terminological cul-de-sac involved in some anthropological uses of the word *culture* (for example, "humans have it; other animals don't"). Termites have habits that are apparently mostly inherited and shared with many or with all other termites. It is unlikely that termites are "aware" of what we call supposi-

FUNCTION AND STRUCTURE

In my experience as a teacher, most young people by the time they reach college have heard of, and frequently talk about, such things as cultural *patterns*, political *systems*, and the like. Unfortunately their notions about these phrases are no more precise than they are about *relativity*. In fact, many such terms and phrases have for them a quality of mysticism or reification that greatly impedes learning. I feel therefore that it would be appropriate, and by no means unfeasible, for the secondary school social studies curriculum to devote some time to the subjects of function and structure as they relate to human habits. There follows a sample of anthropological thinking on these subjects, which might be of some use in planning a curriculum.

Anthropological usage of the concept of function is analogous to the mathematic $x=fy$ in its simplest expression; namely, some change in x results in some change in y, and vice versa. If, for instance, the use of stone axes is superseded by the use of steel ones this change will result in other changes —in technology generally, in social structure, and perhaps even in religious ideology. Or, a change in religious ideology may result in changes in technology, in social structure, and so on. There is certainly nothing new or "anthropological" about this notion; anthropologists have simply been at pains to exemplify it rather than speculate or dogmatize about it, a task greatly simplified by the small sizes of the communities they usually investigate. We are now in possession of numerous studies that demonstrate the general validity of this very general concept of functionalism; but along with this has come

---

tions and norms; but we cannot rule out the possibility, say, of a band of gibbons having such awareness; and it can no longer be denied that gibbons, like many other animal species, have *learned* habits, including perhaps some that are shared, more or less distinctively, by separate communities of them.

the realization that the degree of its applicability varies widely. In some places and times a new kind of tool or idea or technique may revolutionize social structure and cosmology; in others it may do nothing of the sort. The question of degree must always remain a matter for investigation. And in this connection, anthropologists are only beginning to tackle the much more demanding problems of functional analysis expressed in the formulae: x varies directly (or conversely) with y; or x is a *specific* function of y.

Structural statements about habits have to do with their combination, and with similarities between one set of combinations and another.

In most American communities, for example, the marriage of a young bachelor and girl usually consists of the following combinations of habits: announcement of engagement, complete with ring; gift showers for the bride; stag dinner for the groom; nuptial ceremony; reception with cake cutting; escape with feigned chase; honeymoon. (These habits could of course be broken down into smaller elements if desired for finer analysis.) An important characteristic of this combination is that the elements (habits) must take place in fixed sequence.

In many instances statements about habit combinations emphasize less the fixed temporal *sequences* of events than the connections between, say, beliefs, events, settings, paraphernalia—as between Roman Catholicism (one combination of habitual ways of thinking, acting, feeling) in contrast with, say, Shintoism.

Anthropologists call such combinations by various terms: culture patterns, culture complexes, trait complexes, institutions, and so on; but since anthropologists do not share the same habit in this matter (!) it behooves the reader of anthropological writings to ascertain in every case just how such terms are defined.

The search for *structure* does not end here. Efforts are constantly being made to discover combinations of combinations, to learn whether there appears to be any fixed connection between, say, cereal agriculture, village-type settlement, matrilocal extended families, polytheism, and geometric art designs. (Research suggests that this particular combination of combinations is met with less frequently than, for instance, pastoralism, transhumance, patrilineal clans, monotheism, and epic poetry.) The fixity, through time, of such combinations of combinations—or *configurations,* as they are sometimes called—require explanation, which is usually given in *functional* terms already discussed.

In some anthropological writings on the structural relations among habits one comes across the phrase *strain toward consistency*, which implies among other things a steady obsolescence of habits that do not " fit together." This tendency is seen by some writers to have developed so far in some communities that they apply words like Apollonian or Dionysian to summarize a whole *way of life*. More modest and considerably more successful efforts in this direction are concerned with *themes* or *basic orientations.*

Another way in which *structure* has entered into anthropological discussions of habits is that concerned with the degree of congruence, the "fit" between historical habits and suppositions and norms. Marked absence of "fit" in this regard is said by some writers to reveal that the way of life is undergoing radical change.

One aspect of *structure* that deserves a place in a social studies curriculum is that concerned with the connections between a people's language and their other sets of habits, particularly their suppositions. As one anthropologist put it, "Every language is also a special way of looking at the world and interpreting experiences. Concealed in the structure of each different language are a whole set of unconscious assumptions about the world and life in it."[2] While this so-called *metalinguistic* approach is not an easy one to grasp or to teach, my experience indicates that with careful presentation it can leave students with one of their most vivid and lasting notions about human behavior.

While on the subject of *structure* I suggest that those in charge of preparing a social studies curriculum for the secondary schools take special pains to clarify their usage of the seductive but troublesome word *culture.* Anthropologists themselves differ considerably in their usage of this, their most distinctive term. Most commonly, reference in theoretical writings is to learned habits shared by members of whole societies; but within this broad definition there are many different usages. Writers differ concerning the level of reality of the habits included in their usage of *culture*—some including all levels, others only normative, or normative and suppositional. Others differ over the loci of reference—some refer only to those habits or combinations of habits distinctive of the communities studied, others include *all* habits shared by the communities in question, including their universal habits as well. Again, some writers would include under *culture* not only habits but the material products of such habits—not only the method of shaping an arrowhead but the arrowhead itself (i.e., material culture).

In most such usages the habits listed under the term *culture* are implicatively *learned* ones. This may be a perfectly reasonable assumption in the case, say, of most steps in the process of pottery making or divination; but what about such habit combinations as scapegoating or courtship? If *culture* is to refer only to learned habits, then one must be certain that a habit does in fact belong in this class before so labeling it —a decision not always easy to make.

One of the most common usages is the *culture area,* referring to the traits (habits and habit products) or combinations of traits distinctive of whole geographic areas of various sizes; as, for example, the Plains Indian culture area, consisting of buffalo hunting, use of horse, clothing and dwelling made of hides, geometric design, warriors' associations.

No one can legitimately object to variation in usage of *culture* for general purposes of indicating a whole range of phenomena; but anthropology has reached a point of development at which sharper terminological tools are needed. Also the word *culture* has become so central in anthropological discussion that it sometimes becomes a distinctive, almost substantial "thing" that students attempt to describe and analyze and explain.

BIOLOGY AND BEHAVIOR

Faith is one thing; blind faith quite another. I take it to be one of the objectives of our educational system to remove the blindness so that citizens' convictions may be arrived at rationally, on the basis of fullest available knowledge. In this connection, there are probably few areas of thought so dominated by myth as that concerned with connections between man's anatomical-physiological nature and his habitual ways of thinking, feeling, and acting. It is probably safe to say that every person past infancy has views about this connection—views that underlie religious, political, social, even aesthetic attitudes; it is probably just as safe to assert that most such views are based on half truth and myth. The character of this connection is a central concern of anthropology—perhaps *the* central concern—and its views on the matter constitute one of the principal contributions anthropology can make to a program of social studies in the secondary schools.

There are numerous facets to this subject, but consideration of three of them will suffice for present purposes. One of these concerns the *biological imperatives* involved in all forms of human social life. Another concerns the kinds and degrees of interdependence between body and behavior as revealed in the evolutionary record. The third concerns the corollary matter of *race*.

1. No conception of mankind, however soaring and "spiritual," can ignore the fact of his irreduceable physiological needs

—for certain kinds and quantities of food, for water, for air, for evacuation, for rest, and for avoidance of extreme heat or cold and of extreme pain and injury. There is also accumulating evidence in support of the theory that extreme or continuous anxiety may destroy the healthy functioning of the human organism.

It is abundantly clear that the individual erect, featherless biped cannot become *human* save in interaction with other humans; that is to say, many and perhaps most of the habits that distinguish a human from other animals have to be learned from other humans. This being so, it is probably safe to add that most of *Homo sapiens* could not even survive without such humanization—so short are they in the instincts and physical strengths that help other animals to survive.

In this connection, there may well be some distinctively *human* psychological processes—ways of perceiving, generalizing, etc.—quite apart from, and prerequisite to, other and more specific kinds of human habits; but isolating these involves methodological difficulties of great complexity. The question of the so-called *drives* is also complex. Some writers have attempted to account for many features of human activity in terms of individual and sexual differences in dominance drives, but most such attempts end in tautology. The case with sexual activity is somewhat clearer. There can be no question about the existence of a sexual drive, but an individual's physiological survival does not necessarily require its satisfaction, however important it may be for the continuity of the species.

And finally, given all the above—including the indispensable fact of human *sociality*—all societies of humans must develop habitual adjustments to the coexistence of male and female, of neighbor and stranger, and of older and young, including the presence of helpless infants and senile elders. No human community can ignore these situations, and all of them reveal some similarities in dealing with them. Some of these similarities are also shared with communities of other animals, but some are distinctively human.

2. The most telling evidence for the interdependence of body and behavior in mankind's evolutionary past has been discovered in East and South Africa, in geological contexts dating some half million years ago. It is there that archaeologists have found skeletal remains of creatures with ape-sized brain cases but with pelves adapted to bipedal locomotion. Also these hominid australopithecines had smaller canine teeth —with concomitant changes in the direction of more manlike faces, jaws, and skull, which suggests that they no longer depended upon their teeth and jaws for attack and defense. A plausible explanation for the change is that these African hominids had begun to make and use *tools*—not as exceptional solutions to exceptional problems, as individual apes occasionally do, but as common and *habitual* behaviors. Support for this explanation has now come to light; pebble tools, crude but undeniably shaped by or for constant use, have been found in direct association with these African hominid remains. Also, numerous broken bones of small animals have been found associated with these creatures, suggesting that they augmented their diet of wild-plant foods with some meat. It seems quite clear that these hominids, despite their small brains, were well along on the road to the condition we call human.

Our next glimpse of human evolution comes from the Middle Pleistocene epoch. Skeletal evidence from Java, China, Southwest Europe, and Northwest Africa shows the existence of hominids with much larger brains, greatly reduced masticatory apparatuses, and near-human locomotion. Although intermediate forms are still lacking, some specialists infer that these late hominids were evolved from the African hominids, some of whom probably dispersed into other habitable parts of the Eastern Hemisphere after the retreat northwards of the Pleistocene's first major glaciation. By this time the crude pebble-tool industry had developed in two directions: a very slow-changing chopping-tool tradition associated with East and Southeast Asian forms; and relatively fast-developing hand-ax, flake, and blade traditions found in Africa and Europe. Other evidence from this same epoch points to the unsuccessful hunting of large game animals for food and to the use of fire, possibly for the cooking of food.

Slow as these changes may appear from the vantage point of today, they marked an extraordinary acceleration over the pace of previous epochs in terms of both physical evolution and of subsistence techniques. And the explanation for this acceleration probably lies in the word *both*. With the evidence now available it is not possible to say which was the more crucial behavior: more bipedal locomotion or more use and manufacture of tools. But once the interdependence and the selective advantage of these behaviors had become established, subsequent developments seem to us today to be irreversible. Forelimbs freed from walking and clinging became more specialized and skillful in the making and using of tools, leading to an increase in the size and complexity of that part of the brain governing the use of these forelimbs, made possible, in turn, by a release in pressures upon the brain case through the reduction of those muscles operating the progressively smaller jaws. The invention of cooking may have speeded up this development, by tenderizing food and reducing mastication.

This is about as far as one can extend the reconstruction on the basis of direct evidence from bone and stone and signs of fire, but it is far enough to demonstrate the interdependence of the hominid's body and his habits in the evolutionary process. Beyond this, it is not unreasonable to infer that successful hunting of the larger game required new kinds of social ties, involving new forms of communication—all of which would necessitate still larger and more complex brains.

In time, the kinds of selective pressures favoring the survival and reproduction of this or that physical mutation were greatly reduced as human societies improved their control over the physical environment (including other animals). In other words, for a few tens of thousand years habitual behaviors may have slowed down cumulative physical change. But recently the situation appears to have taken a new turn, involving a different kind of connection between body and behavior. As a result of an increase in ionizing radiation from industrial and military activities, mutation rate appears destined to accelerate. Meanwhile, although *natural* selection continues to operate, it is qualified by *social* selection and subject to increasing limitation by societies' protective measures, which promote the survival of genes, including deleterious ones, that might otherwise not be reproduced.

3. And finally we turn to the matter of *race*, which demands a large share of attention in any curriculum aimed at encouraging attitudes essential not only for domestic social health but even for national survival. In view of the importance of this subject for citizenship education—that is, for secondary school treatment—I offer the following summary of points around which instruction might be organized.

All erect, bipedal primate populations—that is, all humans—now inhabiting the earth appear to have the capability of interbreeding; in other words, they constitute the same species, and as such they differ markedly in many respects from all other anthropoids: in size and shape of bones and teeth, in form of body covering, etc. Placed side by side with, say, a chimpanzee or a monkey, all humans look and act remarkably alike. (The contrast would of course seem much less striking if the intervening forms were arranged in evolutionary sequence between these extremes, but such forms are now extinct.) No one can however deny that humans also differ physically among themselves. Place an African pygmy beside a fat blond Swede and a lanky citizen of Peking, and no person in his right mind can deny their differences; even arranging numerous intervening forms between these extreme types—and such forms could easily be found from among the living population—cannot obscure these differences. The arguments swirling around the subject of *race* have to do with the definition, the causes, and the consequences of these differences.

Pick up almost any history book or newspaper and one will find statements about, say, "the English (or Chinese) race" or "the dark (or white) races" or "the backward races." On the surface there is nothing wrong about some of these popular usages except their lack of precision—it being more informative to speak of "the English nation" or "Chinese-speaking peoples" or "technologically primitive societies." But none save the most naïvely zealous anthropologist believes himself capable of reforming popular language. All one can do is insist that when anthropologists now use the word *race* they refer to people sharing certain biological characteristics.

Physical characteristics in humans, as in all living organisms, are controlled in part by genetic structures within the organism and in part by environmental factors acting upon the organism. Race has to do with those physical characteristics controlled by the former; specifically, "a *race* is a population sharing a distinctive combination of physical traits that are the result of distinctive genetic combination."[3]

Unfortunately there is a considerable disagreement among anthropologists concerning where to draw boundaries and what traits to stress in setting up their schemes of racial classification. Some insist that distinctions be based only on genetic constitution (i.e., the *genotype*). Others continue to classify mankind on the basis of measurement and sorting of external features (i.e., the *phenotype*). The genotypists have biological logic on their side, but can deal only with the minute number of gene patterns for which inheritance laws have been demonstrated (e.g., blood groups, ability to taste phenylthiocarbamide). The phenotypists base their classifications on such criteria as skin color and hair form, body shapes and sizes, which are assumed to reflect genetic constitution despite complications standing in the way of proof. Because of the personal element involved in judgments of the latter they often differ on what criteria to stress, with the result that there are many different schemes of race classification, some containing as few as three major races (Mongoloid, Negroid, and White), others as many as ten or more.

We shall summarize here one recent scheme of race classification, while adding the caution that future discoveries of fossils and future developments in human genetics will almost certainly require some changes in this formulation.[4] This scheme postulates seven major races: Early Mongoloid (typified by American Indians), Late Mongoloid (typified by northern and eastern Asians and by Eskimos), Negro, Bushmen (the short, yellow-skinned, pepper-corn-hair peoples now inhabiting the deserts of Southwest Africa), Australian (the dark-skinned but wavy-haired Aborigines), Pygmy Negroids, and White. In connection with this or similar schemes of man's racial characteristics it should be borne in mind that during the last ten millennia the total number of humans has increased about five hundred fold, resulting in extensive "racial" interbreeding and a universal blurring of race boundaries that will probably continue to accelerate.

It is not yet known whether contemporary mankind evolved from one or from several of the major varieties of hominids living during the middle and late glacial epochs, but it is certain that dissimilarities among the present races of *Homo sapiens* involve differences in total genetic composition of ten per cent or less. The important question concerns the meanings to be attached to these differences; it is probably safe to say that this is one of the most fateful questions facing the world today. At one extreme are the answers provided by such doctrines as Nordic supremacy, anti-Semiticism, and Apartheid—here and abroad; these doctrines themselves have proved calamitous enough, and violent reactions to them may prove just as calamitous. At the other extreme are those who would deny the biological reality of race differences in order to refute the evil sociological fictions about them.

Certain modern races may resemble the older hominids more closely than others in specific features, but averaging out such resemblances leads to the conclusion that no modern race is, overall, more physically *archaic* than another. To some Europeans, blond hair and straight thin noses may be aesthetically more pleasing than woolly brown hair and flat broad noses; but it must be kept in mind that with most Africans the reverse is probably true. To call one variant of a physical trait better than another invites the query, *Better for what?*

Natural selection has unquestionably played a part in race differentiation—heavily pigmented skin, for example, being better adapted to tropical sunlight than light skin, and dumpiness being superior to lankiness for conserving body heat. That is to say, other things being equal, Negroes have a better chance to survive and to perpetuate themselves in the tropics, as do Eskimos in the arctic. Similar adaptive advantages can be demonstrated for several other racially distinctive physical traits, including inherited immunities to certain kinds of disease; but for many others the advantages, if any, are not clear.

Even more crucial is the question: Do human race differences in genetic composition include *behavioral* traits? We know that individual members of any population differ in innate behavioral capabilities; but does this extend to whole populations? It would be logical to assume, say, that a long-legged white man could run faster than a Pygmy; but how do whole races compare with respect to behaviors less obviously and less directly associated with physical differences? What about such notions as "Negroes are naturally better musicians," that "Indians are naturally stolid," or the insidious belief that some races are mentally superior to others? It may someday be discovered that there is a connection between distinctively Negroid anatomy and the resonances so many of us admire; or it may be found that the nervous systems of Mongoloids have higher thresholds to pain; but until such connections can be established notions like these must be relegated to the realm of unprecise identification or myth. As for the notion that some races are in general mentally superior to others, it must be emphasized that no experiment has yet been devised that provides an impartial test for this thesis. One community's way of life, including education for that way of life, may stress memorization, another may stress concrete-object discrimination, still another generalization and abstraction. And it is conceivable that social selection has favored the survival and proliferation of persons with genetic equipment better suited to the acquisition of one or another of these kinds of mental skills. This is an intriguing hypothesis, and methods may someday be discovered to test it; but if it is found to be correct it will still be difficult to demonstrate that any of these kinds of skill is "superior" to another—except in the context of particular ways of life.

1. See, for example, the more adequate evolutionary analysis of animal communication presented by Charles D. Hockett, "The Origin of Speech," *Scientific American*, Vol. 23, No. 3, Sept. 1960, pp. 88–96.
2. Clyde Kluckhohn, *Mirror for Man*, Fawcett, 1960, p. 124.
3. Adapted from E. Adamson Hoebel, *Man in the Primitive World*, 2nd ed., McGraw-Hill, 1958, p. 116.
4. William W. Howells, "The Distribution of Man," *Scientific American*, *op. cit.*, pp. 112–27.

Sociology

Gresham M. Sykes / *Dartmouth College*

I. Introduction

Many professional sociologists have watched the rapid growth of sociology over the last several decades with unquestioning approval. After all, an intellectual specialty demonstrates its health in the expansion of research, school enrollments, and the scope of application in every-day concerns.

However, such growth has created a number of problems for sociology—and this has happened in other disciplines as well, I suspect. Recruitment of competent personnel has become more difficult; speculative assertions of the classroom have sometimes been translated into policy too quickly in some areas; and it seems that a passion for growth for the sake of growth has sometimes taken the place of a desire for more solid advances. I suppose all this is familiar enough since many bodies of knowledge recurrently suffer from the pains of irregular development. But I think the problems of expansion are particularly marked in relatively new academic disciplines such as sociology; and among their various manifestations these growing pains are apt to show up as a lag between the presentation of sociology in the college or university and the presentation of sociology in the high school. There is a serious danger that the current substance of a rapidly developing field such as sociology will be reflected imperfectly in current teaching in the secondary schools.

It is true, of course, that few high schools have programs in sociology as a separate subject, but many courses in social studies do embrace important sociological issues. Since a variety of sociological topics appear under the name of social studies and since these topics are supposedly viewed from a sociological perspective, the question of whether sociology should be taught in the high schools and preparatory schools as an independent course can be put to one side for the moment. The difficulty is that many teachers of sociology in colleges and universities doubt, at the present time, that their discipline is adequately represented in the high school, regardless of whether it is called social studies or something else —and regardless of whether the work in the high school is a preparation for more advanced training or the end of academic schooling.

II. The Study of Society: Means and Ends

What does the teacher of sociology in the college expect of the high school? There's no easy answer to the question, of course, since as one writer has said, "The social sciences are too fluid and too varied to warrant neat generalizations about their nature and their methods. . . . Social scientists, moreover, even within their respective disciplines, have varied approaches."[1] And finding a worthwhile answer to the question may be made still more difficult because the question is often fobbed off, in effect, with a too easy statement about the purpose of teaching sociological topics under the heading of social studies. "Educating citizens for democratic intergroup relationships," "educating citizens for responsible individualism," "educating citizens for world responsibilities"—all are praiseworthy ends, but they come dangerously close to what Professor Hager once called an "apostolic laying-on of words."[2]

Now I have no desire at this point to resurrect old debates about teaching values in the secondary schools, subject teaching versus a concern with over-all growth, and so on. But the plain fact is that many college and university teachers of sociology are not primarily interested in "educating citizens" and many believe that the high school can perform a disservice by placing too heavy an emphasis on the utilitarian aspects of social studies. For the professional sociologist, his discipline is —or at least is in the process of becoming—a science of human behavior.* I am sure that the professional sociologist is happy if a student becomes a better citizen or acquires responsible individualism by learning something about society. But the professional sociologist is also convinced that if his discipline is treated mainly as a means to an end (no matter how lofty that end may be), his discipline will eventually be weakened and the student will be shortchanged. The spirit of free inquiry and objectivity is the foundation of sociology, just as it is the foundation of all other liberal arts and sciences; and it cannot help but be undermined if the study of society is curbed and channeled by the demands of an ideology, even a democratic one.

The reluctance of the college teacher to convert sociology into a tool for the production of good citizens is coupled with qualms about stressing the immediate, material benefits of so-

* The problem posed by the fact that sociology is a science in the making will be touched on below. For the moment, I think it is enough to point out that if sociology is not fully mature as a science, the problem is ill met by falling away from the standards of science. Poor science is made better by better science, not worse.

cial studies for the individual. If an examination of the community's occupational structure becomes a form of instruction for the techniques of job seeking, if an analysis of the family is transformed into a course on better family living, or if the study of the American economy is seen as a sort of consumer's guide, the professional sociologist is apt to feel that his field is being subverted. Again, I should stress the fact that the professional sociologist may think these are worthwhile aims; his quarrel is not with vocational guidance, aid in personal adjustment, and so on. Rather, his argument is that nothing but confusion can result from equating the objective study of society with a means for securing the good life. A knowledge of society may prove useful to the student. But this is not necessarily the result, and an excessive concern with this result carries the danger that the content of sociology will be distorted.

In short, I think there is apt to be an important disagreement between the college and the high school about the purpose of teaching about society. It is a disagreement best brought out into the open. The study of society at the college or university level, from the viewpoint of the professional sociologist, is primarily a matter of transmitting a systematic knowledge of a scientific discipline. The study of society in the high school, it seems to me, is likely to put its heaviest emphasis on instilling pieces of knowledge and attitudes that will adapt the student to the society in which he will live.

I realize that the contrast may be overdrawn. I realize that the college teacher of sociology will also resort to an "apostolic laying-on of words," if driven, and will justify his work not as an end in itself but as a means of elevating the human mind and spirit. And I realize that the high school does not claim to provide a comprehensive view of sociology. But differences do exist between colleges and high schools in their treatment of sociological topics. As one college teacher has said, "The notion that a college or university is designed to equip and train its graduates for fruitful occupational and societal equilibrium is a demeaning one."[3] I doubt that the majority of social studies teachers in the secondary schools would agree with this statement as far as their own work is concerned and it seems to me a great mistake to ignore this fact or disguise it.

III. The Content of Sociology

If the college teacher of sociology is concerned that the high school student should learn to analyze society objectively, he is no less concerned that the high school student's knowledge of society be something more than a grab bag of isolated facts. The college teacher will argue that the student should have an integrated view of society, of social processes, no matter how elementary this view may be. Only thus can a student gain an idea of a science of society as a coherent body of thought.

Now, despite the many different theoretical positions in sociology, there is one theme on which most sociologists are likely to unite. Society is to be viewed as a system, as a set of interacting parts. Two questions then emerge that are central to the concerns of sociology: What keeps this system going through time, as generation replaces generation and the society interacts with its physical environment and other societies? And—as the other side of the coin—what makes this system change through time, transforming the society into new patterns?

The view of society as a system and the two basic questions about the system seem to me to form the core of what is called the *functional orientation* in sociology. We want to know how the activities of men function to maintain or change the social system in which they live. It is this functional conception that unites the diverse inquiries of sociologists and provides a common framework into which we can fit the many theories and empirical studies of social behavior. Without some such focus, sociology is apt to appear as a random assortment of facts and notions, meaningless to both teacher and student.[4]

The important point, for our present purposes, is that the functional orientation in the study of society provides a logical scheme for tying together many diverse sociological topics that now rattle about under the heading of social studies in the high school. At the same time it can make for far greater continuity in the treatment of these topics in both the high school and college.* The functional orientation tells us, in effect, the major topics to be covered in the study of society, why these topics are important rather than others, and how these topics are interrelated.

Now as we look at societies in different times and places (and here sociology must and should shade off into anthropology and history), we can see that men everywhere engage in a common set of activities. We can call these activities, these patterns of behavior, *functional requisites,* i.e., the activities that function to insure the survival of society or that are requisite for the survival of society.** Various lists of functional requisites have been constructed, but I think the following would win wide acceptance.[5]

* I do not believe that I am engaging in any special pleading by proposing a functional treatment of sociological topics in the high school since there is widespread agreement that a functional analysis of society is essentially equivalent to sociological analysis. See, for example, the presidential address of Professor Kinglsey Davis read at the annual meeting of the American Sociological Association, Sept. 1959, printed in the *American Sociological Review,* Vol. 24, No. 6, Dec. 1959, pp. 757–72.

** There are some sociologists who might argue that these activities are not in fact requisite or essential—they simply happen to be universal. Such sociologists, I suppose, would prefer to speak of universal social institutions. I'm not sure it makes much difference. The important thing is that we can distinguish a limited set of activities that we must understand if we are to understand man in society.

PHYSIOLOGICAL NEEDS

First, in every society men must of course meet their basic physiological needs for food, clothing, and shelter. As we know, the particular way this gets done varies. It varies from one part of the world to another and it varies through the years as the environment and technology and fads and fashions change. But the critical issue is that the student can now be directed to studying in a systematic way how these needs are met, why they are met in a particular way, and what are the forces at work to maintain or alter the patterns that are observed. It is not enough to show that architectural styles differ from one region of the United States to another, that different societies have different tastes in food, that the dress of one century becomes the costume of the next, and so on. Rather, the student must be brought to an understanding of the general principles that underlie the variation—the limits and possibilities posed by the physical environment, the forces generating cities and suburbs, the requirements of health, and so on. I doubt very much if I am urging anything new in the way of subject matter. Many courses in world history take into account the geographical setting of ancient and modern societies; many courses in world and United States history examine the industrial revolution and the growth of cities; many courses in civics, United States history, and government include material on the way in which American government provides social services. What may be new is the argument that such topics should be studied as part of a science, within the context of a larger theory.

REPRODUCTION

Second, in all societies men and women are faced with the problem of replacing themselves, of producing children to insure the continuity of the society as members of the society die. This functional requisite of reproduction thus leads into two areas of fundamental importance: First, into demography with its study of birth rates, death rates, and migration. And second, into the study of the family as a social group that performs the function of reproduction. Again, I think it important to stress the idea that the study of these topics should not dissolve into an unconnected set of observations—or, what is worse, into vapid moralizing. The study of the family, as far as the sociologist is concerned, is not a study of marital adjustment or parent-child relationships or the problem of adolescence, although these may merge as legitimate subsidiary questions. Nor is it simply the description of the curious customs of "other" people, distant in time or space. Instead, it is the systematic analysis of how and why the family gets organized in different kinds of ways and the consequences of these various modes of organization for other parts of the social system. Only by placing the study of the family in a larger intellectual framework—the stability and change of society—can the student see the sociological significance of his work.

SOCIALIZATION

Third, we now know that very little human behavior is innately determined, and so in every society there is the problem of teaching children the values, skills, knowledge, and other requirements for the survival of society. As Professor Waller once said, every society is faced with the threat of being engulfed by a wave of barbarians—the next generation—and somehow these barbarians must be converted into adult members of the social order. The function of socialization is performed in part by parents, in part by peers, in part by formal agencies such as the school; and we now have a fair knowledge of the major features of the process. And since the process of socialization is an activity in which the student is caught up, in immediate and direct terms, a functional analysis of the situation is apt to take on an added bite. The significance of educational opportunity, the determinants of school performance, the learning that takes place in adolescent groups—all can be illuminated by viewing them as part of a larger, crucial activity.

PRODUCTION AND DISTRIBUTION OF GOODS AND SERVICES

Fourth, in all societies men must work out a method to produce and distribute the goods and services that they require. The production of goods and services may range from the crudest forms of hunting with a rudimentary division of labor to the most complex industrial organization; and the distribution of goods and services can be founded on age, priestly rank, amount and type of labor performed, etc. Yet behind all this variation and the specific studies to which it may give rise (such as occupational distribution, patterns of social class, types of business organization, and so on) the student must be made to see the main issue—the structuring of a major social function, its causes and its consequences.

SOCIAL CONTROL

Fifth, in every society there is the problem of social control or the problem of power. The issue can be analyzed in its more obvious terms, such as the power of the state over the citizen in particular forms of political order, the power of the parent over the child, or the power of the clique leader over other clique members. But there are other, more subtle, manifestations of power or social control, such as gossip, ridicule, and the internalized voice of society. And I might suggest that here as elsewhere the teacher is confronted with the difficulty of keeping his own values free from the facts that he is trying to teach. The teacher must have a preference for a particular form of political order and I think his preference will inevitably show up in the classroom. But he is duty-bound to keep his values and facts separate in his own mind *and* in the minds of his students.

MEANING AND MOTIVATION

Sixth and last, there is the question of meaning and motivation. I have talked about other functional requisites, the activities that must be performed if the society is to maintain itself. There remains, however, the question of how and why people are in fact motivated to do these things. And thus we can recognize that every society has the problem of instilling values and goals that will insure the performance of necessary tasks. This is not simply a matter of short-run aims, but also includes those larger considerations that inform an individual's life and give it meaning and coherence. Religion, systems of ethics, the arts—all can play a role in creating that elusive sense of significance that men in all societies seek beyond their mundane affairs.

Every society, then, can be analyzed as a social system made up of interlocking activities that are solutions to the problems of the maintenance and development of the system. The solutions can be adequate or inadequate—occasionally societies do die out or, more often, change their form as well as persist; and the solutions that a society offers, such as its particular form of stratification, family structure, or methods of production, can be judged in terms other than those of stability and change. But it is the job of sociology, as a scientific discipline, to discover the requirements of a social system, the principles that determine how these requirements are met, and the nature of the influence that the solution to one requirement has on another.

The six functional requisites or six major forms of social activities I have described are crucial for our understanding of man in society. They are not simply an *ad hoc* listing of topics that might be covered in the study of society. They are essential and interdependent elements that make possible the maintenance of human groups. They are not selected because an understanding of them will create good citizens or adjusted personalities; they are selected because they are basic to a science of society.

But at this point the student—and the teacher—must run headlong into a serious difficulty. Sociology is not yet so far advanced that it can state with certainty all or even most of the answers to the fundamental questions about human behavior that concern us. The neat sureness of mathematics or the natural sciences is lacking. It might be argued that the often-cited certainty of these disciplines is somewhat spurious: In this age of inquiry, advanced workers in all fields find their basic assumptions being called into question. But this isn't much help to the teacher of sociological topics in the high school—nor, for that matter, to the teacher of sociology in the college or university. The teacher finds himself being forced into the position that is so difficult for a teacher, of having no choice but to say "maybe" or "we don't really know." What happens, I'm afraid, is that the teacher, in order to feel assured, falls back on obvious tautologies and the student recognizes them for the banal statements that they are. Perhaps it is this fact that accounts for an attitude common among students both in the high school and the college—the attitude that the social sciences or social studies are "soft" or "easy" in contrast to "tough" or "solid" subjects like physics, chemistry, and mathematics.[6]

I think there is a solution to this problem, a solution that is in fact an invaluable aid to the student's intellectual development. The student must learn that many of our statements in the social sciences (and in all sciences) are made not with full certainty but as provisional explanations based on bodies of evidence more or less adequate. The student must learn that our knowledge does not appear out of nowhere but is accumulated in a process of research, and that our knowledge is no better than the research on which it is based. And this is to say that the student should learn about methods of inquiry as well as the content of a discipline.

In talking about methods of research, I do not mean a rather narrow consideration of specific techniques. Rather, I have in mind the general form of research procedures:

First, the rooting of an issue to be studied in a theory and an existing body of knowledge

Second, the development of hypotheses to be tested

Third, the choice of a population to be studied or the choice of the sources of data

Fourth, the development of procedures for collecting valid and reliable data

Fifth, the analysis and interpretation of data

Sixth and last, the presentation of results in clear and precise language

The value of learning these procedures (and I think the student can learn about them only by using them) does not lie only in the knowledge gained about the issue chosen for study, although such knowledge should not be discounted. Nor does the major benefit spring from acquiring a skill for investigating sociological topics, although this too has its advantages. Instead, I think the most important thing for the high school student learning methods of research is that he is provided with a standard of judgment by which he can evaluate logically and critically the principles of sociological thought and the evidence on which they are based. All this is to say that, at the present time, we recognize that the student of biology, chemistry, and physics needs the experience of laboratory work, even though it may be elementary. It is time, I think, to recognize that the same is true for the student of the social sciences.

It is true, of course, that many textbooks in modern social

studies for the high school are filled with suggestions for projects to be undertaken by the student and they are defined as laboratory work in the social sciences. I am sure that when these projects are carried out carefully (and carefully supervised) many of them fulfill the need for learning methods of research. There are, however, three points to be noted. First, there is the danger that many of these projects will remain purely descriptive, and while the knowledge so gained is of value, it is not the sole aim of research. Second, there is often little time in the school year for the teacher to weed out irrelevant projects and to supervise carefully those that are carried out. And third, there is the possibility that some of these research projects will laboriously assemble information that is readily available in standard reference works or elsewhere. The important point, then, is that if attempts are made to teach high school students the methods of social research, such efforts require a careful fitting to a coherent program. Then, perhaps, we can develop that intelligent skepticism essential for scientific inquiry.

IV. Conclusions

The college teacher's view of sociology in the high school really boils down to a simple argument. Sociological facts and ideas are now being taught in most high schools in the United States. However, it seems doubtful that the treatment of these matters at the present time takes sufficient advantage of the unique contribution of sociology as an academic discipline—namely, the scientific study of social behavior within the framework of systematic theory and accepted methods of research. The study of society, in the college or university, is not "current events," it is not an examination of social "problems," and it is not a system of polemics to fit the student to the *status quo*—or any particular *post status quo*. It is, instead, the objective analysis of a coherent body of principles concerning the crucial aspects of social systems. The student going on to college will be badly misinformed if he is led to believe that the study of social behavior involves mere description, disconnected studies of social phenomena, or a tool for individual and social adjustment. And for the student not going on to college, the need for acquiring an adequate perspective of sociology is no less acute.

Undoubtedly there are many barriers to the importation of the college and university teacher's view of sociology. The existence of "taboo" subjects, the competing claims of other disciplines included in social studies, the problem of finding good textbooks, the reluctance to examine emotion-laden issues objectively, the difficulties of preparing teachers, the limitations of students' ability—all would play their part. The existence of these barriers makes difficult the widespread adoption of sociology as a separate course in the high school. Yet I think it is possible and desirable (1) that sociology should be made available as an avenue of study for the academically talented high school student; and (2) that a much more thorough treatment of sociology should be incorporated in existing social studies for all students. Only thus, I think, can we correct a disturbing discontinuity in the study of society.

1. Pendleton Herring, "Toward an Understanding of Man," in *New Viewpoints in the Social Sciences*, ed. by Roy A. Price, Twenty-Eighth Yearbook, National Council for the Social Studies, 1958, p. 1.
2. Don J. Hager, "Some Observations on the Relationship between Social Science and Intergroup Education," *The Journal of Educational Sociology*, Vol. 23, No. 5, Jan. 1950, pp. 278–90.
3. Charles A. Fenton, "The Sweet, Sad Song of the Devoted College Teacher," *AAUP Bulletin*, Vol. 46, No. 4, Dec. 1960, p. 362.
4. See, for example, Robert K. Merton, *Social Theory and Social Structure*, Chap. 1, The Free Press, 1949.

5. Cf. John W. Bennett and Melvin M. Tumin, *Social Life,* Chap. 4, Alfred A. Knopf, 1948.
6. Milton M. Klein, *Social Studies for the Academically Talented Student in the Secondary School,* National Education Association, 1960.

Psychology*

W. J. McKeachie / University of Michigan

ALTHOUGH COURSES IN PSYCHOLOGY are not in the main stream of high school curriculums, a good deal of psychological content finds its way into the high school. Psychologists have had some uneasiness about psychology's role in the high school. Many psychologists would prefer to reserve psychology to the college curriculum; most worry about the effects of "psy-

* In preparing this paper the author has drawn from L. Cronbach, "Psychology," a talk delivered at the National Education Association Disciplines Seminar June 15–17, 1961; from a report of the Social Science Study Committee of the University of Michigan, 1960; from W. J. McKeachie, R. L. DeValois, D. E. Dulany, Jr., D. C. Beardslee, and Marian Winterbottom. Objectives of the general psychology course. *American Psychologist*, 1954, pp. 9, 140–42; from W. J. McKeachie. List of objectives of the general psychology course. University of Michigan Department of Psychology, Mimeo, and W. J. McKeachie, and J. E. Milholland. *Undergraduate Curricula in Psychology:* Report of the Michigan conference supported by the National Science Foundation, Scott, Foresman, 1961. Helpful comments have been received from Stanley Ratner, Sherman Ross, and Stephen Kaplan.

chological" advice presented with little scientific content by teachers whose college training often includes only a couple of courses in academic psychology.

Yet, the growth of psychology has been so rapid and psychological research and applications so widespread that psychology is now an important part of our culture, and its role in the social sciences cannot be ignored in the public school curriculum. Whether or not psychology should be presented as a separate course is not at issue in this paper. What I shall try to do is to indicate desirable outcomes, irrespective of the manner in which they are fitted into the curriculum.

Before entering upon a discussion of these objectives, however, I should like to wander aside for a moment to discuss some background considerations. First, let me clarify my role. Decisions about objectives are value questions that should not, I believe, be determined by authority. I can contribute a psychologist's view of his subject matter and its educational values, but specific course objectives need to be formulated as the product of interactions between an instructor, his students, and other parties concerned (such as subject matter specialists and school administrators or curriculum committees).

The social science teacher has a resource that this author lacks. That resource is the possibility of learning from his students what they already know, or think they know, in the area of psychology. Psychology has been prominently featured in educational programs on television and in articles in popular magazines. Thus the typical high school student probably has a much greater awareness of psychology than did his predecessors a generation ago. He has expectations of psychological content that may facilitate or interfere with achieving certain objectives, and in some cases an important objective may be simply to reduce the subjective confidence level of existing psychological "knowledge."

Because the background and abilities of students in differing high schools at different times are different, and the qualifications and interests of the teachers vary, objectives should not be formal, rigidly unchanging statements, but rather continuously evolving guides for teaching and learning. Articles such as this can only provide background material to assist the local decision makers in setting their own goals.

With this prologue, let us turn to the objectives themselves.

I. Attitudes and Skills

The social sciences tend to differ from the humanities largely in terms of method, attitude, and approach, and from the natural sciences largely in terms of subject matter. In contradistinction to the humanities, social science attempts to discover regularities of relationships and processes through experiment, controlled observation, analysis, or other forms of study. It is the distinctive task of the social sciences to discover regularities in the world of man and his institutions, a world that takes its characteristic form from the human ability to interact through meaningful symbols.

The body of dependable generalizations in the social sciences is still small. At present the dynamic features of these disciplines called the behavioral sciences lie not so much in major bodies of theory and fact as in the methods being developed to study human behavior. During the student's lifetime, one of the significant aspects of his culture will be the application of those methods to more and more complex problems. It will be important to him as a citizen, whatever his status, to have some basic understanding of these methods so that he will be better able to evaluate and make use of their outcomes. Moreover, because the frontiers of science in the social sciences are so close to the students' own position, they may provide a more understandable introduction to science generally than do the more highly developed biological and physical sciences. Psychology is a particularly appropriate introduction because scientific methods have been used more fruitfully in some areas of psychology than in other social sciences; yet the content necessary to introduce methodology has a good deal of interest for most students. Goals in this area may be achieved in relationship to each of the behavioral sciences, but I shall discuss them with particular reference to psychology, grouping them in two categories: attitudes and abilities.

A. ATTITUDINAL GOALS

1. *Curiosity about human behavior.* To me this is our most important goal. Everyone deals with other people. The variations and regularities in their behavior are of direct personal importance to each of us. But their behavior is also fascinating as an object of observation and thought. We want students not only to study psychology because it will help them solve their own immediate problems but because it is interesting in itself. Students in any field develop new sensibilities—new appreciations. The student of psychology should become aware of many more factors accounting for the behavior he observes. The ideal student is one with a lively curiosity. Curiosity about people, their behavior and experience, their relationships to other organisms and to their environment, is a spark that may be easily kindled by psychological material, and this spark may spread into curiosity about other aspects of our physical, biological, and social environment.

2. *Appreciation of scientific methods and their applicability to problems of human behavior—with awareness of their limitations.* Curiosity about people is a fundamental objective of our teaching, but the sort of behavior motivated by curiosity can vary from window peeping and back-fence gossip to attempts to conceptualize and test major hypotheses about learning or motivation. Certainly our goal is not an increase in window peeping or palm reading. Understanding of behavior can be obtained from many sources and in many ways. One

of the most important of these is scientific research. We would hope that high school work in social science would develop favorable attitudes toward this method of gaining understanding—attitudes not of blind faith in statements of white-coated scientists and of statistics like "4 out of 5," but rather an appreciation of the potential contributions of the scientific approach as well as some understanding obtained from literature, art, philosophy, or religion. The approach of social scientists is relatively new in the history of attempts to understand human behavior, and the idea that human nature can be studied by objective empirical methods is revolutionary.

Laboratory experience is accepted as an important method of teaching physical and biological science, and it should be equally accepted in some areas of the social science curriculum. High school students can carry out studies requiring systematic observation of human behavior, careful planning and execution of a sample survey, empirical testing of hypotheses about learning, as well as many other interesting and meaningful laboratory studies. From such studies they can gain appreciation based upon direct experience with psychological methods.

3. *A critical attitude toward generalizations about human behavior.* We cannot and should not try to make our high school students complete behavioral scientists, of course. What we should try to do is to develop an appreciation of science. We are faced with the problem of wanting our students to have faith in and to support psychology and other behavioral sciences as these disciplines use the scientific method to discover "truth," but not to have such faith that they blindly accept all the claims and generalizations of pseudo-scientists. They should begin to realize the difficulty of establishing the truth of a proposition; yet they should recognize the possibility of developing generalizations that give us increased ability to predict and understand what people do. We want them to ask, "What is the evidence?" We want them to have respect

for good, hard, empirical facts. Among the most frustrating moments in the life of a social scientist are those when he must quietly listen to heated arguments about matters that are questions of fact rather than of values or interpretations. We would hope that students would have an increased tendency to try to get empirical evidence relevant to decisions they participate in making.

4. *Increased skepticism about the finality of our present state of knowledge. Greater ability to get along without absolute answers to every problem. Recognizing that all scientific generalizations must be viewed as tentative in nature, subject to modification in light of new evidence.* Among our objectives, this is one of the most difficult to achieve. We have such a great need for simple answers to the problems of human behavior, so much investment in particular ways of dealing with our fellow man, and such an aching yearning for some stable frame of reference with which to orient our own lives that it is very difficult to give up our cherished "principles" and to base our view upon statements of probabilities. Yet unless one can do this, he may be unable to benefit from the discovery of new perspectives with greater generality and power.

5. *Recognition of the influence of needs and cultural values upon the acceptance of generalizations about human behavior and a desire to separate values from observation.* If we could get this one idea really accepted, we would save hours of fruitless debate, numerous disappointments, and a great deal of wasted research.

6. *Willingness to recognize one's own needs and values as sources of error and bias—the fallibility of man as a student of man.*

7. *Appreciation of the importance in the scientific process of fresh perspectives, of creative imagination, and of freedom as a factor influencing creativity.* Psychological studies of creativity are beginning to untangle the tangled web of the relationship of creativity to heterogeneity of groups, to diver-

gence in thinking, and to freedom in the situation. This material together with actual examples of creative research should indicate to students the dangers of oaths, dogma, restriction of scientific communication and travel, and other barriers to fresh, flexible approaches to scientific problem solving.

8. *Increased objectivity in approaching social problems.* I list this late, not because it is least important, but because it is so fundamental that it takes some temerity to suggest that it should be an objective of high school social science courses. Yet, we must communicate some sense of the importance of objectivity, of the subordination of personal preferences to observable evidence, and of willingness to discard assumptions and hypotheses that are infirmed by data.

9. *Attitudes toward people.* One of the common misconceptions about a scientific study of human behavior is that it leads toward a lack of respect for man's individuality—that the scientific attitude is incompatible with human warmth and sympathy. It is true that an understanding of psychology does not inevitably lead toward an increased humanity, but it can and should contribute to *a heightened sensitivity to the feelings of others and to an understanding of their needs.* While changes in social attitudes and personality characteristics cannot be the primary goals of teaching psychological material, our goal should be to teach in such a way that the content is related to students' attitudinal structures.

B. PERSONAL ADJUSTMENT

Psychologists differ greatly in the degree to which they believe psychological knowledge is able to contribute to personal adjustment. While I recognize that the gap between content and personal application is great, I lean toward the view that psychology does have some knowledge that could contribute to the productivity, happiness, and social effectiveness of the average person. Moreover, there is valuable psychological knowledge that is concrete enough to be communicable to students who lack the maturity or ability to comprehend some of our more elegant abstractions. Ojemann, for example, has demonstrated that children in elementary school can learn and use the concept of motivation. Psychological concepts can be presented with concrete, real-like materials that make the generalization to everyday life possible. In fact, one of our goals should be to develop habits of thinking as psychologists do.

"Thinking as psychologists do" does not mean voyeuristic prying into the unconscious reasons for others', or one's own, behavior, nor does it mean a coldly analytic attitude toward human hopes and fears. Rather it means an acceptance based on an understanding of the complexity of the determinants of behavior, and a warm involvement in working toward the basic values of our society.

This does not mean that the study of psychology will necessarily reinforce the student's values, but neither will it be as destructive as some laymen fear. Nor can it avoid value questions as some psychologists and teachers would wish. Psychology deals with basic human problems, and we cannot duck the likelihood that if we teach well, students will relate what they learn to their values. This re-examination may be painful both to students and their parents, but in the long run it seems to me a healthy and desirable outcome.

Yet, despite my faith in the relevance of psychology to personal adjustment, and my belief that we should teach in such a way as to maximize transfer, I do not believe that this should be a major goal of psychological materials in the social science curriculum. One telling argument against this goal is the self-evident fact that psychologists themselves seem to have the usual human quota of personal problems. Although I personally think the psychologists I know are, on the whole, better people than the average, our ability to apply our knowledge to our own lives is certainly not obvious. Thus it seems unlikely that a single course will achieve major changes in adjustment. A second argument against "Personal and Social Adjustment" courses is that this sort of goal is not best approached directly. Assuming that we have learned defense mechanisms to protect our egos, a frontal attack may be the most difficult way of achieving any real impact. A third argument is simply that psychology's major contribution to the curriculum lies in the systematic knowledge and methods that characterize it as a scientific discipline. Courses oriented toward adjustment are likely to be inadequate in achieving the major values to be derived from the study of psychology. Thus, changes in adjustment should be a welcome by-product rather than a primary goal of the inclusion of psychological material in the high school curriculum.

C. UNDERSTANDINGS AND ABILITIES TO BE DEVELOPED

1. *Understanding of the elements of scientific methods as applied in social science.* The experimental method has been a tool of tremendous power in the physical and biological sciences. Thus far, its use in the social sciences has been more limited, but it still is one of the major methods used in behavioral science, and it provides a paradigm for understanding other methods of testing hypotheses or discovering relationships. Because of the difficulties of applying scientific methods in social science, the rational structure of scientific method is probably more apparent and is more easily teachable here than in the physical sciences. From a study of psychological experiments the student should derive such elementary understandings as:

a. Recognition of the importance of control of variables in research.
b. Knowledge of some of the important variables to control in research on human behavior, e.g., motivation, past experience.
c. Understanding of some of the terms used in describing

experiments, viz., assumptions, hypotheses, variables, sample, control group, independent variable, dependent variable.

d. Understanding that science involves drawing inferences from data, and that scientific statements are thus inevitably abstractions and generalizations that lack flesh and blood vividness.

2. *Increased ability to formulate testable hypotheses about behavior.* One can investigate questions about human nature only by defining relevant observable behavior.

3. *Increased ability to recognize assumptions involved in generalizations about behavior.*

4. *Increased ability to discriminate between reasonable and unreasonable generalizations in terms of the evidence upon which they are based.*

a. Recognizing stereotypes and clichés.
b. Recognizing bias and emotional factors in a presentation.
c. Distinguishing between verifiable and unverifiable data.
d. Distinguishing between relevant and nonrelevant data.
e. Distinguishing between the essential and the incidental.
f. Recognizing the adequacy of data.

5. *Awareness of some of the major tools and methods of psychology and other behavioral sciences.* Psychology uses a variety of methods: observational, experimental, correlational, sample surveys, etc. No method is equally useful for all purposes; each has its peculiar advantages and limitations. Most of these methods involve the use of statistics. Because probabilistic knowledge is often viewed as inferior, it is important that students understand the nature of its contribution to the social sciences.

6. *Understanding the purposes of the behavioral sciences, the nature of their subject matter, and their limitations.*

a. A major purpose of the behavioral sciences is to explain social phenomena, not to judge their goodness or badness nor to define ultimate objectives.
b. A related purpose is to give order to facts; to integrate findings into a coherent body of concepts and principles.
c. Human institutions and behavior tend to pattern themselves into objectively identifiable forms.
d. Human institutions and behavior express cause and effect relationships that are susceptible to discovery.
e. Human institutions and behavior are ordinarily so complex that they must be explained on the basis of multiple rather than single causes.
f. The society within which a social scientist operates may influence and limit the problems on which he works, the data that he collects, and the conclusions that he reaches. Here some examples of history of thought and research in some area of psychology (such as personality) may be pedagogically helpful.
g. Social phenomena can be adequately understood only in relation to the unique environment or context in which they take place.
h. The interaction of the social scientist and the system that he purports to study may appreciably distort the system itself.
i. Contingency factors—presently unpredictable discoveries, events, or personalities—limit the predictive value of the social scientist's generalizations.
j. A sample that is inadequate or unrepresentative yields unreliable scientific generalizations.
k. No amount of statistical refinement in treatment of data can overcome inadequacies in the data themselves. Social science thus depends upon measurement.

II. Knowledge

When we turn from general attitudes and understandings to the concepts of psychology that seem most important for the education of the high school graduate, I feel strongly that our goal should be far beyond that of attainment of some recognition or knowledge of these concepts. We would hope that to some degree the student would not only know something of psychology but that he would also be able to apply it in new situations, that he would be able to predict behavior from theory and choose a course of action on the basis of his knowledge. With this in mind let us turn to some of the central themes that the social science teacher might draw from psychology.

A. THE BIOLOGICAL BACKGROUND OF BEHAVIOR

It may seem incongruous to suggest that one of the basic contributions of psychology to a *social* science curriculum should be to give students an understanding of the significance of the biological background of behavior. Yet it seems to me that unless this link to the biological sciences is emphasized, the student's understanding of such processes as socialization, cognition, learning, and performance is likely to be one-sided and distorted. Thus one would hope that a social science student would learn at least the following basic generalizations:

1. All of the bodily systems are involved in behavior, particularly the receptor, nervous, and muscular systems.

2. As animals develop, the bodily systems increase in complexity of organization. This is associated with greater variability and modifiability of behavior.

3. The higher the animal in the ontogenetic scale, the more complex is the organization of the nervous system, and therefore the more variability and modifiability there is possible in behavior.

4. As the higher brain systems develop in size and complexity in the phylogenetic series from a fish to man, there is a

progressive shifting of dominance to the higher centers of the brain and more behavior is determined by learning and problem solving.

5. Psychological processes such as perception, motivation, and learning may be studied through much of the phylogenetic scale.

B. PERCEPTION

In understanding man as a social being, one of our fundamental concepts has been perception. Understanding something of the nature of perception not only helps one understand why other people behave as they do but also should contribute toward a more probabilistic attitude toward one's own view of the world. In his dealing with other people the student of perception should be characterized by a humility produced by knowledge that his own view of the world is not complete and correct.

The following generalizations from the field of perception should be helpful:

1. The needs of individuals influence their perceptions and cause them to see and interpret the same phenomena differently.
2. Language and attitudes affect perception.
3. Perception is selective.
   a. There are certain stimulus determinants of selectivity. That which is different from its context, or changing, is perceived.
   b. There are certain determinants of selection in the nature of the sense organs. Sense organs are sensitive to a limited range of physical energies.
   c. Motivation, learning, and set affect selectivity.
4. Perception is characterized by organization of stimuli into figures, patterns, or perceptions of objects.
   a. There are certain stimulus determinants of organization, such as proximity, continuity, and similarity.
   b. Motivation, learning, and set affect organization.

c. The properties of a substructure are determined in large measure by the properties of the whole structure of which it is a part.

5. Stimuli not only provide information but also maintain arousal or alertness of the organism.

6. In addition to his perception of the world, the individual develops a concept of himself, the self.

C. LEARNING

Learning is fundamental to an understanding of man as a social being. It is also an area in which psychological research has been especially sophisticated. Thus the introduction of content on learning provides an excellent opportunity to combine important content with the illustration of scientific methodology.

Following are some generalizations appropriate for high school courses:

1. Behavior is determined by the interaction of genetic-physiological factors and experience.

2. Learning is a continual process, not limited to school studies.

3. Conditioning is one important way of looking at learning processes.

4. Memories change over time.

5. Interference causes forgetting.

6. Learning in one situation may generalize to other similar situations.

7. Mediating processes influence the transfer of learning from one situation to another.

D. MOTIVATION AND EMOTION

The area of motivation and emotion is not only of great theoretical importance but also is of much interest to students. It is a particularly good area in which to introduce concepts of scientific method because there are good experiments on problems of human motivation close to student interests.

Illustrative of generalizations from this area are the following:

1. Motives and rewards are learnable.

2. A person may be unaware of his motives.

3. Most behavior is determined by the interaction of several motives.

4. The "self" becomes a value around which many motives are integrated.

5. The organism seeks an optimal level of stimulation.

E. PERSONALITY

Personality is the area that is most closely related to the layman's conception of psychology. Psychologists would like students to be aware of other important areas studied by psychology. Nevertheless concepts of personality are important for an understanding of Social Man. Because mental illness and delinquency are such important social problems, some understanding of deviant personalities is important for all members of society. One effect of such understanding should be a significant change in attitudes toward the mentally ill.

The following are some concepts and generalizations important in this area:

1. The study of our own personalities, lives, and cultural institutions is aided by the study of other peoples and sometimes other species, among whom there are great but predictable variations that permit us to form and test many hypotheses that also apply to ourselves and our culture.

2. The latent inherited potentialities of the individual are drawn out and shaped by environmental factors and in turn help select from the environment factors relevant to their development.

3. Childhood is an important determiner of adult personality.

4. The groups of which the individual is a member are particularly important in influencing his developing personality.

5. The family is the primary group affecting the individual's socialization.

6. The developing individual may experience conflict between different behavior possibilities.

7. Conflict and frustration may produce strong tension that the individual attempts to reduce. As a result of conflict, new behavior patterns may result. Some typical ways of reducing this tension have been classified, such as avoidance, aggression, repression, denial, and substitution.

8. Behavior disorders are attempted resolutions of conflicts that are maladaptive for the individual in society. In some cases there is observable organic damage. In some cases not. Behavior disorders are frequently classified into:

a. Psychotic reactions: in which the individual does not usually realize that he is behaving abnormally, and there is lack of orientation in reality.

b. Neurotic reactions: in which the individual may realize that he is behaving abnormally and be oriented in reality, but lacks insight into the causes of his behavior.

9. Physical symptoms may be caused by psychological conflicts.

10. In our society adjustment is defined in terms of such criteria as:

a. *Self-esteem.* Well-adjusted individuals are likely to be able to recognize and accept their own characteristics both good and bad.

b. *Self-actualization.* Good adjustment is characterized by development of one's talents and abilities.

c. *Integration.* The adjusted individual is able to reconcile and order his motives. He has relatively few unresolved conflicts.

d. *Independence.* Our society expects an adult to be able to stand on his own feet and make decisions for himself.

e. *Realism.* The well-adjusted person seeks, and uses, checks upon his own perception of the world.

f. *Environmental mastery.* In our society adjustment depends upon being able to work and interact with other people productively.

F. ABILITIES AND TRAITS

One of the areas in which psychology comes closest to the average man is that of the measurement of human abilities and traits. Everyone has some experience with psychological tests and it is important that he know something of what they can do and what their limitations are. Moreover, the concept of individual differences that underlies this area is important not only in awakening students to differences between people, but because the study of individual differences also reveals the similarities between oneself and others. To the adolescent, who sometimes feels that no one else has ever been as ugly, or stupid, or faced such difficult problems of adjustment, it is a big step forward to become aware of the degree to which his problems are shared by others.

This area also has important implications for our basic goal of developing respect for the dignity and worth of individuals. Studying the effect of cultural background on test scores, the data on racial differences in abilities, and the evidence on correlations between abilities should have relevance for the students' acceptance of other groups and his commitment to the ideal of equal opportunity.

1. Psychological tests are simply samples of behavior collected in standardized situations.

2. Psychological tests may be used to sample many different kinds of behavior such as motor skills, sensory acuity, intelligence, motivation, personality, and attitudes.

3. Test scores are affected by situational factors as well as by the more enduring characteristics of the individual tested.

4. Heredity and environment interact in determining ability.

5. Individual differences in ability are distributed normally.

6. The overlap between abilities of different racial and cultural groups is so great that there is no justification for policies of differential opportunities.

G. SOCIAL PSYCHOLOGY

Some of the most interesting problems in social science lie in the area in which psychology and sociology overlap—social psychology. This rapidly developing area now has produced a number of generalizations of importance to all men, as well as extending concepts drawn from its parent disciplines. The study of social psychology is not only of value in its own right but also should be of practical value in providing knowledge basic to skills of effective group participation and to effective participation in society.

1. Groups are formed for many different functions.

2. Society is a complex system made up of lesser units like kinship groups, communities, social classes, and formal associations integrated by ties of interdependence, mutual understandings, and agencies of control.

3. Group behavior and institutional forms are invariably systematized, so that the acceptance by the group of change in one sort of traditional behavior initiates, in a systematic way, still other changes away from the traditional behavior of the group. The processes by which society solves its problems create new problems. All behavioral responses are multiply determined.

4. The attempts by individuals to achieve their objectives commonly involve some degree of competition and co-operation between them; mechanisms must be developed to control or direct this interaction into socially acceptable channels.

5. Individuals within a group perform different functions.

The behavior characteristic of a person performing a particular function is called a *role*.

6. Technologies, with their economic systems, profoundly influence the structure and functioning of societies, and there are important personality correlates of these social structures and function.

7. Groups have certain fundamental objectives and values (e.g., security, freedom, status), which underlie their activities and which give to these activities some logical (i.e., in the eyes of the groups involved) rationale.

8. The capacity for symbolic thought, expressed in speech, is basic to the life ways of every human group, creating and organizing the techniques, social arrangements, ideas, beliefs, and values (i.e., the culture) of the group.

9. The individual's attitudes are anchored in the norms of *reference groups*, groups with which the individual compares himself.

10. Social factors interact with individual factors determining behavior.

The list of generalizations above is obviously a limited selection biased by my own view of psychology. Many of them might equally well be contributed by other disciplines. But at this point it is probably more important to be sure to cover the breadth of psychology than to be concerned about overlap with other fields. While these generalizations and concepts might be worded differently by someone from another social science, the general view of man represented by them is one that is widely shared by social scientists, and most people looking at contemporary problems would grant that in the remaining decades of this century the contributions of the social sciences are going to be greatly needed.

This implies a final objective of our teaching—to present a view of social science that will be stimulating and appealing to the gifted young people who have the potential to make contributions to social science themselves. Social science is not often seen as a potential career choice by high school youth. The widely publicized needs for physical scientists, medical doctors, and engineers are likely to drown out the faint murmurings of those communications suggesting careers in social science. Thus it is particularly important that social science in the high school not only be sound in content but that it also be well taught. Not that we want high school students trained to be future psychologists. We can take care of the training in graduate school. But we do want students with an orientation to and an understanding of the scientific approach to human behavior.

Teaching about Asia

Hyman Kublin* / *Brooklyn College

THE REVOLUTION in the technology of transportation and communications of the past decade or two has given rise to the platitude that the world grows daily smaller. Today it is easy to fly by jet aircraft from New York, Rome, or Tokyo to almost any land on earth in far less time than was required a generation ago to travel from Washington to San Francisco by conventional means of transportation. Scientific achievements, moreover, promise that within the foreseeable future people everywhere will have at hand the facilities to establish well-nigh instantaneous oral or audio-visual contact with the principal centers of the globe. The age of space and electronics bids fair to make Earth a planet of neighbors.

From the perspectives of science and technology, particularly as they impinge upon universal social relationships, the world may well be contracting like a rapidly deflating balloon. In another sense, however, namely that of education, the globe is expanding at incredible speed, becoming increasingly and bewilderingly complex literally with the passage of each month and year. Since the founding of the United Nations in 1945 the number of member states has more than doubled, dozens of new and independent nations have come into being, and the United States has simultaneously become politically, economically, and culturally involved with the peoples of more than one hundred countries. The frontiers of knowledge are advancing at a constantly accelerating rate and the unknown of yesterday has become the truism of today. As a result, the demands imposed upon those who must learn and teach about the world in which we live have probably never before been so formidable.

Amidst the numerous changes in the conditions and requirements of living during the past generation educators have, on the whole, been sensitive to the emergence of new and fundamental challenges to their *raison d'être*. The very liveliness and, at times, acrimony of the debates and disputes within the teaching profession, joined with increasing gusto by the public at large, should not be misconstrued as mere bickering and carping and be permitted to obscure the larger fact that the purposes of education in the United States have been under continuing, searching review. The constant re-evaluation of the American public school system and its functions has, to be sure, been accompanied by considerable confusion and much misguided effort. Yet, heavy as the cost of re-appraisal has and will continue to be, the thought that the American people are insistent upon an ever improved educational effort is comforting. In few, if any, countries in the world is sound education accorded as high a social value as in the United States today.

In the many statements formulated in recent years on the aims of American education it is not difficult to detect several common and widely upheld concepts. Allowing for differences in terminology and variations in emphases, most teachers and informed citizens apparently agree that the development among students of facility in the basic skills of learning, the inculcation of concrete and healthful attitudes and habits of good citizenship, the promotion of respect for knowledge, the nurturing of critical thinking, and the fostering of a sense of taste and an appreciation of values should be cardinal objectives of education in the public schools. These objectives are doubtless extremely ambitious but they are, nevertheless, worth pursuing. Much of the innovation and experimentation in the American educational system since the end of World War II has, in fact, been concerned essentially with the perfection of new techniques to facilitate the attainment of these goals. But, equally as important, educators have ceaselessly wrestled with the staggering task of aligning the purposes of their endeavors with the problems and implications of life and learning in the middle of the twentieth century.

In the secondary grades especially, after the two- or three-year "pause for adjustment" in the junior high school, the student first begins to feel the heavy impact of an interminably expanding world of knowledge. It is in the high school that a severe strain is placed upon the more sophisticated normative aims of education. At the risk of oversimplification it may be stated that the humanistic subjects in the secondary school curriculum—music, art, English composition and literature, as well as foreign-language study—have deviated least from their traditional tracks. But though the teacher of English today has at his command unprecedentedly rich techniques and insights to stimulate latent humanistic sensitivities, he must, willy-nilly, devote inordinate time and energy to undisguised remedial work in the basic skills of reading and written expression. And the foreign-language instructor, caught by the impulses of the cold war, now all too frequently slights his proverbially humanistic function in an attempt to respond to the practical needs of the prevailing international situation. Problems of a different type, however, have arisen in the areas of the sciences and of the social studies. In these fields epochal breakthroughs have occurred in the accumulation and organization of knowledge, reflecting to a large degree the political, technological, and cultural imperatives of our times.

If an important aim in the current teaching of the sciences in the secondary schools is to bring up to date and reorganize subject matter, still presented nonetheless under familiar rubrics, as well as to encourage improvement in actual instruction, the social studies have been subjected to other pressures. It would not be too much to say that in no other sector of American education has there arisen so urgent a need for self-criticism and re-evaluation of aims as in the field of social studies.

With the growth of informed opinion that knowledge of the world, in its proper meaning, has become a prime responsibility of the American citizen, there is no need to argue at length that the role and purposes of the social studies in the educational process must be submitted to penetrating and thoughtful review. Not merely does current teaching in history and related subjects fall far short of the stated aims of American education but it continues to reveal the outlook of an age and tradition in which the American people could indulge without great loss in political isolation and intellectual parochialism. The time for a grass-roots change is long overdue.

No social studies teacher would seriously dispute the proposition that a primary mission of the public school system is the development of a sound understanding of the history, traditions, and way of life of the American people. Since it is a reasonable presumption that for years to come the overwhelming majority of graduates of the secondary schools will continue to fulfill their personal needs and social responsibilities within an essentially American environment, the teaching and learning of the American heritage, including its European origins, must certainly continue to be a major function and rationale of the social studies. The corollary of this observation is self-evident: understanding of the purposes, concepts, and techniques of analysis in the social studies must be basically instilled through instruction largely given over from the earlier grades on to the treatment of the social phenomena of the United States and Europe.

To contend that the high school graduate should be familiar with his own social and cultural background, both in its historical and contemporary dimensions, does not mean, however, that he may be deemed properly educated for having been exposed to a social studies curriculum preponderantly devoted to Western civilization. Today as never before it is both necessary and possible to encourage the study of peoples, cultures, and ways of life different from our own. The justification and value of this intellectual experience cannot be too strongly stressed. As a practical matter, it is apparent that the United States has elected to undertake a major role in international affairs and the American people have, as a consequence, begun to feel the backlash of events throughout the entire world. A reasonable familiarity with the history and cultures of peoples living beyond the pale of Western civilization has certainly become mandatory for citizens expected to participate, directly and indirectly, in the vital decision-making processes of their country. There is, in addition, a dawning awareness that the study of the heritages of peoples in other parts of the world is not only intrinsically important but also provides immeasurable opportunities for personally rewarding intellectual experience.

When the social studies curriculum in countless secondary schools is examined, it becomes painfully evident that the constantly emphasized need to understand other peoples rarely proceeds beyond lip service. Teachers continue to present traditional courses in history, government, economics, and geography, painfully and at times embarrassingly aware of their outmoded character. Even when the standard offerings on Western civilization have been revised in recent years in attempts to justify such grandiloquent course titles as "World

History" and "Our Contemporary World," they rarely provide for more than enhanced coverage of Western imperialism in modern times or for deeper treatment of American foreign policy toward non-Western areas of the world. However worthwhile such courses might otherwise be, they are intellectually shoddy and not even the most expert instruction can fully atone for the illusions and pretensions that are fostered by these misbranded academic packages.

The widespread presence in the curriculum of high schools of course titles implying concern for the non-Western world is in itself a tacit admission of the need for and value of such study. But that little more than nominal treatment of Asia, Africa, and Latin America is provided in the American high school today is too well established to necessitate further documentation. The reasons for the neglect are, of course, clear. Most important is the fact that a large majority of social studies teachers are themselves the products of a college and university system that generally slighted the study of peoples and cultures beyond Europe and America. In addition to the gaps in their own academic training, teachers with the best of intentions have been discouraged in expanding the scope of social studies because of the lack of suitable texts, bibliographical guides, teaching aids, and the common run of audio-visual materials. Fortunately, these handicaps are in many instances rapidly being overcome and the problems of training and teaching are now not so insuperable as they seemed only a few years ago.

Among the areas of the non-Western world, most promising for introduction into the social studies curriculum of the secondary school is Asia. It is on this continent that more than half of the peoples of the world live, that one finds as nowhere else all the races of mankind, that all the major religions have originated and continued to endure, that great and complex civilizations have evolved and persisted, and that incomparably rich stores of social and artistic experience of endless inspirational quality have been accumulated over the entire span of the history of man. If the more highly educated and better informed citizen is cognizant of these matters and is also acutely aware that the problems of Asia and the foreign policy of America have converged during the past generation, not even the man in the street is totally oblivious, as he once was, to the influence of Asian affairs upon his own life. From the viewpoint of the educator, it should be evident that Asia offers almost limitless opportunities for motivation towards learning in the realm of the social studies.

Assuming that the study of Asia is to be introduced into the secondary school as an integral component of the social studies curriculum, what should be the aims of such an educational effort? What are some of the principal problems that may generally be expected to arise in modifying the more or less standard programs of study so as to provide for the harmonious accommodation of substantial amounts of new subject matter? What approaches are the most promising in facilitating the achievement of stated aims of study and how are these approaches to be reconciled with the concepts and techniques employed in the study of Western civilization? And in view of the many other demands upon the learning time of the student, what may one, normatively at least, expect the student to have learned about Asia before his graduation from secondary school? The answers to these basic questions will understandably vary from school to school in keeping with peculiar conditions and requirements. Yet a few general propositions may be postulated, with the caution that they should be considered imaginatively and flexibly.

At the outset it cannot be too strongly stressed that the study of Asia, or any part or aspect thereof, be undertaken primarily in terms of its intrinsic worth. If the purpose of introducing subject matter on Asia is to be the inculcation of some intelligent understanding of the history and peoples of that part of the world, only marginal results may be anticipated if the subject be dealt with as an additional dimension of Western civilization or as a target of American foreign policy. Students should rather be led into several of the main streams of the past and present of Asia where alone they may discover that flow of human affairs, once so separated from but now so intimately related to our own. It is only by learning about the great historical events and the outstanding historical personalities, about the essence of social and religious value systems, about the structure and functioning of the social and economic systems, and about the routines of daily living, now and yesterday, that the student may acquire a knowledge of Asia worth having.

Sound understanding of the present is predicated upon some insight into the past. The attainment of this aim necessitates, in so far as the introduction into the social studies curriculum of subject matter on Asia is concerned, considerable reliance upon the historical approach. The advantages of this procedure are numerous. Not only is the student given opportunity to develop in a more sophisticated manner a technique of studying social phenomena, in which he has progressively received training throughout the lower grades, but history also enables him to integrate effectively the content of related social studies subjects. An approach to the study of Asia in reasonable depth helps furthermore to demarcate the scope of subject matter on Asia, a matter that cannot but be of grave concern to the curriculum-maker.

In courses on European history the social studies teacher ordinarily employs the principle of selectivity. Efforts are rarely, if ever, made to give either equal or proportionate attention to the history of all nations and peoples from Ireland to Russia and from Sweden to Italy. To a greater or lesser extent coverage is sacrificed to the need for depth. The loss in coverage has never been any cause for deep regret, since a prescription for country-by-country treatment in such courses as history, government, or geography is at best pretentious and at worst unworkable. For similar, if not necessarily identical reasons, a useful study of Asia in the secondary schools—or even in the college and university—must rest upon the practice of selectivity.

In the determination of the area coverage feasible for the study of Asia in the secondary school, experienced teachers of the subject would probably not be hard put to reach a consensus. There is wide agreement that China, Japan, and India, as distinct and cohesive historical and cultural complexes of primary importance in the far greater world of Asia, warrant the interest and concern of educators in the field of social studies. Study of any or all of these three major centers of civilization must surely be the *sine qua non* of any program devoted to Asia in the secondary school. In addition, a tenable case, with qualification, may be made for the extension of areal coverage to include Southeast Asia.

The vast expanse of territory south of China and east of India poses peculiar problems for study and teaching. Southeast Asia, it has been maintained, is a distinct region largely within the conceptual framework of the geographer, geopolitician, the theoretician of the economics of underdeveloped areas, and the military strategist. But the very idea of Southeast Asia is of extremely limited usefulness in many other academic respects and is, moreover, of dubious worth as a realistic proposition in the domain of American foreign policy. Southeast Asia not only raises peculiar challenges for the principle of selectivity in social studies teaching about Asia as well as elemental problems of instructional manageability, but also necessitates an unusual degree of skill in social science concepts and methodology. There is too a general lack of suitable teaching aids as well as study materials for the secondary school level. In view of these various considerations, it is a moot point whether the high school youngster should be required to undertake the study of the Southeast Asia area and peoples. Such instruction should perhaps be undertaken only when qualified teachers and suitable materials are deemed to be available.

Provision for the study of China, Japan, and India may be considered the optimum in social studies programs concerned with Asia in the secondary schools. Though it might well be rash to strive after greater area coverage than is suggested in this pattern, the goal recommended may nevertheless be considered possible of achievement where adequate opportunities for curricular modification exist. It is, on the other hand, likely that some schools may not be able to afford the luxury of such extended coverage because of competitive demands upon the student's time or because of a wish to encourage study in greater depth than breadth. In either of these circumstances it would be wise to establish as an irreducible minimum the study of either China and Japan or of China and India. In justification of this proposal it may be noted that the study of the history and culture of more than a single nation or people is vital in underscoring the vast heterogeneity in Asia and in coping with the omnipresent danger of facile generalization.

Whether the optimum recommendation be adopted or one or another of the various alternatives be selected, it is essential to strike some balance between the requirements for study in breadth and the desideratum for study in depth. But whatever the choice of coverage may be, it is preferable to avoid either extreme concentration in depth or excessive emphasis upon the purely contemporary era. For the purposes of the high school student, precocious as he may be, there is no reason to immerse him in the long and involved currents of Chinese, Japanese, or Indian history or to divert him with the fascinating but tangential problems encountered in the study of the evolution of civilizations. Such intellectual matters are more properly the concern of higher education. Conversely, inordinate attention to the passing scene, while theoretically providing training in social and political problem-solving of immediate significance, and fostering so-called critical thinking, is possible only at an exorbitant cost to the construction of a more or less permanent residuum of knowledge. Long after the passing scene has passed there will always be need for a store of basic concepts and information that cannot be acquired in the analysis of current events.

Provided the student has been grounded in some basic ideas and data, there is no compelling reason why the study of Asia may not be focused upon the period since the early or middle nineteenth century. As late as this era in history the major civilizations in Asia still retained their "traditional" character, the impact of the West and the onslaught of imperialism being forces yet to come. By about 1800 the Chinese still basked in the glory and magnificence of their cultural heritage, the Japanese were still hidden from the world by their barrier of national seclusion, and in India the British stood only on the threshold of an incomparable empire. Save for the Philippines and Indonesia (the East Indies), under Spanish and Dutch rule respectively, all other states in Asia were at this time largely in control of their own affairs. This was the dusk of old Asia.

From the standpoint of the teacher and the student in the secondary school there are numerous advantages in basing the study of Asia upon the last one hundred to one hundred and fifty years. First of all, a convenient and valid point of entry is provided into the "traditional" civilizations at a time when they had not as yet been significantly influenced by the power, technology, and ideas of the culturally alien West. Without some acquaintance with the nature of traditional life in the countries of Asia, it is impossible to acquire proper perspective and insight into the nature of the subsequent breakdown of social and cultural systems of long standing. Failing the essential background, it is most likely too that the more profound and lasting effects of the tide of imperialism that swept over most of the Asian continent during the late nineteenth century will not be tenably interpreted. And without knowledge of the legacies of the Asian past it is futile to strive for acute insight into the dynamics of the nationalist and revolutionary movements as well as of the drives for modernization that have increasingly dominated life in Asia during the twentieth century.

Before considering specifically the scope of concepts and subject matter relating to Asia that might well be posed as goals of learning in the social studies curriculum of the secondary school, several general matters must be raised. In any program devoted to the study of the lands and peoples of the non-Western world, especially of Asia and Africa, it is vitally necessary, and preferably in the initial stages of the teaching-learning process, to clarify the meaning and implications of popularly employed jargon. Nothing is more important for the establishment of proper attitudes. Most students entering the secondary school possess to a greater or lesser extent illusions and biases about Asia and its inhabitants. Not only must these uncritical and deplorable thoughts be corrected but accurate and objective terminology and frames of reference must be actively encouraged.

A stimulating way to inaugurate the study of Asia or any of its component parts is to engage in an analysis of the meaning of Asia itself. As an exercise in critical thinking no beginning lesson could be more instructive. The implications for the study of other parts of the world in a social studies program should be evident.

Asia, it may be pointed out by techniques familiar to most teachers, is largely a meaningful designation when it is used by geographers, geopoliticians, and military strategists. As such, it refers to that vast part of the Eurasian land mass extending from the Arctic Ocean in the north to the Indian Ocean in the south, and from the offshore islands in the far western Pacific in the east to the Ural Mountains and the Mediterranean Sea in the west. Though the term is useful in locating and identifying a large part of the territory of the globe, lending itself to fairly precise delineation, its applicability is extremely limited for the purposes of the historian, anthropologist, and political scientist. As history and cultures in the border lands of western Asia demonstrate, peoples from remote antiquity to modern times have ceaselessly intermingled, disregarding the lines of continental demarcation agreed upon by centuries of cartographers. Asia, in short is an idea, a concept, and an attitude of mind, useful for the organization of some types of data but meaningless or constrictive for various other purposes.

More important, indiscriminate use of the term *Asia*, not to speak of such vague synonyms as "the Orient," "the East," and "the Far East," only serves to foster misconceptions about a unity and homogeneity of the continent that have probably never existed save in the domain of political mythology. Though, to be sure, philosophers, littérateurs, and sociological theoreticians have for a century and more manipulated the idea of a uniform East, it should be borne in mind that the more lasting consequence of their speculations has been the construction of a possibly more tenable image of a dissimilar but culturally integrated West. It may be worthwhile to seek, through the approaches of comparative history and through social scientific analysis, common sectors in the configurations of Asian cultures, but these efforts should not be permitted to obscure the existence of equally profound differences. Awareness of these latter characteristics, it may be argued, justifies the generalization that no generalization about Asia is perhaps complety valid.

In singling out the principal similarities and differences among the major civilizations of Asia, the methods of anthropology may be employed to great advantage. Primary social institutions and values may be dealt with as peculiar responses to particular social and natural environments, as common or alternative solutions to the basic problems of living and life that men have faced everywhere from ancient times to the present. Emphasis may thus be placed upon governmental processes, economic systems, social organization, value patterns, and religious ideals, to name but several of the fundamental categories of anthropological analysis. The dissection of societies and cultures in order to illuminate their basic features and to identify their similarities and differences, when compared with other ways of life, should, however, not be aimless. What should not be lost sight of is the total configuration, which has and still does give distinctive quality to the civilizations of China, Japan, India, or any of the other main complexes of culture in Asia.

When configurations of culture are taken up for inquiry, either on an advanced or elementary level, it is appropriate to consider patterns of behavior and national character or personality structure. In a social studies program these aspects of culture should not be neglected. They provide an incomparable means of infusing the study of other peoples with the element of vibrancy so frequently lost in mechanistic analysis and dynamic theorizing. The task of teaching the basic concepts necessary for the understanding of variously different patterns of behavior—why other peoples behave the way they do—and of providing pertinent illustrative material as course content should not be beyond the faculties of the average social studies teacher. Somewhat more challenging and obviously more sensitive is the problem of dealing with national character.

Essentially the social studies teacher has a twofold challenge in dealing with national character in an Asian setting. On the one hand, by the time the student enters the secondary school he has accumulated a standard stock of stereotypes concerning the nature of Chinese, Japanese, Indians, and other peoples of Asia, many of which are probably held by the teacher himself. These popular images, favorable and unflattering, are, moreover, continuously reinforced, even if inadvertently, by all the media of communications, "learning," and entertainment to which the public of all ages in the United States is exposed. What American does not encounter sooner or later such hackneyed and "loaded" expressions as "the mysterious East," "the inscrutable Oriental," and "the Asian mind"? It is the responsibility of the teacher to lay this nonsense to rest by exposing it for what it is—namely, the product of ethnocentrism and sheer ignorance.

Unwarranted clichés about the character of ethnic groups will most likely not be expunged by mere exhortation. What is rather called for is the development of processes of critical thinking and of control over the basic concepts of anthropology that make possible intellectually defensible generalizations about national character. This entails learning that national character is properly the pattern of behavior and attitudes practiced and sanctioned by the overwhelming number of members of a society. This pattern of behavior is, furthermore, not congenitally acquired but is culturally learned. The Chinese may thus be considered a "cruel people" only if it may be satisfactorily demonstrated that cruelty is behavior practiced or condoned by the social group. Failing this proof, which must be based upon an examination of enduring values and mores, cruelty among the Chinese or any people may only be deemed aberrant or atypical. This analytical approach will doubtless help many students to re-examine their conventional images of unfamiliar peoples and also instill some necessary checks against the absorption of new and equally faulty stereotypes.

With the preceding cautions in mind it is now possible to consider the primary concepts and the scope of subject matter that may realistically be set as curricular goals in a social studies program partly devoted to Asia. No attempt is made here to establish the levels in the secondary school at which the concepts and course content are to be introduced, nor is any definite recommendation made with respect to organization of new courses as opposed to modification of existing offerings. The objective is rather to suggest the range of conceptual and substantive data on Asia that the student may be expected to master without inordinate difficulty during the course of his secondary school education.

Knowledge of the pertinent geography and related concepts is fundamental for the proper understanding of the history and civilizations of China, Japan, and India. Though it cannot be denied that the learning process is facilitated by the typological presentation of subject matter, it must simultaneously be stressed that considerable flexibility is required if the lessons of geography are to be mastered by more than mere rote memory. The common danger in the use of highly schematized approaches in the teaching of geography is that meaning is too often overshadowed by sheer data. Specific information about the geography of the three countries under study should hinge upon some basic and general ideas serving simultaneously to elucidate the essence of historical and cultural problems and achievements.

In undertaking the study of China the student must at the very outset acquire appreciation of the immensity of the land. Without entering into the historical particulars, it will suffice for him to learn that the country currently known as China has grown over the course of almost four thousand years from a relatively small center of civilization in the Yellow River region to embrace during the past few centuries the vast territory delineated upon the conventional maps of today. The tremendous geographical sweep of modern China may easily be underscored by comparisons with the size of the United States and of Europe, and, if it be desired, with other familiar territorial expanses. The student's approach to the perennial problems and unique accomplishments of the Chinese people cannot but be strongly influenced by the realization that all of the United States or the entirety of Europe may be comfortably tucked within the borders of China. He will indisputably be astonished to discover that the distance from the eastern to the western frontiers of China is almost as great as that between New York and London. Other appropriate comparisons may easily be formulated by the teacher.

Some major historical and cultural implications of China's size may be suggested by reference to the correlated factors of time and technology. Because of the huge distances frequently involved, communications, transportation, and ordinary travel have from early times to the present required the expenditure of considerable time. Though facilities for the movement of men and goods were perhaps technologically as well developed in China as in the United States and Europe until about the early or middle part of the nineteenth century, the West was on the whole to draw rapidly ahead during the next one hundred years. Even today, despite the intensive efforts of the Communist regime during the past decade, China still does not possess a network of communication and transportation facilities adequate for many of the primary needs of the state and people. For many years to come traditional devices will surely continue to exist alongside the ultramodern.

The idea of China's territorial immensity may serve effectively as a pivot for the consideration of additional primary characteristics of Chinese civilization. It is not difficult to relate the Chinese solutions to problems of political organization and administration partly to the challenges raised by a society spread over many hundreds of thousands of square miles. Similarly, patterns of demographic distribution, the social foundations of life on the basis of family and village, and the principal economic mechanisms may to a large extent be explained in terms of China's vast domain. And, in combination with other factors, the continental dimensions of an imperial China that endured for two thousand years should help to reveal how tens of millions of people had opportunity to sustain themselves in impressive economic self-sufficiency.

The geographical extent of China should not be allowed to obscure the prevalence of substantial diversity. Covering from north to south more than thirty degrees of latitude and from east to west about seventy degrees of longitude, it is not surprising that an extremely rich variety of land forms, terrain, vegetation, and animal life is to be found. With its forest lands, steppes, plains, deserts, marshes, subtropical jungles, and lofty mountain ranges China is physically more comparable to the United States than to Europe, more akin to an Africa lying upon an east-west axis than to the Soviet Union. Climate ranges from patterns similar to those of the northern United States and southern Canada to cycles suggestive of Central America and the Caribbean. Soil types and volume of rainfall vary substantially from north to south and from east to west, with the consequence that types of basic crops and dietary patterns differ significantly. For purposes of instruction the spectrum of diversity within China may be aptly illustrated by reference to human physical types, linguistic and dialectical variations, housing forms, or whatever cultural features may be fruitfully considered in particular classrooms.

The most impressive historical achievement of the Chinese is that, despite the plethora of regional differences that has and still does characterize the vast area of East Asia, they succeeded in developing a way of life homogeneous in its essential features. A hard core of widely shared traditions, mores, and values, comprising the ethos of Chinese civilization, has not only persistently prevailed amidst regional and local particularities, but it has also functioned as a source of cultural influence radiating into the peripheral lands and societies. It is this historical and cultural heritage, shared directly and vicariously by almost countless numbers of mankind over the past two or three thousand years, that has given the Chinese people cohesiveness and their way of life a unique and distinct quality. It is this Chinese way that has given its practitioners their sense of cultural identity and the yardstick with which they have differentiated themselves with understandable ethnocentric pride from the remainder of humanity.

An integral component of the heritage of China as well as the vehicle by which it was transmitted through the ages is the mode of writing. The Chinese character system is one of the oldest instruments of literacy in the world still in everyday use. Complex and in many ways cumbersome as Chinese writing is, it has been a culturally unifying force for more than thirty-five hundred years. The system, or at least the elements of its morphology, is not only intrinsically worth knowing but its indivisible relationship with many of the basic cultural forms of the Chinese way of life may not be too strongly emphasized. It is exceedingly doubtful that any other system of writing ever devised by man has had so pervasive an influence. In addition to being a means of communication and expression, Chinese writing has powerfully affected the nature and purposes of education, the composition of history, the formulation of philosophy, and expression in literature, poetry, and painting. The written word reveals the "soul of China."

It would obviously be too demanding to compel students in the secondary schools to acquire familiarity with Chinese writing. Still, it may be urged that, even if it be in an elementary and superficial way, a unit or two of teaching on China be devoted to the construction of simple and basic characters. Students would thereby secure a faint glimpse of an important aspect of Chinese civilization that cannot otherwise be easily comprehended. Equally as important, young men and women may in a small number of isolated cases be encouraged to learn a language capable of providing personal intellectual satisfaction and contributing to the fulfillment of a vital national need.*

* Teachers interested in acquiring a glimpse of the nature of China's writing system should consult the useful brochure by Herrlee G. Creel: *Chinese Writing,* American Council on Education, Washington, D.C., 1943. Less useful but equally worth reading is Rose Quong, *Chinese Wit, Wisdom and Written Characters,* Pantheon, 1944. But by far the best introduction for the serious beginner is Bernhard Karlgren, *The Chinese Language,* Ronald, 1949.

Until very recent times literacy in China was indelibly associated with Confucian learning. Deeply influenced as it has been by other philosophies and religions, particularly the Buddhism derived from India and the indigenous school of Taoism, the Chinese way of life has been most profoundly pervaded by the teaching of the sage of antiquity, Confucius. As a secular philosophy rather than a religion in the more conventional sense of the term, Confucianism has been the wellspring of Chinese thought and values in matters concerning social relationships and social ethics. The function of the state, the structure of society, economic thought, patterns of behavior, the purpose of learning and scholarship—all derived their rationale from the repositories of Confucian wisdom. Acquaintance with the main outlines and the spirit of this social philosophy is literally the *sine qua non* for an understanding of Chinese civilization.

Though Confucianism was the state cult for two thousand years, its well-nigh unshakable position in Chinese society and life rested upon more than official approval. It is not enough to state that the teachings of Confucius provided a force for social harmony and stability. What is also necessary is an appreciation of the institutional forms through which Confucian thought and ideals were transmitted and perpetuated. Etiologically these various institutions may be ascribed to the continuing need of the state for a class of political administrators willing and competent to oversee dynastic interests throughout the far-flung imperial domain. Having learned from their own long history to distrust military and paramilitary subordinate governors, China's rulers turned long ago to the literate Confucian scholars. As civil bureaucrats they were to be an elite class of political administrators for almost twenty centuries.

The Confucian scholar-bureaucrats, as men of power, prestige, and influence, were extremely successful in fostering and maintaining a peculiar view of society generally accepted by the rank and file of Chinese. Rejecting the arbitrary and rigid determinant of class status in accordance with either birth or law, the Confucians emphasized social function. In their idealized conception all members of society were not only assigned but also thought of themselves as belonging to one of four classes: scholar, peasant, artisan, and merchant. A suborder was reserved for the nominally despised soldier. If the realities of life did not always allow most Chinese to alter their class status through change in social function, there is no denying that, in comparison with most other major social systems, the Confucian scheme was relatively fluid and permitted an appreciable amount of social mobility.

The rise and fall in social status in traditional China may be most aptly illustrated by reference to the scholar and peasant classes respectively. Insofar as the Confucian scholar-bureaucrat is concerned, he was recruited for administrative service by means of regular competitive examinations sponsored by the state. Theoretically at least, these civil-service tests were open to all subjects of the emperor. Since the examinations themselves were based upon knowledge of the Confucian classics and commentaries as well as upon related subjects and arts, education in China was fitted to the Procrustean bed of Confucianism. If an aspirant for the imperial bureaucracy were successful in passing the intellectually rigorous tests, he became eligible for civil-service appointment. Once he received his official post he became, regardless of his prior social and economic standing, a member of the elite and enjoyed the status and emoluments of the aristocracy of the mind for the duration of his life. Scholar-bureaucratic status not being hereditarily transmissible, each new generation ostensibly had to make its own way in life.

While the scholar-bureaucratic system reflects an important aspect of the social values of traditional China and also points up a channel of social mobility, different lessons emerge from a consideration of the peasantry. Comprising eighty per cent and more of the population, the tillers of the soil were, for all practical purposes, the "people" or the "masses." The continuing fluctuation in the social status, economic circumstances, and community influence of the peasant, his family and household, is one of the persistent if immeasurable dynamics in the long span of Chinese history.

Generally speaking, it may be said that a very large portion of the Chinese people has rarely enjoyed more than a low and, at times, marginal standard of living. Subsisting in a social system upholding the private ownership of land but rejecting in law the principle of primogeniture, the Chinese peasant has periodically been brutally caught between the millstones of land fragmentation and population growth. Though a small minority of peasants was always able to withstand these pressures, which were intensified by official corruption, mounting tax burdens, and the ruinous workings of nature, and actually to improve its lot, an even larger number was gradually pressed beyond the limits of human endurance. It was under such circumstances that the agrarian rebellions, chronic in Chinese history, broke out, ultimately swelling into gigantic upheavals that swept away the prevailing regime. This pattern of distress, conspicuously evident from the middle of the nineteenth century on, was, when further aggravated by the disruptions of Western imperialism, to underlie the revolutionary wave that burst over modern China.

While dynasties, both native and alien, were to come and go in China during the course of more than three milennia, one institution was never entirely shattered by either human or natural force. This was the family, whose preservation was the first and ultimate responsibility of all its members. Resting upon the pre-Confucian ritual of ancestor worship, by which the past was intimately linked to the present and future, and reinforced by the values of Confucianism, the family was the social focal point of loyalty, obedience, and interest. Not only were the needs and hopes of the individual subordinated to those of this elemental group, but each familial member was explicitly cognizant of his particular position in a hierarchical arrangement resting upon the criteria of sex and age. The requirements of personal and social relationships were well understood. Group cohesiveness, harmony, and stability were acquired at the cost of individuality, youthful initiative, and creative nonconformity. It may easily be understood why the Chinese Communists of our day have dedicated themselves to the destruction of this virile competitor of the state and its interests.

The preceding concepts and the corelated subject matter, which may be tailored to fit particular curricular specifications, will most likely help to establish a basis for an intelligent understanding of Chinese civilization. Taken comprehensively, they will also provide a strong base of departure for the study of modern Chinese history. If, as a wag has put it, the trouble with Chinese history is that there is so much of it, the study of the modern era alone, it may be maintained, presents many difficulties, and not only for secondary school pupils. Without an integrating element, it may be anticipated that Chinese history since the early nineteenth century will be viewed by the beginner as a jumble of unrelated and meaningless data. What is needed, above all, is a fundamental theme enabling the student to maintain a constant focus during his historical study.

In the past century the main currents in the history of China converge sooner or later upon the course of revolution. The vast human drama of one-quarter of mankind, the people of China, caught in the throes of a collapsing civilization and drawn, voluntarily or otherwise, into struggles and movements of titantic proportions for the renovation of their way of life, is indisputably the main strand in modern Chinese history. Given the historically unprecedented interrelatedness of human and international affairs more and more typical of the past one hundred years, it has perhaps been inevitable that the effects of a China in decline and, more recently, of a resurgent China be felt throughout the world. In view of the trends of our own times it is obvious too that the unfolding Chinese revolution will continue far beyond the foreseeable future to be one of the grand themes of global history. If no other aspect of Asian affairs be studied, the modern Chinese revolution alone is worthy of consideration in any educational effort in the area of the social studies.

Manifestly so confusingly complex a social and historical process as is embraced so simply but deceptively under the rubric of the "Chinese Revolution" or of the "Modern Chinese Revolution" cannot but raise difficult problems for teachers in the secondary schools. It would be foolhardy to call for high school students to trace in detail the evolution of China's upheaval over the span of a century or to probe into the numerous aspects, important as each may be, of the national transformation of China. The subject matter must be kept within controllable and definable limits. This would seem to suggest the wisdom of a topical approach to content and of the use of the block-and-gap method in teaching. This procedure should make it possible for the student to secure an intelligible overview of the revolutionary movement as well as a fairly deep perception of some of its more important aspects and problems.

Since the beginner will need some orientation before launching his study of modern China, a general discussion of the conquest of the Chinese Empire by the Manchus in the seventeenth century and their establishment of the last of the imperial dynasties, the Ch'ing (1644–1911), is advisable. In this survey the principal elements of Chinese civilization might be reviewed and some of the main features of the Manchu regime should be outlined. In particular, emphasis may be placed upon the geographical extent of the Empire, the collaborative government by the Manchu conquerors and the Chinese scholar-bureaucrats, and the relations maintained by the imperial court with the surrounding states through the medium of the tributary system. This last topic presents an opportunity for consideration of China's ethnocentric attitudes toward foreign peoples, deemed "barbarians," and of the basis for the tensions that later developed between the dynasty and the Western powers.

The breakdown of the Manchu Empire and of the Chinese way of life, commencing in the early nineteenth century and reaching a point of political crisis with the revolution of 1911, is best treated as the interaction of domestic and foreign pressures. This theme, pivotal for the interpretation of modern Chinese history, is extremely delicate and requires the allocation of proper emphasis to each of the pertinent forces. On the one hand, due consideration must be accorded to developments within China itself that contributed to mounting agrarian crisis and the concomitant decay of traditional social and political institutions. The topical focus for these problems is the rash of peasant uprisings of the period from 1850 to 1875, especially the gigantic Taiping rebellion (1849–64). On the other hand, account must be taken of the gradually intensifying impact of alien political and military power, of the intrusion of Western technology and ideas, and of the growth of foreign trade and economic influence. These disruptive factors, generically designated imperialism, may be typically examined in the so-called Opium War, in the onslaught against China's tributary system and its final destruction in the Sino-Japanese War (1894–95), and in the Boxer uprising of 1900. The synthesis of these domestic and alien forces undermining Manchu China is concretely observed in the anti-Manchu, republican movement of Sun Yat-sen and the revolution of 1911.

The history of China under the Republic reveals not only a continuation but also a deepening and broadening of the crisis that was not and could not be solved by the mere overthrow of the Ch'ing dynasty. In addition to the struggle for the political unification of the country, ripped apart by contending war lords, and for the destruction of imperialist controls abridging China's sovereign rights, the social, economic, and intellectual ferment was increased by the rapidly spreading movements for modernization. In the midst of the rampant strife, confusion, and despair, the paramount note of hope was sounded by the new national revolutionary movement led by Sun Yat-sen and, after his death in 1925, by his successor, Chiang Kai-shek. For a brief while (1923–27) the newborn Chinese Communist party nominally supported the Kuomintang (Nationalist party) in the drive for political unification but, after the split in 1927, the two organizations openly vied for leadership of the country. The invasion and conquest of Manchuria and further encroachments upon North China by Japan after 1931, leading to the outbreak of war in 1937, fatefully affected the course of events within China. They hindered especially the unification efforts of Chiang and the Kuomintang.

There is obviously a tremendous range of suitable topics for the study of Chinese history during the years 1912–37. Probably the subjects that may be pursued most profitably by students in the secondary schools are: the launching of the national revolutionary movement after World War I, with emphasis upon Sun Yat-sen's Three Principles of the People (Nationalism, Democracy, and the People's Livelihood); the uneasy alliance between the Kuomintang and the Chinese Communist party, supported by Soviet Russia and culminating in the split of 1927; Chiang's efforts to achieve national unification during the following decade; Japanese aggression in China from 1931–37; and the vicissitudes of the Chinese Communist party under Mao Tse-tung during this same period.

The history of China from the beginning of the war with Japan in 1937 until the final triumph of the Chinese Communists in the fall of 1949 is without question most difficult to interpret and to teach. What should be the problems of scholarship have too often been made the issues of politics.

The all-pervading question, which may never be answered with exactitude, centers upon responsibility for the decline and fall of the Nationalist regime on mainland China and the ascendency to power of the Communists under Mao Tse-tung. From the point of view of the educator the soundest procedure in treating this entire matter is to single out what may tenably be considered the most relevant factors. In this respect such themes as the heroic resistance of the Nationalist government against the Japanese aggressors for eight long years and the simultaneous disintegration of China under the cataclysmic pressures of war; the expert political exploitation of the nation-wide distress by the Communist party; and the highly controversial roles in China of the United States and Soviet Russia, particularly from 1945 to 1949, might well be studied.

There is, needless to say, no dearth of topics on China worthy of study since the establishment of the People's Republic in October 1949. The policies and programs of the Maoist regime may be investigated in their numerous aspects and dimensions. The extension of the Communist apparatus of power, the reorganization of social life, the manipulation of the agrarian system, the frenzied drive for industrialization, the expansion of the educational system, and population problems and trends are but a few of the significant subjects in which secondary school students have demonstrated consuming interest. At the same time developments and issues in the realm of foreign policy and international affairs such as the Korean War, Sino-Russian relations, Chinese-American tensions, China and the United Nations, the issue of recognition of the People's Republic by the United States, and the quandary posed by the Nationalist government on Formosa may be studied and pondered with great advantage.

Whether one studies China as one of the great civilizations of mankind or as one of the foremost powers of the twentieth-century world, the subject cannot but be of absorbing interest for both young and old. For teachers and citizens of an older generation it is still not too late to remedy some of the gaps in education about China so characteristic of our public school and collegiate system of not so long ago. But for students now making their way through the successive grades of the primary and secondary schools, continued neglect to study China is inexcusable. Knowledge of the land and way of life of almost seven hundred million people must be an earmark of the American student who has completed a secondary school course of education.

Most of the reasons adduced for the study of China are pertinent in the case of Japan. Not only is the Japanese an old and rich culture, many facets of which have been in vogue in the United States in recent years, but Japanese and American history have been closely intertwined during the past generation. As one of the ranking industrial powers, moreover, Japan may be expected to play a prominent role in international affairs for many years to come. And not to be overlooked is the fact that Japanese culture, though strongly influenced in the past by the Chinese, has nevertheless continued to retain a unique quality sharply distinguishing it from its continental neighbor.

In discussing the geography of Japan many teachers tend to point out certain characteristics of the archipelago that, though true, are apt to be misleading. Thus, it is commonly noted that the total area of the Japanese islands does not exceed that of the state of California or of Montana. As a country, however, the United States is not "typical" in its size. A more realistic comparison for students is that the Land of the Rising Sun is about as large as the British Isles or somewhat smaller than France, Germany, Italy, or Spain. It is also pertinent that the Japanese islands lack the compactness of many other countries of equivalent size, being spread over some fifteen degrees of latitude. Fifteen hundred miles separate the extremities of the island chain, comparable to the distance from the Great Lakes to the Gulf of Mexico. The relationship between the factor of distance and political, social, and economic problems in Japanese history may be imaginatively explored by the social studies teacher.

The distance factor in Japan has been strongly magnified by the unusually mountainous character of the land. The rugged terrain has also had other far-reaching effects. About eighty per cent of the islands' area has been unsuitable for either habitation or agriculture. As a result, the search for arable land was for centuries one of the dominant forces in Japanese history. The scarcity of good cultivable soil compelled the Japanese people to turn long ago to intensive methods of farming, thereby consolidating the primacy of wet-field rice among the several cereal grains raised for food. If Japan's mountainous terrain has sharply limited the extent of the arable domain and conditioned the patterns of agriculture, the earth has also been niggardly as a source of raw materials. Deficiencies of this critical nature have powerfully influenced the character and direction of Japan's industrialization in modern times and have necessitated her strong reliance upon international trade during the past several generations.

The implications of her insularity is another aspect of Japan's history and culture that may be fruitfully explored. Though the Japanese people have probably never been completely cut off from cultural and commercial relations with adjoining Korea and China, except when any of the governments involved has so decreed, the difficulty of access to the islands from the continent most likely reduced the threat of alien political domination and military conquest for many centuries. And while Japan did not hesitate to dip deeply into the rich store of Chinese culture to her own lasting benefit, her insular position enabled her to stand apart from the empire's far-flung system of tributary states. The insularity of Japan also heightened consciousness of her isolation from the mainstream of world culture, as represented by China, and paradoxically stimulated tendencies to cultural borrowing as well as to cultural parochialism. Japanese culture has, as a result, been both worldly and particularistic.

The insularity of Japan is reflected most pronouncedly in the cultural homogeneity of the people. Though the ancestors of the Japanese immigrated to the archipelago from various areas of the Asian continent and while strong cultural waves have periodically rolled into the islands from abroad, the Japanese have successfully and successively reduced the many diverse influences to a common cultural denominator. For more than a thousand years a relatively common way of life has been pursued throughout the many parts of the land. Localisms may, to be sure, be found at most times and in many parts of the country, but these may, for all practical purposes, be considered variations on the theme of homogeneity. From the north to the extreme southwest the similarities in language, social and religious values, customs and mores, social and political institutions, economic practices, and modes of artistic expression have been sufficiently widespread to outweigh the existence of differences. Few other major societies in Asia or in the world have ever achieved such cultural homogeneity as the Japanese.

When the problem of the nature of the Japanese way of life is raised, a common illusion is frequently evoked. Because of much uncritical writing on things Japanese, particularly during the decade of the 'thirties when Japan was widely scorned and feared for her aggressive policies, it has been alleged that the civilization of the island people has historically been nothing more than a carbon copy of the Chinese and, in modern times, a poor facsimile of the Western. It is not enough to dismiss this widely shared belief as a demonstrable canard. Of far greater consequence is the fact that this illusion deters understanding of one of the elemental traits of genius of the Japanese people, namely, their facility at cultural manipulation.

From the point of view of the anthropologist no eyebrows

need be raised because the Japanese have acknowledgedly been cultural borrowers. The patterns of life in all societies throughout the world have from time immemorial been profoundly affected by the processes of cultural transmission and diffusion. In the case of a people like the Japanese, dwelling off the mainstreams of civilization and confined to an ultima Thule, cultural enrichment from alien sources cannot but have necessitated intelligent and deliberate effort. Stubbornly to have resisted cultural stimulus and inspiration merely because they were of alien provenance may well have led to arrested development and even stagnation. The purposive introduction of Chinese and Western civilization into Japan should, it may be suggested, be viewed as the response of a people sensible and practical enough to recognize and appreciate ways of living superior to their own. To use the parlance of our times, the Japanese have periodically attempted to modernize, somewhat in the fashion of the underdeveloped nations of the twentieth-century world. Today one would scarcely deride the many governments of Asia and Africa for pursuing policies of social and cultural renovation that are intrinsically old hat to the Japanese.

It must furthermore be stressed that, while Japanese cultural borrowing has had its share of faddists and dilettantes, the practice of selectivity has rarely been absent. The introduction of numerous aspects of Chinese and Western civilization was and still is designed not only to fulfill momentary enthusiasms and vogues but also to serve more basic political, religious, and artistic requirements. In this more discriminate type of transplantation of foreign institutions, ideas, and artistic forms the Japanese have invariably revealed a rare capacity to mold derivative culture to their own particular needs and tastes, a process that has been summed up simply but aptly as "adopt, adapt, adept." It is this behavior and the underlying attitudes that have given the Japanese way of life its singular character and enabled the island people to adjust more rapidly than all other societies in Asia to the demands and pressures of the late nineteenth- and twentieth-century world.

The social studies teacher may illustrate the symbiotic nature of Japanese civilization by reference to many features of the traditional way of life. In the area of political institutions it may be noted that, while the very concept of an emperor with a court comprised of a finely ranked peerage was derived from China in the seventh century, the entire rationale of the imperial family has differed profoundly from the Chinese. In the political traditions of the Middle Kingdom the emperor was considered to be a mortal intermediary between all-powerful Heaven and the people, and susceptible to displacement by revolution. That the popular "right" was often exercised is indicated by the existence of twenty-five dynasties in the official line of China's ruling houses. But in Japan, where there has been only one dynastic family, the claim of the emperor to his throne has rested until recently upon a generally accepted belief by his subjects in his divine descent from the mythological sun goddess. The emperor of Japan always reigned but rarely ruled, and the prime objective of the politically ambitious amongst his subjects was, accordingly, to control the occupant of, but not to seize, the throne.

Again, in contradistinction to the vaunted Chinese practice, political administration in premodern Japan was never based upon a scholar-bureaucracy recruited from the people at large. On the contrary, in Japan an aristocratic tradition prevailed for many hundreds of years after it had disappeared in China. Administrators were enlisted from the ranks of the imperial courtiers and, from the twelfth to the late nineteenth century, from the dominant samurai, or knightly class. These courtiers and warriors also played in Japan the intellectual and creative role reserved in China for the Confucian scholar.

The individuality of Japanese society is especially well observed in the composite of religious beliefs and social values. In the same way that Buddhism from India never succeeded in overcoming indigenous Confucianism and Taoism in China but was rather absorbed by them, so too the teachings of Gautama and generations of his disciples were never able to displace the native cults of Shinto in Japan. The so-called Way of the Gods, rooted in ancient rites of ancestor worship and in a commonly held respect for the forces of nature, was never obliterated but only complemented by alien social and spiritual creeds. Both Buddhism and Confucianism exercised a spiritual, moral, and humanizing influence upon the Japanese people, but Shinto, above all, continued to satisfy through its myths, traditions, and concern for the wonders of the natural universe the emotional needs of the people both high and low.

Shintoistic rites and beliefs, orienting the Japanese toward the natural world, powerfully conditioned and sharpened their aesthetic sensitivities. Constantly alert to the variegated phenomena of their physical environment and delicately attuned to its changing faces and moods, the people of Japan made beauty a cult and art a philosophy. But the Japanese have not only been concerned in their literary and artistic forms with the delicate and subtle delineation of the marvels of nature. They have also sought to capture and retain, in their poetry and painting especially, the finely shaded nuances of human emotion evoked by the microcosmic aspects of the natural world, whose essence was to be sensed rather than explained. If the Japanese way of life, which developed in keeping with peculiar problems and needs, has made any lasting contribution to the evolution of civilization in the over-all sense of the term, it has doubtless been in the area of applied aesthetics exemplifying the play of good taste and judicious simplicity.

Students of Japanese history and life have frequently been puzzled by the seeming paradox of a society upholding values emphasizing refinement, grace, and propriety and a pattern of behavior frequently characterized by harshness and violence in human relations. This apparent enigma may be partially explained by examination of the long social and historical experience of the island people. In the first place, it may be surmised that, because of the persistent influence of Shinto, not to speak of their own peculiar temperament, the Japanese adopted some portions of Buddhist and Confucian teachings but remained cool or indifferent to other aspects. In particular, they did not accept entirely the personal and social ethical requirements of the foreign faiths. Japanese behavior has, as a result, been adapted to what has been called situational ethics, or adjustment to the special circumstances of social problems and relationships. In other words, the Japanese have not in the past behaved in conformity with the general ethical norms of Buddhism or Confucianism but rather in compliance with what their own social group has deemed proper and permissible. In their own familiar social environment the Japanese have been acutely cognizant of what is sanctioned and forbidden; but in a different social milieu, where they have few psychological and philosophical anchors, they have fluctuated between the extremes of painful uncertainty and embarrassing excess. The same Japanese, proverbial for their politeness and thoughtfulness, could, thus, horrify the world during World War II by their atrocities in many foreign lands.

It must also not be forgotten, when seeking understanding of the behavior of the Japanese, that during at least half of its recorded history the nation lived under the heel of an uncontestedly dominant military class. If the values of this elite group, later idealized under the designation of *Bushido* (Way of the Warrior) and also manipulated for the indoctrination of Japan's modern army and navy, provided guidance for the sword-carrying samurai, they also fostered distinct behavioral attitudes and practices among the great mass of downtrodden people. The peasant as well as the more cynical and sophisticated townsman was able to share with the warrior his esteem for such virtues as bravery, loyalty, and obedience, but, given their lower social stations, they simultaneously could not but develop traits of fear, suspicion, evasiveness, and, understandably, the need for circumspection in their relations with their social superiors. These latter qualities were considerably strengthened during the two and a half centuries of authoritarian rule under the Tokugawa Shogunate or military dynasty (1603–1868).

A grasp of the aforementioned concepts, reasonably elaborated, should contribute to an understanding of modern Japanese history, culture, and life. The basic ideas themselves as well as the substantiating subject matter may be culled from the broad range of excellent studies on Japan published in the last decade or two. The subject of Japanese history, however, is, as in the case of China, apt to be somewhat confusing for the secondary school student if it is undertaken in too ambitious a manner. Here again it would be advisable to follow a highly selective topical approach, focusing upon a variety of significant but interrelated problems, achievements, and trends.

The point of entry into the study of Japanese history in the secondary school might well be the first half of the nineteenth century. At this time the Tokugawa Shogunate had already begun to decline, the feudal system of life upon which it was based crumbling under the pressures of an expanding commercial economy. At the same time the policy of national isolation and seclusion, upheld since the middle of the seventeenth century, was being subjected to increasing challenges from the Western powers searching for new international markets for the commodities of the industrial revolution. By 1868 the feudal regime of the Tokugawa having been successfully overthrown by a coalition of discontented samurai and the emperor having recaptured the position and powers he had anciently enjoyed, the political ground was broken for the construction of a modern centralized state.

The topics during this period of history that might be

usefully examined by the secondary school student are: the principal features of Japan's isolation policy under the Tokugawa, with some consideration of the activities of the Dutch who alone among European peoples were permitted to carry on trade with Japan during this era; the expedition of Commodore Matthew Calbraith Perry of the United States and the opening of Japan to international relations; the fascinating experiences of Townsend Harris, the first American consul-general and minister to Japan; and the main characteristics of the Imperial Restoration of 1868. This last topic should offer the basis for suggestive comparisons with the issues of the American Civil War and the movements for national unification in the contemporary Italy and Germany.

During the half century after the accession to the throne of the Meiji Emperor in 1868 Japan engaged in a relentless drive for modernization of her state and society, striving also for a position of equality and security in the international arena. Japan's efforts in this respect might be fruitfully compared not only with the reactions and responses of other peoples in Asia and Africa to the impact of Western might but also held up for comparison with the world-wide quest for modernization and security so characteristic of our own age. In exploring the processes by which the Japanese labored to draw apace of the politically and technologically advanced nations of the West, attention might be given to several areas of Japanese life where concrete successes were scored. In addition to the history of the struggle for the introduction of constitutional, parliamentary government, about which adequate studies are available, such topics as industrialization, the construction of a modern army and navy, and the introduction of a mass compulsory education system are extremely promising. In the field of foreign policy and international affairs Japan's participation in wars with China and Russia as well as her part in World War I may be considered, together with specific problems in American-Japanese relations.

For purposes of the secondary school student the emphasis in Japanese history during the 'tween-war period (1918–41) is best handled within the context of international affairs. This entails the treatment of such subjects as the pattern of Japanese foreign trade, characterized by growing reliance upon the export of manufactured goods and services to pay for imports of raw materials and foodstuffs; the military solution to Japan's dilemmas epitomized by the invasion and conquest of Manchuria and subsequent encroachments upon China; and the general and specific background of the attack against Pearl Harbor in 1941. If the vital question of the atomic bombings of Japan is to be discussed in the classroom it is absolutely necessary, if the student is to acquire a fairly full view of the many dimensions of the matter, to evaluate it within the political and military context of affairs during the summer of 1945 and not simply as a moral issue.

Developments and affairs in Japan since her surrender in 1945 offer rich and varied fare for study. Topics that may be examined selectively are the policies, achievements, and failures of the Occupation forces; the quest for a democratic way of life; the reconstruction and expansion of Japan as one of the foremost industrial powers of the world; Japanese attitudes and policies on the issues of war, peace, and neutralism; the transformations in Japanese society, especially in the behavior and values of the younger generation and in the role and position of women; and the changing patterns of living stimulated by new tastes, values, and expectations. In all of these themes there are boundless opportunities for the development of comparisons between the traditional and modern in Japanese life.

Subtle and profound as the similarities and differences in the Chinese and Japanese ways of life have been and are today, taken individually or collectively as integral parts of a much broader Sinitic area of civilization embracing East Asia, they are quite distinct from the great complex of peoples and cultures known as India. No detailed brief is really called for in justification of the study of India at any level of American education. India is not only the oldest functioning civilization in the world today and a peerlessly rich storehouse of human experience but her rapidly increased importance in world affairs during the past century is either known or assumed by most American people.

It is only fair to point out that, while an extremely high priority should be accorded the study of India in the secondary schools, there are numerous difficult problems to overcome. Though the humanistic aspects of Indian civilization have attracted the attention of both scholars and laymen in the United States and abroad for many years, Indian studies, as opposed to the more narrowly based Indology, have evoked somewhat wider interest in American colleges and universities only during the past decade. In contrast to the teaching and research on China and Japan, which have been carried on in an ever increasing number of academic institutions since the end of World War II, Indian studies have yet to penetrate into the curriculum of an appreciable number of schools. Lacking widespread opportunity for formal study of India, it may be anticipated that many social studies instructors, otherwise convinced of the need to include India in their teaching, will have to resort to self-study. The intellectual returns of such an effort would, nevertheless, be very rewarding.

For purposes of study, teaching, and research, India with its profuse diversities, striking contrasts, and bewildering complexities poses problems of a unique nature. In comparison, the study of either China or of Japan seems encouragingly simple. If India has not been a mere geographical expression for the past several thousand years neither has it been a civilization in the sense the term is ordinarily applied. Within the huge expanse of the South Asian subcontinent, as large as all of Western Europe, there has existed since ancient times a cultural heterogeneity that may in some ways be compared with that of continental Asia itself. Misleading as it is to generalize about Asia with its many variegated peoples and cultures, the pitfalls are apparent in the case of India alone.

As a political entity India is largely the creation of the great English empire builders of the last two centuries. Since 1947, when the republics of India and Pakistan were founded through partition of the subcontinent, the territorial proportions of India have been substantially reduced. But whether one has in mind the former British Indian Empire, the vast and constantly changing congeries of empires, kingdoms, and petty states that comprised India before the arrival of European merchants and conquerors, or the postpartition nation, the fact remains that India has historically always been huge. Within this extensive territorial domain there has been more than adequate latitude for the growth and perpetuation of heterogenous cultural elements.

The social studies teacher must exercise considerable care in developing the theme of the heterogeneity of India, being as certain as possible of the purposes this pivotal idea should serve. Merely to consider one or another of the multitude of diverse features of the land, peoples, and cultures of India as learning goals in themselves is likely to lead to confusion. The idea of heterogeneity should be used to establish a key frame of reference for the study of India as a whole. The concept may be employed to underscore not only a conspicuous characteristic of Indian history and life but also to impress upon the student the remarkable achievement entailed in fashioning a general way of life amidst such formidable diversity. The factor of heterogeneity is furthermore vital for a proper appreciation of the various achievements and manifold problems of the people of India in their recent struggle to construct a modern nation-state.

In selecting geographical and cultural features and forms to illustrate heterogeneity in India the social studies teacher has a wide area of choice. But whatever topics that may, because of special interest or individual feelings of competence, be elected for treatment in the classroom, there are several that should not be overlooked. Though the degree of emphasis may well vary, the subjects of physical geography, language, and race must be discussed. The crucial problem of religion is best handled within a separate context.

From the point of view of physical terrain there are few countries in the extensive Eurasian land mass possessing as broad a range of contrasts as India. Only China is comparably rich in its geographical diversity. Relatively isolated from the remainder of Asia by the towering mountain ranges of the north and northwest, by the jungles of the northeast, and by the oceans to east and west, India has been penetrated during the course of her long history only by the hardiest invaders. This is not to say that India has not had continuing cultural and commercial contact with peoples beyond the frontiers of the subcontinent; it is rather to suggest that because of isolation the intensity of these contacts has historically been reduced. In addition to the singular and varied features of her borders, there are few major land forms that are not to be found within India. Long ranges of mountains and hills, broad and almost impenetrable deserts, fertile river plains, rich alluvial deltas, extensive upland plateaus, and thick jungles and forest lands have indisputably conditioned the features of local cultures and strongly fostered regionalism and particularism.

The geographical regionalism, which has for centuries been typical of India, has been greatly confirmed by the numerous languages and dialects. Though the various tongues spoken throughout the country are almost two hundred in number, the large majority are either dialectical variations or languages used by minor ethnic groups. Yet, since the great mass of people speak one or another of about fifteen major languages, the difficulties of comunication on a country-wide basis are evident. The principal languages, moreover, differ more significantly than the European, which, for philological purposes at least, are related through their Indo-European base. But in India not only are languages as similar or different as French, Spanish, and Italian spoken in and within adjoining areas, but totally different linguistic families dominate the speech of large portions of the subcontinent. North and South India especially are distinguished from each other in this vital respect. The multilingual character of India, typical, to be sure, of other parts of Asia, presents a sharp contrast to China but more particularly to Japan.

In recent years racial differences in India have doubtless not loomed so large as during ancient times. The persistence of distinct racial types, not to be confused with ethnic groups, through many centuries has lent an additional dimension to the range of heterogeneity. The overwhelming number of Indian peoples are Caucasian and, hence, are racially related to the peoples of Southwest Asia, North Africa, and Europe. Within the Caucasian element of India's vast population of more than four hundred million there may be found all the variations in skin coloration, physical appearance, and size characteristic of the racial type as a whole. In addition, pockets of peoples of Mongolian and Negroid ancestry are situated in many parts of the country, notably in the far north and northeast. The resourceful social studies teacher should be easily able to illustrate pictorially the profuse variety of human types represented in the ethnology of India.

Perhaps the most fascinating aspect of India's diversity is her many religious faiths. No other civilization in the history of the world during the past two thousand years has been exposed to a greater variety of spiritual teaching and practice. Almost all major religions that have arisen and flourished in the course of man's quest for spiritual guidance have at one time or another been represented by a following in India. Some of these faiths—Hinduism, Buddhism, Jain, and Sikhism —have originated within India itself; others such as Christianity, Judaism, Islam, and Zoroastrianism (the religion of the

Parsi), have been transmitted to the subcontinent by immigrants, missionaries, and conquerors. For pupils interested in studying the checkered scope of the religious experiences of man, Indian civilization offers unparalleled riches.

Though each of India's many religions has contributed in one way or another to the formation and enrichment of India's civilization, none has ever lastingly rivaled Hinduism in its hold upon hundreds of millions of people for a hundred generations and more. Hinduism may be considered the all-encompassing way of life of India during her entire history, other major religions, notably Buddhism and Islam, being meaningful within the context of Indian civilization largely as major challenges to the dominant faith. Even more so than in the case of Confucianism in China, a familiarity with Hinduism or, at a minimum, of some of its principal teachings and features is indispensable for an understanding of India's past and present.

Hinduism is so infinitely complex as a religion, a philosophy, and a way of life that it literally defies definition. Far-ranging in its concerns, it is sufficiently flexible and all embracing to accommodate without serious strain a spectrum of belief ranging from the most noble and elevating thought ever perceived by man to the crassest superstition that has governed the behavior of people. The genius of Hinduism and unquestionably the principal cause for its survival through the centuries in the face of innumerable challenges, both religious and secular, has been its capacity to provide spiritual, intellectual, and emotional satisfaction on all levels of human need and understanding. Hinduism has sufficed for the occasional philosopher and saint as well as for the far more multitudinous masses.

Regardless of their many differences, Hindus have, one and all, believed in rebirth of the soul. The life of the individual has not been considered fixed in time but rather a single phase of a continuing process of being, extending through many life spans in the course of which the soul seeks union with the all-pervading oneness or Brahma. Death is final for the physical body but not for the soul, which is reborn into a new life. The lot of the soul is determined by karma, not to be confounded with fate or destiny but meaning the summing up of the moral consequences of past behavior. The worthiest goal of man is, consequently, to strive to fulfill his dharma, the moral law and his ultimate duty, and by his karma to move progressively from one life span after another to the ultimate reward—namely, liberation of the soul from the trials of life, death, and rebirth.

The implications of the Hindu conception of the purpose and meaning of life are observed in the well-known but not always understood caste system. It is one of the oldest systems of social organization in the world. Originating perhaps as a color bar established by ancient invaders of India, the caste system has evolved over the past three thousand years into a highly elaborate and ramified pattern of social differentiation dominating all areas of Indian life. Born into the particular caste of his parents, the Indian has accepted his status as the consequence of his karma and has sought to fulfill the concomitant requirements. Caste, prescribing the range of permissible and sanctioned behavior, is unchangeable during the lifetime of the individual. Only when the soul is reborn into a new life, the Hindu has believed, may he anticipate an alteration, for better or worse, of his caste position.

Study of the Hindu caste system should be of deep interest to Americans of high school age, who are ordinarily not familiar with forms of social organization different from their own. In the classroom it would be advisable, however, for the social studies teacher to concentrate more upon the functions of the caste system and less upon its philosophical rationale, though a minimum understanding of the latter is necessary. More particularly, examination of the caste system should be approached as a historically evolving process for the determination of occupational differentiation and assignment that has, for all practical purposes, blurred the lines of demarcation stratifying Hindu society in the four or five classes discussed in the literature of antiquity. For many centuries and even today the general class divisions of priest (Brahmin), warrior, merchant, peasant, and outcaste have been far less meaningful for everyday social and economic purposes than the hundreds of subcastes into which the world of Hinduism has been divided. It is the subcaste, rather than caste per se, that has prescribed the patterns of behavior, the character of human relations, and the type of occupational function of the Hindu.

To reduce the caste system from the levels of purely descriptive treatment and abstract analysis its workings should be studied within the context of some of the primary social institutions of Indian life. These ends may be excellently fulfilled by examination of the Indian village and family. Fortunately, there is available an appreciable volume and variety of suitable reading material on these subjects in the form of popular and semipopular sociological and anthropological treatises, biographies, autobiographies, and works of fiction not beyond the capacity of secondary school students. Excellent use too may be made of the various documentary films and film strips concerned with these aspects of Indian life.

India has been called a land of villages, a designation that might with almost equal validity be applied to all countries in Asia save perhaps modern Japan and Israel. In the case of India, however, it is the staggering number and variety of villages that is so impressive. There is no need for the secondary school student to be concerned with the nature of the many differences among the Indian villages; these problems are more consequential at higher levels of learning. But it is important for the student to secure some insight into the earthbound nature of Indian civilization. In the life of the peasant village, wherever it may be found in the subcontinent, he may discover the routines of daily life, the time-old problems and methods of wresting food from the land, the occupational divisions on the basis of subcastes that reveal the methods of fulfillment of elemental social and economic needs and services, the expression and performance of social relationships, and the structure and functioning of the family. The village and family are, in short, the key to an understanding of Indian society for the past several thousand years. Without this background it is literally impossible to fathom the immensity of the problems entailed in India's current struggle to uplift her vast population and to establish a modern way of life.

In considering the caste system, village, and family in India the social studies teacher must be careful to establish a sound frame of reference. All too often these subjects are approached from the point of view of Western civilization and its peculiar value system. As a consequence, hypercritical assessments of Indian social forms are not uncommon. Care must be taken to ensure that the purposes of these social institutions are understood. Though the life of the individual has been greatly circumscribed in tradition-bound India, though opportunities for social mobility have been greatly restricted, and though ambition and creative impulse have been sharply limited, the benefits of social stability and of social and psychological security have been ceaselessly emphasized by all careful students of Indian society.

While the beliefs and outlook of Hinduism have penetrated deeply into all areas of Indian life during the past three millennia, account must also be taken of the influences of two other great religions, Buddhism and Islam. The secondary school student should acquire at least a minimal familiarity with their principal tenets.

Buddhism arose in north India almost twenty-five hundred years ago, partly as a reaction against a Hinduism that was becoming dominated more and more by Brahminical caste and ritualism. Though the founder of this new religion, Gautama (sixth–fifth century B.C.), accepted many of the principal doctrines of the Hindu faith such as karma, dharma, and rebirth of the soul, in his attitude and behavior he implicitly rejected the caste system. Troubled by the perpetual misery that seemed to be the lot of mankind, he attributed human sorrow and suffering to man's desire and vain attachment to the things of life. To achieve liberation from his wretchedness, man, Gautama taught, had to conquer and extinguish his inner desire. By pursuing the good life or the Eightfold Path through many life spans man might ultimately attain the only worthy goal, namely, nirvana, or absorption of the soul or ego into the all-pervading cosmos. The end of all human endeavor was the annihilation of self.

Buddhism, with its promise of the possibility of escape from the confines of caste and its exaltation of humanitarian virtues, had a profound appeal for the peoples of India. But by about ten centuries ago it gradually succumbed to the superior strength of both Hinduism and the newly introduced Islam, popularly but inaccurately called Mohammedanism. Still, Buddhism with its various schools of thought was successfully transmitted by missionaries to the many peoples of Central, Eastern, and Southeast Asia where it has continued to thrive. Today the teachings of Gautama the Buddha, modified by local tastes and needs, remain alive in such lands as Japan, Thailand, Laos, Cambodia, South Vietnam, and Burma.

As opposed to Buddhism, which was of indigenous provenance, Islam was brought to India by invaders and merchants from Southwest Asia. And contrary to common belief, the message of Muhammad was not thrust upon the peoples of India at the point of the sword. Islam's success in winning a multitude of converts was largely due to the power of its monotheistic creed, social egalitarianism, and rich philosophical and cultural heritage. But not to be discounted is the patronage provided by successive dynasties of Muslim conquerors. The contribution of the Mogul (Mongol) emperors, who ruled over a large part of the Indian subcontinent during the sixteenth and seventeenth centuries, is very pertinent in this respect.

As in the case of Buddhism the gospel of Islam was transmitted eastward far beyond the frontiers of India. From the fifteenth century on, the teachings of Muhammad were carried by merchants into Southeast Asia, where new and notable successes in conversion were scored. Sweeping through the world of Malaysia, Islam struck deep roots in the East Indies, Malaya, and the southern Philippines. Today far more Muslims live in the lands from Pakistan to Indonesia than in the entire Arabic Middle East.

For the study of modern Indian history, a suitable theme, as in the case of China and Japan, is called for. If China's history in recent times is best approached through the long and protracted nationalist revolution and modern Japanese history through the struggle for modernization and the quest for international power, the history of modern India should be focused upon the theme of struggle for national independence. Among the three societies recommended for the study of Asia in the secondary schools, India is the only one that completely lost its independence in early modern times and furnishes, accordingly, lessons for the study of nationalism and imperialism in modern Asia that cannot be entirely derived from a consideration of either China or Japan.

As a preliminary to the study of India's struggle for national independence from the mid-nineteenth century to 1947 there is some merit in reviewing the broad outlines of Indian affairs since the early seventeenth century. This survey should be designed to reveal the gradual ascendancy of England to paramount political power as a consequence of its triumphs over Muslim, Hindu, and French opposition and competition. It should serve to point out the circumstances of British succession to the mantle of the imperial Mogul dynasty, which dominated much of the Indian subcontinent before its collapse in the early eighteenth century. And it should seek to clarify the nature of the structure of the British Empire in India, a complex of many hundreds of princely domains and directly administered states, on the eve of the great Sepoy uprising in 1857–58. These were the formative years of the British raj in India.

From the outbreak of the Sepoy Rebellion until the end of World War I British power was increasingly extended throughout India. For a half century and more the technology and ideas of England were transplanted to the "jewel" of the British Empire, posing challenges and creating conflicts in the traditional way of life. During these years India became one of the foremost markets for industrial England and one of its primary sources of wealth. Here one may see a model of British imperialism in action. But regardless of the conflicting interpretations of the purposes and effects of British policy in India during these times, it would seem that India's emerging political leaders were less grieved by matters of economic exploitation and more concerned with issues of governmental and administrative processes. The primary goal of Indian nationalist leaders before the close of World War I was to secure a measure of self-government.

For the initial period in India's movement from rebellion through political struggle to ultimate independence several topics lend themselves well to study in the secondary schools. The unfolding of the Sepoy uprising as well as its suppression and aftermath; the introduction of one or another of British institutions, preferably educational facilities; the founding and early history of the Indian National Congress; and Gandhi's early career in South Africa and India as well as his teachings of nonviolence resistance commend themselves for the attention of the student in the secondary school.

The period from the end of World War I until the attainment of independence in 1947, necessitating partition of the subcontinent into the republics of India and Pakistan, was characterized by the growth of bitterness and strife, not only between Indian nationalists and Great Britain but also among the nationalists themselves. On various occasions formulas for the extension of powers of self-government were presented by the imperial regime for the consideration of nationalist leaders and the hereditary rulers of the princely states. Unfortunately none of the basic solutions was considered acceptable by the many interested parties, while the possibilities of agreement were greatly complicated by the emergence during the decade of the 'thirties of a Muslim League alarmed by the prospects of a Hindu-dominated India. The rejection by Indian National Congress leaders, symbolized by Gandhi and Nehru, of any program for self-government falling short of their expectations is summed up in their refusal to support England during World War II. The outcome of the entire dispute was the decision of England to withdraw from India in 1947 at the cost of political cleavage in her imperial domain.

The struggle for self-government in India after 1918 may be studied in the careers of Gandhi and Nehru. A number of fine biographies as well as the principal writings of these giants of Indian nationalism are currently available and, in most instances, may be handled without undue difficulty by students in the secondary schools, especially on the junior and senior levels. Other manageable topics are India's role in World War II, the partition of British India in 1947, and the dispute between India and Pakistan over Kashmir.

As in the case of postwar China and Japan, there are literally innumerable worthwhile topics for the study of Indian affairs since the achievement of national independence. The governing theme for this period should doubtless be India's struggle to create a modern nation-state. From the many choices possible the following subjects might well be considered: programs to promote democratic institutions, ideas, and behavior in a strongly tradition-bound civilization; efforts to raise abysmally low standards of living, entailing the fostering of industrialization and the encouragement of change and reform in agrarian life; problems and trends in the expansion and modernization of education; the problems and prospects for modification of the caste system; and the challenges of population growth. When possible, a comparison of the modernization efforts of India and Communist China might be made. Needless to say, some attention must be given to India's role and influence in international affairs, particularly in the United Nations.

The aforementioned concepts and topics may be considered realistic goals of learning about Asia for the secondary school student. Whether the scope of study be highly concentrated or spaced out over the course of several years in various social studies classes, there is no reason why a student of normal intelligence and intellectual capacity should not be able to achieve the proposed objectives. Judging from scattered experience to date, it is a fair presumption that the secondary school student will not only be greatly enthused by his glimpses of ways of life different from his own but that he will thereby be so much the better educated.

Teaching about Russia and Eastern Europe

Michael B. Petrovich / University of Wisconsin

I. General Statement of the Problem

THERE HAS BEEN a notorious lag between new advances in scholarship and their appearance in our elementary and secondary schools. However, the impact of World War II and the global responsibilities of the American nation in a world fraught with tensions are tending rapidly to close the gap in many fields. One of these fields is the study of the non-Western areas of the world. In view of the international situation, it is hardly surprising that Americans should be especially concerned with the Soviet Union, not only as an expanding great power but as a leader of the world-wide Communist movement.

The specific question before us here is: What kinds of knowledge, what concepts and attitudes about the Soviet Union in particular and Eastern Europe in general, should American school children have acquired by the end of their senior year in high school?

We should specify at the outset the problems that we have deliberately chosen to ignore in our discussion, though we are painfully aware of their existence. We feel no need to differentiate between the "terminal" student (a ghastly term) and the college-bound student inasmuch as we shall be dealing with those minimum understandings that we consider appropriate to both groups. Furthermore, we shall consciously avoid being swayed by our acquaintance with such griefs as the inadequacy of teacher training in this field, the dearth of suitable teaching materials, the demands of an already overcrowded curriculum, local pressures and taboos, and similar obstacles. We must assume that once agreement has been reached on the necessity of teaching more, and more effectively, about Russia and Eastern Europe in our schools, these problems cannot be regarded as deterrents, but only as challenges to be met by those best qualified to meet them. Thus we shall address ourselves solely to questions of approach and content. In so doing, we shall not presume to suggest at what point in a child's education, in what grades and courses, he should be exposed to any part of the material to be discussed here, though we insist that certain kinds of knowledge cannot be grasped without certain prerequisites.

While this study deals with the Russian and East European area, it is hoped that most of the underlying assumptions and approaches here will be found applicable to the study of any other major world area.

II. Some Basic Assumptions

It is, of course, possible to learn a great deal about Russia and Eastern Europe through disciplines outside the social studies. Literature, music, art, physical geography, and still other subjects can each contribute to the student's knowledge of the area, and this should never be forgotten in planning a curriculum. However, given the nature of our interest in the

Russian and East European area, it is reasonable to suppose that the school child will acquire his knowledge of the area largely through the social studies. Therefore, we feel obliged to state our position on the role of the social studies in our education.

The social studies have both an ideal and a practical function in our educational system.

Ideally, the social studies provide the pupil with the means to acquire a more perfect knowledge of himself and his potentialities through and understanding of the social groups of which he is a part and with which he must deal—from the family to all of humanity. To understand these social groups the pupil must see them as dynamic institutions or systems that have a historical development and that contain elements of both continuity and change. The pupil must comprehend the interaction of these institutions or systems, their relation to him and his relation to them.

The practical role of the social studies is to provide the kinds of knowledge that will develop effective members of society who will be able to make decisions and to act with understanding.

It will readily be noted that these are the basic aims of a liberal education as traditionally understood in our society. The learning human himself is our first concern, and then the present state of the world. Naturally, it is hoped that the improvement of the one might lead to the progress of the other. Yet we must insist on the primacy of the pupil as our chief concern because the values of a liberal education are universal and permanent, whereas the state of the world is highly unstable. Our education must be not only for today's problems but for ever. If we recognize this clearly, we shall be less apt to expose our children to a consideration of the unsettling crises of the day before they have had a chance to gain the stability that comes with a knowledge of past experience and the basic workings of human society.

We hold with the view that regards the pupil, the developing human achieving self-fulfillment, as the center of a series of concentric circles—the family, the community, the state, the nation, Western civilization—all of which encompass him physically and all of which he in turn must encompass intellectually and emotionally before he can participate effectively within them. Our particular concern is simply that the pupil be led beyond these traditional limits into the whole world with which his society, in all its parts, is increasingly involved.

III. The Area as a Unit of Study

How is the student to learn more about world areas other than his own? Obviously the most direct and immediate way is to introduce more material about these areas in appropriate places within existing courses, and this should be done, though with great discretion. However, if this is all that is going to happen, if existing courses are simply going to be crammed with more bits of information hither and yon, something crucial will be lost—the educational opportunity to see another part of the world as a whole, as an integral socio-cultural system. Thus we envision the study of Russia and Eastern Europe as a unit (whatever material about the area will find its way in other courses), and we regard that unit as one of several in a special course devoted to world areas.

What are the advantages of such an area approach? We should like to advance four:

1. The area approach is well suited to the stated basic aim of a liberal education—a deeper knowledge of self and of one's own society.
2. It provides information of practical value about an important part of the world which concerns us.
3. It gives the student an awareness of cultural relativity.
4. It makes possible and necessary the integration of all the social sciences.

It is well known that American education has been traditionally ethnocentric and Western-oriented (if anything can be occidentally oriented). The writer teaches in an otherwise fairly progressive state where the only required social studies course is United States history, and where many students obtain little organized knowledge of the world except what they glean in the hours devoted to current events, if that can be called organized. It is by no means solely or even primarily the exigencies of the present world crisis that require the extension of our understanding beyond the borders of our nation and of the Atlantic Community. The demands of a liberal education summon us to break through the sound barrier of our ethnocentrism, and to hear and to comprehend the voices—the official and the unofficial, the friendly and the hostile, the loud and the muffled—which emanate from all the major world areas that engage our attention. We need to do this, not only for urgently practical reasons, but also because this extension of the limits of our knowledge will surely teach us more about ourselves and the more lasting meaning, purposes, and values of our own society. The student of a culture area different from his own is forced by the very nature of the study to make comparisons with his world; he must make judgments of some kind that will necessarily proceed from his own experience and background. We are, of course, not concerned here primarily with the study of other peoples by children in the elementary grades; it is presumed that information on this level will not be of the kind that will demand sophisticated soul searching and consideration of principles (though it can and must lead to positive attitudes, such as acceptance of differences without intolerance). However, as the older student learns more about the basic principles of Russian (Soviet), Chinese, Indian, or Arab society, he is increasingly nudged into seeing his own society, and himself, in a constantly changing light. We must make certain that this confrontation with other worlds will not lead the pupil to reject his own society but to seek to improve it with a growing appreciation for what is his own, what is distinctive of others, and what is common to all.

It follows that the study of Russia and Eastern Europe, or any other major world areas, should certainly not be undertaken at the expense of studying our own nation and Western civilization. Rather than a diminution of an already weak and neglected program, we require a renewed emphasis on the study of Western civilization in our schools as a prerequisite for area studies. Indeed, nothing might be healthier than to correct the labels on our "World History" courses, tighten up and strengthen the content of these courses, call them what most of them really are—courses in Western civilization—and then require all students to take them. The day is past when the study of the history of the white race and its expansion over the globe can be decently described as world history. On the other hand, there is a greater need than ever for us to understand the history of our own culture area and the extent and nature of its impact on the world at large.

Surely we need not belabor the second of the advantages that we have ascribed to area studies—their practical value—particularly with respect to the Soviet Union. The U.S.S.R. is a great power of vast territory and resources whose expanding influence is a major problem in international affairs. It is a planned society whose Communist principles are antithetical to the bases of a free enterprise system or even a mixed system such as that common in the West. As so dramatically illustrated by the Sputniks, this Soviet society has been successful in producing impressive advances in the material culture of a vast area that was but yesterday an economically underdeveloped society consisting largely of an illiterate peasantry. Moscow is still the leading center of the world Communist movement. Furthermore, both the old Russia and the new have made outstanding contributions to the arts and sciences. Finally, it is clear that the future of mankind depends in large measure on the modus vivendi our own society and the

Soviet can reach, despite their differing ideologies, and this will call for the active understanding of our entire citizenry.

Despite the urgency of the global crises that have triggered so much of our interest in other areas of the world, especially the Soviet Union, we can do ourselves a grave disservice by studying this or any other area solely in a spirit of utilitarian present-mindedness. Exaggerated preoccupation with the daily headlines can lead only to a disconcerting crisis hopping in a cold-war atmosphere. We must not permit the daily headlines or present atmosphere to dominate curriculum planning or course objectives. The trouble-spot approach can only lead to diffusion and distortion.

An exaggerated present-mindedness in dealing with the Soviet Union, for example, can lead to the know-your-enemy philosophy. It seems incredible that educators reared in the traditions of liberal education would even consider such an approach. Yet, given the intensity of American popular anxiety over the Soviet Union and Communism, this attitude may attract the militant, or at least serve the timid educator or school board as a cover for a legitimate educational interest in the subject. Whether the Soviet Union is or is not our friend, now or forever, is irrelevant here; we are also against the know-your-friends approach with regard to any area. Such approaches lead to a dogmatism that divides the world into the "good" and the "bad," truth and error. It measures all men by their real or presumed attitudes toward us in the cold war. Such a dichotomy is not only unrealistic, for real life is never that simple, but it is harmful in assuming the conflict of irreconcilables when experience teaches otherwise. We do not suggest for a moment that it is good educational policy to hide the fact that there are basic ideological differences between the democratic conception and the totalitarian. On the contrary. But we do object to the emphasis on knowing-your-enemy because this is not good education: it is indoctrination. It hinders the student from searching all the facts, from delving into the rationale of an opposing point of view, from testing one's own values, and from earning an opinion. Where there is mere acquiescence there can be no education.

Still another danger that can result from an obsession with present problems is the attitude that it is the existence of Communism and the threat of Soviet power alone that makes the U.S.S.R. and Eastern Europe an important subject for study. Somewhere lurking in our minds is the suspicion that all these countries cannot have been very significant before 1917 because few Westerners were interested in them. We hope that it is not necessary to expose here the fallacy of this opinion. Let us merely state our underlying assumption that Russia and Eastern Europe would be worth studying as a significant part of world civilization and a major culture area even if Communism never existed and nobody believed our national security to be at stake. We wish to make clear that we regard knowledge of Communism, both its theory and practice, a vital part of American education. Furthermore, we think it entirely appropriate to undertake a comparative study of Communist regimes. While we are aware of many difficulties involved in teaching about Communism, we insist that the importance of the issue makes it impossible for us to shirk this responsibility in the face of taboos or other problems. Yet it must be recognized that the practice of Communism in any country does not take place on a clean slate erased by revolution but rather in a socio-cultural system that still bears the imprint of the past. It is a decided error to suppose that one can study the past half century of Soviet Communism without reference to the total Russian environment that gave rise to and stamped that movement.

An awareness of cultural relativity, the third advantage listed, involves recognition of the fact that all cultures are self-consistent and distinctive systems that have evolved from a unique past and environment. Different challenges have produced correspondingly different responses, within a certain set of culture patterns. Nothing betrays American ethnocentrism more than the benign assumption that everyone in the world would like to emulate our "way of life," and that those who do not are either hopelessly backward or pernicious. Many Americans have little conception of those elements in Western civilization that finally produced our type of political democracy, and so they assume that any society can, by fiat, attain that kind of democracy even when the prerequisite elements are absent. In our dealings with other areas we are often oblivious to, or impatient with, certain attitudes or procedures distinctive of that culture, while we are apt to be easily hurt when our own ways are misunderstood or criticized. An important goal of area studies should be to instill recognition that there are other ways of life besides our own and that the differences among them are not only, or even primarily, to be ascribed to simply different stages of material development (as Marxists would claim). India is not different from America because it is "backward"—though it certainly is behind us in many aspects of life—but because it is India; and even if it were to advance beyond our material standards, India would still be India in that the changes would take place within the Indian cultural patterns. This point can be made even more effectively using the Soviet Union as an example.

American children must learn better than their parents did to accept cultural diversity in the world; indeed, to welcome it, because only thus can we deal effectively with others. This is going to be difficult. There are, of course, millions of Americans who have not yet learned to accept cultural diversity in our own country—hence our minority problems. Besides, the initial impetus of the melting-pot idea in our own society, and one shared by both the melters and the melted despite pronouncements to the contrary, sprang from the desire to homogenize our population. It is not easy, after gearing our educational system to this gigantic task for over half a century, to teach that cultural diversity in the world is desirable and useful. There will always be the patronizing idea that while the customs, costumes, and ways of other peoples are "interesting" and quaint (or horrid), these people would really be like us if they only could or knew any better. I am constantly asked at my public lectures on the Soviet Union: How can the Russians stand it? Why don't they rebel? And the questioners are always surprised to be told that the force of a police state is by no means the only answer, or even the most important answer.

We have stated previously that area studies permitted us to know our own society better insofar as it forced us to make comparisons with other societies. We stand by the argument, but here—in discussing cultural relativity—we must introduce a caveat: we must not study other areas simply for the sake of comparisons, but because it is important for us to learn about these areas as entities in themselves. We are all too well acquainted with the American compulsion to draw comparisons between the American and the Communist way of life, with our side always coming out on top (though the beeps of the Sputniks have injected a disquieting note). It is less known that the Soviets share the same compulsion to compare, and, oddly enough, they find the balance in their favor. This obsession reaches a proper absurdity in the old story about the American tourist in Moscow who failed to be impressed by the marble-lined, crystal-chandeliered subway because the line was too short and didn't go anywhere. "Yes," his chagrined Soviet guide retorted, "but what about the Negro question in America?" Once students learn that culture areas are basically unique, despite borrowings and cross-fertilization, because their environments and histories differ, they will be less apt to attempt comparisons of what is essentially incomparable and they will stop comparing on the assumption that everything ought to be the same to be "normal"; rather they will compare to see if there is anything we can learn about one another, or even from one another. Comparisons made in this spirit will lead to a recognition not only of differences but of similarities. To get the most out of a study of the Soviet Union particularly, pupils must investigate it as they would any other area. If the subject is taught primarily as a vehicle for drawing comparisons favorable to our way of life, this is bound to lead to a didactic tone, an air of self-righteousness, and an almost unavoidable tendency to stack the facts. A perceptive generation of adolescents still not broken by conformity may be quick to expose this. Worse yet, they might succumb. In any case, this is not an ideal learning situation.

A prime aim of area studies is to communicate the concept that each area, if properly defined, is a self-consistent and intelligible whole with a rationale of its own, even though that rationale is different from our own or any other. Area studies offer the student an opportunity to see and to investigate another socio-cultural system as a whole, in all its significant aspects. No matter what area is taught, or by what kind of social scientist, it ought to be a multidisciplinary and even interdisciplinary teaching and learning experience. The concept of an area as a socio-cultural entity demands the study of that area's history, social organization, economic system, religious or ideological basis, geographic environment, national psychology, and forms of artistic expression and technology. Area studies offer a unique opportunity for synthesis among the social studies: history is also theoretically interested in the totality of human existence, but only in the past; anthropology likewise looks at the whole society, but is generally concerned with primitive societies rather than with, let us say, an area such as the Soviet Union. The other social studies are even more specialized.

On the other hand, curriculum planners, teachers, and writers of textbooks must realize that area studies are not a catch-all, a potpourri of all kinds of information. Rather they must integrate various approaches and facts into a comprehensible pattern. The scope and multiplicity of the subject matter is so great that teacher and pupil will be forced to concentrate on those major issues, aspects, or combinations that make that particular culture distinctive and significant. There is no room here for irrelevant or inconsequential facts. Indeed, there may not even be room for many important facts.

This raises the fundamental question: How many areas can be included in the curriculum? We shall not attempt to discuss this problem fully here. For one thing, it would involve consideration of problems which we said at the outset we would avoid. For another, our own concern is with one particular area—Russia and Eastern Europe. Nevertheless, while we would not wish to specify any maximum or even optimum number, we feel obliged to state that the study of one area—even the area of our interest—is not enough. We know that one well-organized, intensive course on the Soviet Union, for example, would have many of the advantages we claim for area studies plus the advantage of depth. We have ourselves been associated with just such a course offered at the high school of the University of Wisconsin and are impressed with the results. However, this was an experimental situation with an unusually well-trained teacher (Miss Beth Arveson), who in turn enjoyed the active participation of area specialists on the University of Wisconsin faculty. In our opinion, the advantage of depth that a single course on one area offers is more than offset by a loss of breadth and a lack of opportunity to compare several quite different culture areas the world over. As a rule we would maintain that no one area is so representative that it alone could offer the student all the important benefits to be derived from area studies. Indeed, even at the university level of graduate study we urge the would-be area specialist in Russian studies to acquaint himself with another culture area. Specialization at the high school level with respect to area studies is not warranted by the pupil's previous experience. Nor should we think of any area study on this level in terms of vocational utility.

Having said this, we should like to advance the contention that, no matter what combination of areas may be chosen for special attention in a curriculum, the Russian and East European area should certainly not be omitted. In addition to previous supporting arguments made here, we add a pedagogical one: the area has the unique advantage of being European but not predominantly Western. On the one hand, it shares with Western civilization so many fundamental institutions that the student need not feel any "cultural shock" such as he might experience with a totally exotic culture. On the other hand, unlike, let us say, Latin America, which is as Western as our own area, Russia and much of Eastern Europe have evolved some institutions that are distinct. Here, then, is an opportunity to observe how two cultural areas may share many basic institutions and still take different paths. Here is also an opportunity to discuss not only differences but similarities between our culture and the Russian and East European, and this should provide a much needed corrective to the popular tendency to dwell only on the disparities. Indeed, there is much wisdom to be gained from the realization that the one institution most Americans think divides us most from Russia, or China—Communism—is an ideology imported from the West.

On the other hand, Harrison Salisbury, New York *Times* correspondent who spent some years in the Soviet Union, once told this writer how he—a harried American "stooge of the Western Capitalist Press" and *persona non grata* to the Soviet authorities—was greeted joyfully by a lonely Russian official in the Soviet embassy in Outer Mongolia as "a fellow European"! There is a profound point to this anecdote that is lost on those who see the world purely in terms of an American-Soviet polarity.

IV. Some Specific Approaches

We will now proceed to suggest the types of knowledge about Russia and Eastern Europe that an American child should have acquired by the time he has been graduated from high school. Since we are not in a position to suggest in what grades this material should be taught, we will not try to outline specific units nor arrange the material in any graded order.

The area of our concern is Russia and Eastern Europe. Covering over a sixth of the world's surface, it includes many states, peoples, and subcultures. There would be as many different definitions of the area as there would be particular emphases or points of view. For practical reasons, let us purposely avoid such questions now and describe the area simply as that part of Europe east of the Scandinavian Peninsula, Germany, Switzerland, and Italy, and extending to the farthest limits of the Soviet Union. To ignore the non-Russian part of Eastern Europe is unjustifiable; to emphasize the Soviet Union is natural.

GEOGRAPHY

No matter how we define the area under question, one thing is clear: Eastern Europe is not a geographic entity; it is not a spatial concept but a cultural one. No physical geographer would ever attempt to draw a line between Eastern and Western Europe. Indeed, American students need to be told that no geographer recognizes Europe and Asia as separate physical entities. The Ural Range as a divider is only an antiquated convenience; the physical geographer recognizes only a Eurasia. Expressions such as "Western Europe" or "Eastern Europe," the student must learn, have a special meaning that far transcends geography, just as "South" and "North" in the American past and present mean much more than points of the compass or physical regions.

Nevertheless, the physical environment of a cultural area is of immense importance, and the student cannot begin to study Russia and Eastern Europe as a whole without a thorough acquaintance with the geography of the area. Year after year this writer has had to explain that Siberia is not an ice-covered waste land relieved only by salt mines. Year after year students in his courses confuse the Baltic States with the Balkan States, and cannot enumerate either. One could offer countless similar examples of American vagueness about Eastern European and Russian geography. As one who occasionally teaches university freshmen general modern European history, I have come to realize that this ignorance of Eastern Europe entails no discrimination whatever but reflects a general lack of geographical knowledge.

Before one can attempt to teach anything about Eastern Europe in general and Russia in particular, he must have students who can identify the countries, and provinces, political divisions, and cities of the area; its chief physical features—rivers, seas, mountains, valleys, plains; its zones of climate and vegetation; its relation to other areas; and so on. Here is obviously a specific body of factual information that must be mastered by the pupil. We cannot overemphasize the need for the full reinstatement of geography in the school curriculum—at some point, perhaps at the junior high school level, where it can come soon enough to provide a solid basis for further work in history and the social studies.

Once the geographical facts are in the students' heads, the teacher of a unit on Russia and Eastern Europe must then relate these facts to the history of the area. Here it would be most convenient to consider the whole area in three parts: Russia, the Balkans, and central Eastern Europe. Certainly Poland's changing borders throughout centuries may be, in part, attributed to that country's lack of real natural borders; the very name Poland is derived from the Slavic word for *plain*. On the other hand, much of the complexity of Balkan history is a reflection of the mountainous terrain that covers five-sixths of that peninsula. The student ought to see through geography why most of the countries of Eastern Europe have been traditionally agrarian states with little or no industry until recent times. Important differences between Western and Eastern Europe can be drawn by comparing such factors as topography, outlets to seas, degree of urbanization and industrialization, density of population, mileages of railroads and highways, and so on. Maps devoted to these factors should be especially effective.

Moreover, the whole region of Europe between the Germans and the Russians has been a "shatter zone," a *Zwischenland* that has borne the brunt of attacks on all sides. The German *Drang nach Osten,* the Ottoman advance (to Vienna itself), and Russian domination or influence have all left their mark on this region, and Russian domination is still a major factor. Undoubtedly, geography has played a major role in all this. The mountains of the Balkans have not hindered conquerors but only provided havens for the oppressed; the conquerors made good use of the river valleys. As for Central Europe, its vulnerability to attack has been demonstrated many times in history—World War II, being the most recent example.

As for Russia, geography teaches us many crucial things about that country's past and present. Russia's position on a vast plain that stretches unhindered for thousands of miles across Eurasia has left that country, too, open to many invasions from east and west—Vikings, Mongols, Lithuanians, Poles, Swedes, Germans, and others. In a period of Russian strength and growth of population, the plain has also invited expansion all the way to the high mountain ranges that form so much of the perimeter of the Soviet Union today. The student must be impressed by Russia's size—one-sixth of the land surface of the earth—but he must also realize that much of this territory became a part of the Russian Empire in relatively recent times, that it is still sparsely populated, unfit for agriculture in many regions and lacking in natural resources. A knowledge of climate and vegetation zones is essential here, especially the lateral belts stretching from northern tundra to southern desert. The student should realize why Russia has been an agricultural peasant country throughout its existence, and that the black soil region of the Ukraine is still one of the most fertile grain-growing regions in the world. The student should see the disproportion between land mass and sea coast in Russia and realize how much of a continental rather than maritime power Russia has been in the past and the Soviet Union still is; the lack of ice-free ports is an important contributing factor. Furthermore, it should be pointed out that Russia's maritime provinces are historically among its most recent acquisitions and that an important part of Russian foreign policy for centuries has been the need for ports and egress to the Atlantic and Pacific via the Baltic and the Black Sea.

The role of Russia's vast river system should be stressed. Today, for example, thanks to a network of rivers and canals, Moscow calls itself the Port of Five Seas, though it is in the heart of Russia. Some historians have even periodized Russian history according to the rivers on which Russia's three capitals —Kiev, Moscow, and St. Petersburg (Leningrad)—have stood: the Dnieper, the Volga (of which the Moskva is a tributary via the Oka), and the Neva. Especially the great rivers of Siberia—the Ob-Irtysh, the Yenisei, the Lena, and others —have played a significant role in Russia's expansion. Though most of these rivers flow in a north-south direction, the westward expansion was facilitated by numerous tributaries.

Certainly the student should see the Soviet Union on a polar projection map or a large globe to appreciate its strategic proximity to the rest of northern Europe and especially North America; it is instructive to realize that our closest overseas neighbor, the Soviet Union, is only a few miles distant from the State of Alaska. Russia's northern clime can also be better appreciated when it is realized that fifty of the Soviet Union's major cities lie on a latitude north of Edmonton, Canada; and that one can comfortably read a newspaper under the sky of Leningrad at midnight during the white nights of the summer. In terms of economic geography, the student must be impressed with the Soviet Union's command of natural resources and ability to be self-sufficient to a large degree, especially in case of necessity. This is not only of present strategic importance but helps explain Russia's relative isolation in the past.

Something ought to be said about Russia's population growth. For example, the sheer size of that population is an important fact. The student should know, however, that for most centuries the Russians were concentrated in so-called European Russia. The final spurt of expansion, like the rapid rise of industrialization in Russia, came with the population explosion in the nineteenth century.

Finally, while it is dangerous to talk about national characteristics, the teacher may point out that many foreign observers have seen a correlation between Russia's vastness and the Russian mentality—a tendency to think in the same broad, expansive terms that characterize most Americans but not most European peoples. It would be a pity, for example, not to compare American westward expansion with Russia's eastward expansion, especially in the nineteenth century; both the parallels and differences in Russian and American frontier life are extremely instructive.

ETHNOLOGY

"How terrible, fantastic, incredible it is," said Britain's Prime Minister Chamberlain during the Czechoslovak crisis of 1938, "that we should be digging trenches and trying on gas masks here because of a quarrel in a faraway country between people of whom we know nothing."

Americans must learn who *all* the peoples of Europe are, not just those of Western Europe. After all, quite apart from other motivations, there is the fact that tens of millions of Americans are of East European stock.

One of the best ways of getting in mind the peoples of

Europe is through the branches of the Indo-European languages. As a university teacher, I am frequently bewildered by this gap in the knowledge of our students. Their knowledge of European civilization, both Western and Eastern, would be much enhanced if they knew who the speakers of Romance, Germanic, Celtic, Slavic, Greek, Albanian, and the Baltic languages were. They could see that culturally speaking, Western Europe consists predominantly of the first three groups, and Eastern Europe of the last four. The exceptions are in themselves instructive: the fact that Romanian, as its name shows, is a Latin language; that Turkish, Hungarian, Estonian, and Finnish are not European languages at all but Asian, and are remotely related; the fact that Basque is still a puzzle. It is also good to know, for example, that there is no Yugoslav language, just as there is no Belgian or Swiss language.

The linguistic approach is especially important in identifying the Slavs, especially since—contrary to some of our new high school textbooks with units on "Slavic Society"—the only distinctive feature that Slavs share is linguistic kinship. The student can help learn who the Slavs are if he thinks of them in their three linguistic subgroups: The Eastern Slavs (Great Russians, Ukrainians, White Russians), the Western Slavs (Poles, Czechs, Slovaks, Lusatian Serbs), and the South Slavs (Slovenes, Croats, Serbs, Bulgars, Macedonian Slavs). It is noteworthy that one out of every three Europeans is a Slav, and one out of every four Europeans is a Russian Slav.

In speaking about the ethnology of the Soviet Union in particular, the teacher should stress two things: the vast number and disparity of ethnic groups in the U.S.S.R., and the numerical predominance of the Slavs. The full implications of Russia as a colonial power, or of the nationalities question in the Soviet Union today, cannot be grasped without realizing the relation between the Russians and the non-Russian peoples in the U.S.S.R.—the Baltic peoples, Poles, Romanians, Georgians, Armenians, the Turco-Tatar peoples, the aborigines of Siberia, the Jews, etc. For example, the Soviet Union contains a Moslem population that equals that of more than one North African or Near Eastern state. The comparison between American westward and Russian eastward expansion is made clearer by remembering that American Indians are originally of Siberian origin and ethnologically related to the Siberian aborigines. Soviet treatment of its nationalities should be studied in itself and against the background of Russian history. Russian oppression of the Poles is not justified by previous Polish oppression of the Russians, nor is Russian rule over the Tatar peoples excused by centuries of Tatar domination over Russians, but one learns more about nationality problems knowing this. Certainly knowing that Stalin was not a Russian at all and spoke the language with a marked accent all his life should help American students understand that the term *Russian* is even less applicable to millions of Soviet citizens than the term *English* is applicable to the Scots, Welsh, or Irish.

Related to linguistic categories is the matter of alphabets. In Yugoslavia, for example, where Serbs and Croats speak the same literary language, the most obvious mark of distinction is the alphabet they use; this is far, far more than a technical distinction inasmuch as the Latin alphabet of the Croats is the badge of their Westernism while the Cyrillic alphabet of the Serbs ties them to their Orthodox Bulgarian, Ukrainian, White Russian, and Great Russian brethren. The Greeks of course use an alphabet made glorious by Socrates, Plato, Aristotle, Euripides, and other luminaries of both pagan Hellenic culture and Byzantine Christendom. The Romanians changed from the Cyrillic to the Latin alphabet in the nineteenth century, thus affirming the Latin origin of their language, but the Romanians in the Soviet Union still use the Cyrillic alphabet. The Roman Catholic and Protestant Croats, Slovenes, Czechs, Slovaks, Poles, and Lusatian Serbs all use the Latin alphabet. Indeed, it would be a helpful rule of thumb if students could learn that, generally speaking, the Latin alphabet is West

European while the Greek and Cyrillic alphabet are East European. It would also be good to point out, for example, that Georgians and Armenians have ancient alphabets of their own, and that the Arabic script has been used by some peoples in the Soviet Union, although the Russians have spread their Cyrillic alphabet to many non-Slavic peoples. Indeed, while Alaska was Russian territory, some Alaskan Indians first learned to write their language in the Cyrillic alphabet!

We should not leave the subject of linguistics without stressing that this approach also offers an opportunity to stress the basic cultural affinity of most European peoples, whether East or West. All the Indo-European languages, from English to Russian, have in common a vast vocabulary. The most obvious examples are the terms denoting kinship—father, mother, brother, sister, etc. Agricultural terms—plow, rye, mill, etc.—also show this common affinity. Words dealing with the Christian Church and its dogma and rites are also similar. There are native words, and not just borrowings from Latin and Greek, in both English and Russian that are so similar, due to a common origin, that even the uninitiated can perceive their kinship when they are written in the same alphabet: to *talk* and *tolk* (*ovat'*), *path* and *put'*, to *beat* and *bit'*, *mead* and *mëd*, *three* and *tri*, *nose* and *nos*, *goose* and *gus'*.

BASIC INSTITUTIONS—EAST AND WEST

It is impossible to study Russia and Eastern Europe intelligently without understanding what institutions give unity to European history, society, and culture as a whole, and what institutions bifurcate Europe into "West" and "East." Once the various criteria are established, it will be seen that it is no easy matter to point to any one line as the divider, but all the lines will go north and south through some part of the general area of Eastern Europe broadly defined.

For example, European culture is the heir of Hellenic and Roman culture, and here we already have a bifurcation, for the Eastern and most Southern Slavs were influenced by the Greek culture in its Byzantine form. Politically Europe was an extension of the Roman Empire, yet there was a West Rome and an East Rome (Byzantium); what the Germanic peoples were for West Rome, the Slavs were for East Rome, and what the Holy Roman Empire was for the West, Byzantium and its successors, the Ottoman Empire and the Russian Empire, were for the East. Europe is essentially Christendom, yet the schism between Rome and the Orthodox churches of the East is crucial, not for theological reasons (there were two unions after the split) but for cultural ones. This is what makes Western ignorance of the Eastern Orthodox churches such a serious gap in our knowledge. It is also important that while the Latin language was the universal vehicle for learned communication throughout the West, Orthodox Eastern Europe had no such unity, for the Serbs, Bulgars, Romanians, Russians, and other Orthodox peoples did not accept Greek as a universal language of learning.

The Tatar and Turkish invasions of Russia and the Balkans are immensely important since they caused the isolation of these peoples from Western Europe for centuries. While the Russians, Bulgars, Serbs, Greeks, and others were struggling to maintain existence under alien, non-Christian, Asian conquerors, Western Europe experienced such vast movements as Scholastic learning, the Renaissance and Humanism, the Reformation and the Counter Reformation.

It will be noted that according to the criteria we have used thus far, the Poles, Czechs, Slovaks, Lithuanians, Hungarians, Slovenes, and Croats are all Western rather than Eastern —in fact, more so than Moorish-dominated Spain. Americans must appreciate the essential Westernism of these peoples for many reasons. Many of the conflicts in East European history arise or are exacerbated by the fact that East and West confront one another precisely in this area. The hostility of Poles and Russians, Croats and Serbs, Hungarians and Romanians, for one another has undoubtedly been heightened by their cultural differences. The satellite states of Eastern Europe that have a Western culture suffer doubly under a Russian-dominated Communism, for there is the conflict not only of ideologies but cultures. We suspect that if the West had always recognized the Roman Catholic and Protestant peoples of central Eastern Europe as their own, the Iron Curtain might not be where it is today.

But there are other criteria. For example, not even the Western-oriented countries of central Eastern Europe participated in the Age of Discovery and Exploration, nor did they establish overseas colonies and outposts. Even more important, the Industrial Revolution that changed the face of the western half of Europe penetrated hardly at all into the eastern half until quite recently. While Western Europe has been and is a region of industrial cities and market-oriented farmers, connected within by a dense network of highways and railroads and connected to world-wide colonies and markets by busy sea lanes, Europe east of Germany, Switzerland, and Italy has been a region of alien cities scattered like isolated islands in a sea of peasantry engaged in subsistence farming. It has been said that even the workers of Russia in 1917 were but "peasants in overalls." Until recently, in many of the countries in the eastern half of Europe capital, large tracts of land, political power, and even cultural life were in the hands of foreigners—that is, people whose nationality differed from the most numerous ethnic group. Whether we are speaking of Imperial Austria, Turkey, or Russia, the pattern has been the same: a multinational empire based on autocracy and run by a bureaucracy, a privileged landed aristocracy lording it over the voiceless peasantry, a dominant nationality suppressing sometimes numerically superior ethnic groups, and all in a state of economic backwardness relative to the West. This situation changed markedly after World War I, but not enough, especially with respect to economic backwardness. It may be said that Communism is the road such countries have taken to achieve the technical results and standard of living of the West. In this respect Communist Eastern Europe is but an example of what is taking place and can yet take place in many parts of the world with similar problems. It is this whole set of circumstances that makes such basically Western peoples as the Poles or Hungarians a part of the East European pattern.

Through this approach to the area, American students can learn to appreciate to what a degree Western democracy is not the result of Magna Charta as much as of an enterprising middle class, the makers and beneficiaries of the Industrial Revolution, and a progressively more educated, better organized, and more prosperous class of workers who insisted on their share in governing their countries. The American students should learn that while the love of freedom is universal, not all areas have developed those objective conditions that permit the establishment of parliaments and the Bill of Rights. Democracy is not a mere matter of volition or absence of tyranny. Eastern Europe, including Russia, can offer many examples of men who wrote as eloquently in defense of freedom as Jefferson, who died for it as bravely as Nathan Hale, who fought for it as hard as Washington. East European history is full of mass rebellions and uprisings for the cause of freedom. But the conditions for democracy as we know it were lacking. While one socio-cultural system can borrow much from another, it cannot obliterate its own past or assume the identity of another socio-cultural system overnight, or in one generation, or perhaps ever. It must evolve its own forms and assimilate borrowings from others in its own way. A powerful state can create an industrial system in one generation, as the Soviet state has done, but the creation of an entrepreneurial middle class is another matter. This is the historic lesson of the reforms of Peter the Great in Russia. In an age of Point Four, the

Marshall Plan, cultural and economic missions to other lands, and so on, it is especially necessary for Americans to realize such fundamentals.

V. Some Basic Concepts of Russian History

The Soviet Union almost fits the rhyme we associate with the American bride's wedding attire—something old, something new, something borrowed, something blue—only the color is red. And even with respect to the color, it is symbolically significant that Red Square bore that name centuries before the Bolshevik Revolution. From the standpoint of an area study, our subject is not simply the Soviet Union—a political entity just past forty—but also the Russia from which the Soviet regime has sprung. To understand the institutions of Soviet life we must dig at their roots, for it is not only change but continuity that makes up the whole picture. Contemporary Russia, for example, does not begin in 1917 but with the industrialization of the 1880's or even the emancipation of the serfs in the 1860's. As Edward Hallett Carr has observed, the chariot of Soviet foreign policy is driven by two horses—not only the red horse of Communist expansion but the older white horse of Russian national self-interest. The historian is around to remind people, for example, that the Soviet intervention in the recent Hungarian revolt had its equally devastating parallel during the Hungarian revolt of 1848–49; that Russian domination over many of the nationalities of Eastern Europe antedates Stalin by centuries, that rule by the few over the many is a historical pattern in Russia, etc., etc. Again we must insist that to explain is not to justify, but knowing such things makes us better able to evaluate the nature of Soviet Communism.

Thus knowledge of the Russian past is indispensible to an understanding of the Soviet present. We, of course, begin with the proposition that even without the Soviet present the

Russian past would be worth studying. However, let us exploit our natural interest in the present without unduly sacrificing the integrity of the past, to show what factors in Russian history before 1917 can illuminate the period that followed. For the sake of convenience, let us restrict ourselves to ten major themes.

(1) *The vast masses of the Russian people have been traditionally disinterested in participating in government and have been politically passive.* The very first central government in Russian history, that organized by the Varangians or Vikings in medieval times, was literally alien to the Slavic masses. The dichotomy between the ruling class and the peasantry has been a permanent motif in Russian history. The Slavophiles aptly described it as the difference between *Rus'* (cultural Russia) and *Rossiia* (political Russia). (Certainly this raises the general question of whether peasants—as distinct from farmers—anywhere are not disinterested in and distrustful of central governments, not necessarily because the governments are despotic but because the very peasant way of life regards anything beyond the village as alien and hostile.) The Tatar invasion of Russia only reinforced the dichotomy by challenging the central government to become stronger, at the expense of the people's rights, so that all might survive. The history of Russia after that is the growth of state power and a corresponding degradation of the enserfed masses. The emancipation of the serfs in the 1860's did not mean the creation of a participating citizenry any more than the Emancipation Proclamation in the United States solved the Negro question. As always, the new regime after 1917 was the rule of the few over the many, and consciously so, perhaps even inevitably so, given the facts of Russian life. To most Soviet citizens the government is still "they" and not "we."

(2) *The Russian peasant way of life is traditionally based on social democracy and communal living.* To understand this, it is essential that the American student understand the bases

of a peasant folk society (which still covers most of the earth). He must see that the difference between an American farmer and a Russian peasant of, let us say, a hundred years ago, is not simply a matter of degree but of kind. It is conceivable that a peasant could be better off than a farmer, far more literate, and able to vote, and still be a peasant. What is involved is a difference in ways of life arising from a difference in role or function in a specific kind of economy. For centuries Russian peasants lived in a communal society based on the large patriarchal complex family and the largely self-managing village community. In a system of repartitional land tenure in which the family did not own and till its own farm but was allotted scattered strips of land that were sowed and harvested collectively with others, the concept of property was sacrificed to the concept of mutual equality. Taxes were paid by the village collectively. The landlord and the government were alien and hostile elements that demanded money, labor, and recruits, and rarely gave anything in return. The peasants themselves were not in contact with the market for which they produced, and felt lucky to subsist. This was their way of life before the emancipation of 1861, after 1861, and—in a modified form—this is generally their way of life now.

(3) *Russian society has for centuries consisted of a small ruling class on top, the vast peasant masses below, and only a thin layer of middle class and workers between, and then only in relatively recent times.* Perhaps the outstanding fact in Russian social history is serfdom. Viewed from the vantage point of Western history, there is a paradox in Russian social development: the Russian peasants were for the most part free in medieval times and became more and more enserfed even as Western peasants were becoming free farmers. Just as the State demanded service from the nobility, so the nobility demanded land and the labor of the peasantry. American students must know the extent and meaning of serfdom; a comparison with Negro slavery in this country would be most

instructive, for the similarities are great, and the differences are often to the advantage of the Russian serf. The task of creating a conscious, intelligent, participating citizenry is difficult under any circumstances, let alone under such conditions. As for the rest of Russian society, the student ought to have a rather more sophisticated idea of the middle class, the dominant majority in his own country, before he can appreciate what the absence of such a class does to a country's history. While Russia had a brilliant class of middle-class intellectuals who were professional people and artists, what Russia lacked was the kind of entrepreneurial middle class that existed in Western Europe and in the United States; the Russian merchant class was more like the Chinese than the French or English. As for the Russian working class, its origins are in serfdom, and its development as recent as industrialization in Russia. And over all was the control of a paternalistic autocratic state.

(4) *For centuries the State has been the prime mover in Russian history, and most of the great changes in Russian life have been effected from above.* Because of the constant danger of foreign invasion, discipline and authority were deemed necessary, and autocracy was long accepted as the best form of government for Russia—even by the peasantry and many liberals. Thus only the State has had the means and power to effect great transformations. Ivan the Terrible crushed the power of the blood nobility. Peter the Great shook Russia to its foundation by his Westernizing reforms. It was a tsar, Emperor Alexander II, who emancipated the serfs because he believed it was better this be done from above than below. It was another autocrat, Stalin, who collectivized Russian agriculture with such wide effect and brutality that this has been called the second Bolshevik Revolution. And even as the Cult of Personality is being denounced, the State goes on controlling everything. The parallel in Church-State relations before and after 1917 is especially instructive. The role of the police

and the bureaucracy in old and new Russia is likewise comparable.

(5) *The Russian State has been ruled like an armed camp for centuries.* The American student who is apt to think of the Soviet Union only as an aggressor, though the United States and the Soviet Union have been allies, ought to understand that the Russian historical memory records many attacks against Russia by foreign invaders, most often from the West. The Tatar catastrophe coincided with the Teutonic *Drang nach Osten* (an early "Crusade in Europe"); then the Polish-Lithuanian onslaughts; the Swedes under Charles XII; the Ottoman Turks; Napoleon in 1812; England, France, and even Sardinia in the Crimean War; Imperial Germany in World War I; the foreign intervention that followed—in which American troops landed on Russian soil, too, to join the British, Italian, Czech, Polish, and Japanese troops; and finally Nazi Germany. It is noteworthy that Stalin used the threat of the "Capitalist Encirclement" to justify the rigors of his regime. Just ten years before Hitler's attack, in a speech to Soviet managers, he recalled all the above invasions of Russia and warned, "We are fifty or a hundred years behind the advanced countries. We must make good this lag in ten years. Either we do it or they crush us." It was the French Marquis de Custine who observed, just a hundred years before Stalin, that Russia was not ruled like a civil body politic but like an armed camp under perpetual siege. The Russia under Peter the Great a hundred years before that was hardly different. Perhaps the present Soviet fear of Western aggression is wrong, but it is not a pose if history means anything.

(6) *Russia has long pursued certain basic aims in its foreign policy that have become a part of Soviet foreign policy.* Despite the jet age, one of these still is egress to and free use of the high seas. Another is to secure Soviet borders, especially vis-à-vis Europe, by dominating the states of central Eastern Europe. The three Baltic States have long been part

of the Russian Empire. Stalin's seizure of Polish territory constituted not the first but the fifth partition of Poland in two centuries. Many of the satellite states of Eastern Europe have been Russia's satellites before 1917. Similarly Soviet policy in the Far East recalls tsarist imperial aims in Korea, North China, and Japan. It may prove instructive to remember, for example, that in the years just preceding World War I, Britain and Russia had a plan for dividing Persia between themselves according to "zones of influence." Soviet Russia used the appeal of Panslavism to rally the Slavic peoples against Nazi Germany just as Imperial Russia appealed to Panslavism in several of its wars. Realization of such continuity in Russian foreign policy should make Americans aware of a certain distinction between the Soviet pursuance of national ambitions and the Soviet stake in the spread of world Communism. Having satisfied so many of its historic national ambitions under Stalin, the Soviet Union today as the bearer of the banner of Communism seems almost conservative by comparison with Red China.

(7) *Russia has long felt the ambivalence of its relation to the West.* On the one hand there has been isolation from the West and even attacks from the West. We have already alluded to the difference in basic institutions between Russia and the West and need not stress that point here. However, there is the other side, the fact that many movements and ideas in Russian history, especially since the time of Peter the Great, do parallel Western movements and ideas. We find frequently that American students who do not know their Western history think of certain aspects of Russian history as being typically Russian when they are in fact common to most of Western civilization in a given stage of development. For example, Ivan the Terrible's campaign to suppress the blood nobility has its parallels in Tudor England and Capetian France. Russian absolutism with Peter the Great is no longer in the Byzantine style but Western, even as to the conscious

substitution of the title *emperor* for *tsar*. Serfdom is hardly an especially Russian institution. The repression under Nicholas I was but the extension of the Metternich reaction in most of Europe, while the ideas of the Decembrists have their counterparts in the American and French revolutions. Russian Church-State relations after Peter I have their parallels in the West, especially in the Lutheran countries. The Russian revolutionary movement in all its aspects—liberal, utopian socialist, anarchist, nihilist, and Marxist—paralleled Western movements. The Russian suppression of other nationalities was matched by similar movements elsewhere in Europe. (The Czechs under Austria in the nineteenth century used to like to talk about the Irish Question since they were not free to discuss their own plight openly.) It was the fiercely Russian Dostoevskii who assured Western Europe of Russian appreciation for the great achievements of Western culture. Any unit on Russian history should be careful, then, to stress not only the unique but parallel developments with the West. The Russians may be "different," but they are far from "exotic." Indeed, in some parts of the world Russians have been and are the carriers of Western material and intellectual culture to non-Western peoples, within the framework of a Western ideology—Marxian socialism.

(8) *There has long been an idea in Russian history that the Russian nation has a mission to fulfill that is destined to go beyond the borders of Russia.* Since the fall of Constantinople in 1453, Russia has thought of itself as the heir of Byzantium and champion of Orthodox peoples everywhere. This idea had its formal recognition, for example, in the Treaty of Kuchuk Kainarji in 1774. In the nineteenth century the Slavophiles preached Russia's mission to improve on the "rotting West" by establishing an example to the world of true brotherhood based on social justice. Since then Moscow has become the capital of a secular universal religion, Communism, which also looks upon the West as doomed by inner contradictions.

(9) *The Russians are and have been an extraordinarily gifted and creative people.* It is essential for American students to learn of the great contributions of Russian culture to the belles-lettres and the arts. This has all the more justification in being included in a social studies unit if the teacher is able to relate Russian artistic expression to Russian society. Students should learn that Russian fiction or painting or even music often gave expression to ideas that in freer countries were expressed in political life. Any effective unit on Russian history should make full use of illustrative material from Russian literature and the fine arts. The teacher should encourage students to become acquainted with Russian music and literature through personal enjoyment. Furthermore, it would be wrong for American students to absorb the rather prevalent idea that the great achievements of Russian science belong to the Soviet age of Sputniks. Pre-1917 Russia has given brilliant men to the sciences and mathematics from Lomonosov to Lobachevskii and Pavlov. Not all Soviet claims to being first in certain scientific fields are absurd, as research on Russian experimentation with airplanes before the Wright brothers may illustrate. This writer remembers how, only a half-dozen years ago, some of his university colleagues laughed at a newspaper report that the Soviet Union had developed television too; today we are not as contemptuous of Russian abilities. But we ought to know that Soviet advances in the sciences, uneven as they are, are not without a solid foundation in the pre-Soviet period and that all these advances were not accomplished overnight. This is not to denigrate Soviet achievements; on the contrary, it should lead to a more realistic appraisal of Soviet potentialities.

(10) *Finally, it is necessary for American students to realize the strength of Russian patriotism, quite apart from Communism.* For centuries the Russian people have suffered oppression under various governments, but whatever they may

have thought of *Rossiia,* they have lived and died for *Rus'*. World War II is but the most recent and most vast example of this. Besides a natural love of homeland, the Russians have a pride in their national achievements and strength, although these might have been achieved under Communism. This is because it is so well realized in the Soviet Union that the Soviet regime is not only a break with a part of the past, it is also a continuation of the past. It is significant that the Soviet regime itself fosters this attitude of ties with the acceptable past. It is highly mindful of the past, especially for a revolutionary regime. During the "Great Fatherland War" of 1941–45 (the name itself is an echo of 1812), Stalin encouraged the revival of Russian nationalism and resurrected many heroes of Russian history whom the Marxists had previously regarded as symbols of the old regime. It is vastly important for American students to realize how natural this patriotism is in the light of the Russian past. On the other hand, the history of the Russian Empire can also indicate to what a degree the non-Russian nationalities have a patriotism of their own that does not find full expression in the Soviet State. Certainly it is time Americans stopped referring to the multinational Soviet State as Russia inasmuch as almost half of the Soviet population is non-Russian.

It should be obvious that we would not advocate constructing a unit on Russian history with these ten examples of historical motifs as sections. However, these are the kinds of conclusions to which we think a study of Russian history can lead. Certainly this approach is entirely alien to any dreary piling up of unrelated facts about "strange people doing un-American things," as a colleague puts it, or to a tendentious recital of Russian history as a tale of horrors and woes, the dark side of the moon. We do not insist that everyone agree to precisely our conclusions, but we do demand that any consideration of Russian history raise questions of this kind. This can be done successfully only if we abandon any lingering idea that history is merely the record of past politics and if we insist on presenting history in the round.

VI. The Soviet Union

The central fact about the Soviet Union is not that it is a great power, though this is extremely important; the Soviet Union is unique in that it is the first state in history based on Communism, and it is still the leading world exponent of that ideology. The central fact about Communism is not that it is another form of dictatorship, though it has proven to be that thus far in its history; Communism is significant because it introduces into practice a different socio-economic principle in the management of human affairs and claims to be the grave digger of a disintegrating capitalism. It is, therefore, unthinkable to study the Soviet Union without a discussion of the Communist ideology.

By the definition of our task, we shall not discuss such material obstacles to the study of Communism in our schools as public attitudes, lack of trained teachers or suitable materials, and so on. However, we must reply to certain objections on academic grounds to the discussion of Communism in our schools.

There is the fear that Communism is too pernicious an ideology to discuss before our children and that exposure to the ideology can lead to more harm than good. We cannot, of course, guarantee what effect anything about which we teach will have on our students, as any teacher sadly knows. Yet the basic principle of liberal education in our country has traditionally been that nothing important should be kept from investigation on principle. To avoid teaching about Communism, as a matter of principle, is a form of censorship that runs counter to the American spirit.

However, some who accept this view still oppose any

consideration of the Communist ideology in our schools on pedagogical grounds—lack of knowledgeable teachers and good materials, and the incapacity of inexperienced young minds to deal critically with so complex a subject. We will admit the former shortcomings in general and hope for a remedy. However, we do not accept the latter objection as a deterrent, though we recognize some of its validity. It is, of course, true that Marxist ideology in all its complexity will be too difficult for most school children, even high school seniors. But we do not insist that school children be exposed to problems beyond their comprehension. Christian theology —for example, the mystery of the Trinity—is a profound and complex subject when treated by theologians; yet Sunday schools all over the country manage to tell their children about the Trinity. Soviet school children take whole courses in *Diamat* (dialectical materialism). There are basic aspects of the Marxist theory that anyone can understand who has any knowledge of history and how the capitalist system works (and we assume all American high school seniors, let us say, should possess this knowledge). It is essential that we know what the Communist vision of the good society is if we are to understand the appeal that vision has for many.

Surely seniors can comprehend such aspects of Marxist philosophy as the conflict of opposites, the stages of human history based on the means of production and who controls those means, class conflict, and so on—if these matters are properly presented. And they should be. The study of Marxist theory is a challenging educational experience that should be discussed in the open and in a disciplined, rational way. Otherwise Communism may be unwillingly lent the appeal of any taboo enshrouded in mystery or disapproval. On the other hand, we must warn against a catechetical tone in which straw men are constructed and then burned at the stake as heretics for the edification of the class. Such autos-da-fé will not produce faith—only smoke. Students must feel that their engagement with the Communist ideology is an intellectually honest one.

Certainly school children should learn something at some point about the various kinds of socialism in Western thought. They should know that Communism is not a Russian idea but a Western idea imported into Russia. They should know who Karl Marx and Friedrich Engels were and what they wrote. (A Washington friend of ours told us just recently how shocked he was to discover that his daughter, a high school junior, had never heard of Karl Marx.) Any unit on Russian history will surely stress the rise of the whole Russian revolutionary movement (carefully avoiding giving the impression that all or even most Russian revolutionaries were Communists).

Marx predicted that Communism would come first to the industrially developed countries of the West; yet it was in the easternmost country of Europe, an underdeveloped agrarian Russia, that the revolution first came. Since then it has spread to countries of a similar nature or even more backward economically. This raises the whole question of whether Communism is not the device which underdeveloped and former colonial areas are adopting to achieve rapid industrialization and a standard of living comparable to the Western.

Any discussion of Communism should stress that no ideology operates in a vacuum once it becomes a working system. It necessarily inherits much of the past. It is a question whether Communism has changed Russia more, or whether Russia has altered Communism. Thus one ought to study both the theory and the practice of any ideology.

How much about the Soviet Union itself should American pupils know? We ourselves are convinced that it is not enough to describe the Soviet scene as it is at the moment, but the student must be shown how things got to be that way. Thus we urge the historical approach, always in the broadest sense of history. We suggest headings such as the revolutions of 1917, Lenin's regime, Stalin's rise to power, the five-year plans,

World War II, the expansion of the Soviet Union, the post-Stalin period, and the Soviet Union as the leader of world Communism. The unit should discuss Soviet government, foreign policy, economy, society, and culture within those headings.

As before, we shall not attempt to fill in this outline here and to give a syllabus. Let us, nevertheless, briefly point to the kinds of issues that could be taken up. Again, we shall arbitrarily take up ten points.

(1) There should be a discussion of the basic and immediate causes of the revolutions of 1917. The student might compare these revolutions with the American or French revolutions. He should be able to define revolution as something more than an uprising or rebellion. He must know that there were two Russian revolutions in 1917, and that it was not the Communists who overthrew the Tsarist government. In this connection it is instructive to know that we were the first major government to grant official recognition to the Russian government that resulted from the February Revolution of 1917, and the last major government to recognize the Soviet government which the October Revolution brought to power. The nexus between war and revolution should be discussed. The student should be able to answer why as small a group as the Bolsheviks were able to gain control of so vast a country.

(2) Through their study of Lenin, American students should learn that Communist leaders are not apt to be peasants or even workers but intellectuals with a theory and the ability to attract through ideas and slogans. Students can follow through Lenin's career how "dictatorship of the proletariat" became in fact dictatorship by a party and its leaders. Lenin's regime shows the techniques of the terror against "class enemies" during the civil war in Russia. Students should learn that there were more sides involved than "Whites" and "Reds." It was in Lenin's time, too, that the foreign intervention took place; students might take stock of America's part in

that episode, as well as in the Hoover Relief Commission during the postwar famine. Very instructive is Lenin's whole retreat from "War Communism" to the New Economic Policy; for one thing, it should prove to students the flexibility of Soviet tactics as distinct from the permanence of Communist ideological objectives.

(3) Stalin's rise to power necessarily brings up the question of the inevitability of dictatorship by one man in the Soviet system. It reveals what can happen in a government with no effective checks and balances. It illustrates, as does the French Revolution, how the revolution can eat its own children. Above all, Stalin's success in attaining power shows what happens when a revolutionary force has become a government that requires stability.

(4) The five-year plans and the drive for collectivization of agriculture should give students an opportunity to study the bases of the Communist planned economy. They should learn, for example, that egalitarianism or common ownership of all property are not Communist goals. Above all, they must observe the impact of rapid industrialization on a traditionally agrarian society, for it is this that makes Communism attractive to many members of underdeveloped countries. The basic question needs to be raised: Is a planned economy under state control effective and desirable? From a teaching standpoint, a plain *yes* or *no* to this question would be unfortunate.

(5) The Soviet Union's role in the events leading up to World War II, especially the pact with Hitler, should illustrate the extreme flexibility of Soviet foreign policy. On the other hand, the magnificent fight that the vast majority (though not all) of Soviet citizens put up against the German invader should demonstrate not only the industrial might of the Soviet Union, but the devotion of the people to their country regardless of the form of government. Communist appeals to specifically Russian nationalism are noteworthy, as is the partial *rapprochement* of the Soviet State with the Orthodox Church.

The American student should be reminded of our alliance and how it worked. He should also realize the cost of the war to the Soviet Union in human and material terms. In any over-all view of Soviet foreign policy in the last four decades, the relationship between any one policy (and there were at least eight) and the domestic situation should be pointed out. Also the question should be raised, at least, whether Soviet foreign policy is determined by ideology or national self-interest.

(6) From our standpoint, the dominant theme in the postwar period deals with foreign relations: the quest for a working world order through the United Nations, and the expansion of Soviet domination, in Eastern Europe especially, as an obstacle to world harmony. American students should learn by what different means Communism came to the Soviet Union's satellites, and what it means to be a satellite. They must also realize that there are differences within the Communist bloc—that Yugoslavia has broken with Moscow though it remains Communist, that Poland is not as rigidly Communist as, for example, next-door Czechoslovakia, and that China is not a mere satellite at all. It should be clear to the student that while Moscow welcomes all unrest against old regimes in the world, especially in the colonial areas, and may even support it morally or materially, it is not the cause of this unrest.

(7) The post-Stalin era is a significant turning point in tactics, though not in aims. The dominant themes are a certain loosening of controls at home coupled with a drive for a higher standard of living, and proclamation of the policy of peaceful coexistence between the Communist and non-Communist world. Students must be given a realistic appraisal of peaceful coexistence so that they will not mistake it for an offer of permanent friendship and co-operation, or, on the other hand, as a mere trick. It is neither.

(8) Any realistic description of the Soviet Union today should recognize that this is a country of extremes—of rapid advances in some fields and a terrible lag in others. To discuss

just the advances would be a false overestimation; to stress just the backwardness is dangerous belittling. We have previously stated the need to show the pre-Soviet foundations of advances in the arts and sciences. Americans ought to learn who the great men of Soviet letters and the arts are and under what conditions, both favorable and unfavorable, they create. We should know more about Soviet science than their success with rockets and space ships. American students might be motivated more if they learned something about the education system in the U.S.S.R. and what it demands of pupils. (They might also get to appreciate our system more!)

(9) American school children should learn about the workings of the Soviet government. They should be able to identify the main agencies of the State and of the Communist party. They should have an idea of what the relationship between State and party is. They should realize how exclusive the party is and that it permits only a small fraction of the total population to join. They should know what the initials U.S.S.R. stand for, what the names of the republics are, and where they are on the map. They ought to be able to compare Soviet federalism with American. They should be acquainted with the main features of Soviet political life: the constitution, election procedures, and the like. There ought to be discussion of the rights of the Soviet citizen in law and practice.

(10) Soviet society today should be studied under several different aspects. The nationalities question needs explaining. So do Church-State relations. The question of the classless society in theory and Soviet practice should be raised. Groups such as the bureaucracy, the military, party members, the managerial class, workers, intellectuals, peasants, need to be defined and described. The machinery of conformism should be described so that American students do not get the idea that the only thing that holds the Soviet Union together is naked terror. It would be good to realize that the Soviet Union is full of people who accept (and even approve of) their way

of life, whose dissatisfaction may consist of nothing more than the desire for a better job, larger living quarters, more leisure, some recognition or status, and a happy family life.

Conclusion

Obviously we are asking for a lot. We believe we have a right to do so. What we ask will demand much more of both teacher and pupil, and this, too, we believe that we have a right to ask. Obviously some basic overhauling is called for. A "crash program" is not enough.

Afterword: Revising the Social Studies

Lewis Paul Todd / National Council for the Social Studies

AS LATE AS THE sixteenth century, alchemists were still pursuing the age-old quest for a method of transmuting base metals into gold and silver and for an even more potent agent; namely, the universal cure for all disease. Times and customs change, but myths die hard and as often as not reappear in strange new guises. The search for magical curative agents is no exception. We cling, many of us, to the belief that there is somewhere a universal cure, a quick and easy remedy, for the frailties that plague education in general or, in terms of the present discussion, the social studies in particular. "What we need . . ." And then the proposals come through, proposals that offer relatively simple formulas for breathing life and meaning into the social studies program.

There are no simple formulas. The social studies are concerned with the whole life of man, with the past, the present, and the future that we "now see through a glass darkly." They seek as their ultimate objective the development of individuals equipped with the understanding, the intellectual skills, and the moral courage to come to grips with the formidable problems facing the human race in this critical moment of its history. Man's fate will not be determined by mouthing empty incantations. The crisis confronting mankind is a crisis of intelligence and will. Only by marshaling to the uttermost our collective intelligence and our moral resources can we hope to emerge triumphant from our present travail and begin the task of building a sane and ordered world.

Such is the job for which the social studies must continue to assume a significant share of the responsibility. Our gravest peril is that we will underestimate the difficulties confronting us, not least of which is the ever accelerating rate of change. Every effort to strengthen the social studies program, if it makes any claim upon realism, must be carried on within the context of Julian Huxley's prediction that "the human species is on the threshold of a new experience as different from ours as ours is from that of the Peking man."

New Dimensions

Although it stretches the imagination to the breaking point, it is not impossible to conjure up a picture of that scene in which a million or so years ago the prehistoric individual we classify as *Sinanthropus pekinensis* crept into the cave near what is now Choukoutien, China, and, his crude stone fist hatchet close at hand, lay down to die. The point at which the imagination *does* fail is reached when we try to visualize a world as different from ours as ours is from that in which the Peking man lived out his days. And yet, as Huxley warned, it is that literally unimaginable world that we are now entering, or rather are being thrust into, with terrifying speed. And it is in this world of almost limitless complexity and bewildering change that the social studies must play their part.

Rapid and ever accelerating change in every aspect of life

is one of the hard facts with which we must contend, and the implications for education are staggering. "How," Margaret Mead asked, "are we who do not know what to do, who do not know how to live in one world, who have no faintest trace of habituated capacity to operate in a world which may actually destroy itself, who do not know . . . how to cope with the spectacle of machines which can do problems which the men who design the machines could not do—how shall we, who are so unfit, prepare a generation which will begin to be fit to face the new problems which confront mankind?"

We desperately needed an answer to the question when Margaret Mead asked it back in 1950. This was before the first hydrogen bomb had been triggered and before anyone dreamed that within a few short years the race for outer space would be on in earnest. We need the answer even more desperately today, not ten years from now, but now, for "things are in the saddle" and driving us hard.

It gives one pause, or *should* give one pause, to reflect that children born in 1962 will be entering kindergarten in 1967, the target date for landing the first United States astronaut or astronauts on the moon. Fantastic though it would have seemed even a decade ago, there is the possibility that some of these children, or if not they then some of *their* sons and daughters, will be among the first settlers to colonize the lunar wastes. This possibility may still appear fantastic to many of us. The government is, of course, betting otherwise with a space program that anticipates the expenditure of a minimum of twenty billions of dollars and an investment of the time and talents of large numbers of the nation's top scientists and engineers. As far as the social studies are concerned, the Government Printing Office has already made available publications that include detailed maps of the moon and, for those teachers who wish to do more by way of preparing youngsters for the "space age," annotated bibliographies on "aeronautics and space" for both the elementary and the secondary schools. Meanwhile, even as we race toward this new dimension of human life, the question Margaret Mead raised remains unanswered.

Unanswered, too, either for us or for future generations, is the question of how to deal with the explosion of knowledge now shaking practically every field of human endeavor to its very foundations. It has been estimated that "every minute, 2,000 pages of books, newspapers or reports are published somewhere in the world . . . enough to fill a thousand feet of bookshelves every day." One may grant that the estimate is probably only the roughest of approximations and that, moreover, the rivers of ink flow largely into warmed-over topics, news of merely passing interest, and trivialities. Nevertheless, imbedded in the whole is a hard core of new knowledge sufficiently large to confound even the most devoted scholars. We have reached the point where the most highly specialized specialists are hard put to keep abreast of new developments in their fields, and the continued improvement of computers and other extensions of man's senses and brain only serves to compound the problem.

Let us be completely clear on one point. We are not suggesting that the reader stand back with us and gaze in awe at the new horizons, physical and intellectual, that science is opening before us. We are suggesting and with as much emphasis as we can command that the rapidly expanding dimensions of human life have drastic and far-reaching implications for the social studies. We are thinking, for example, of the startling discoveries that have encouraged biologists to believe that they are on the verge of revealing the chemical code of inheritance. It is generally conceded that the discovery would constitute one of the greatest scientific achievements of all time. It would unlock doors now closed to researchers in many fields of science, and insofar as it provided a key to the basis of thought itself, the discovery would have incalculable consequences for education, and not least of all for the social studies program.

In the introduction to his classic volume, *Pioneers of*

France in the New World, Francis Parkman takes us back to an earlier age when a vast new world swam into view: "A boundless vision grows upon us; an untamed continent; vast wastes of forest verdure; mountains silent in primeval sleep; river, lake, and glimmering pool; wilderness oceans mingling with the sky." Magnificent though it was, the vision Parkman recalled pales into insignificance when compared with the vistas now opening before mankind. The "boundless vision" of which he wrote embraced an untamed wilderness of continental size; our vision is all-encompassing, guiding us outward to the limitless reaches of space and inward to the infinitesimal but infinitely complex universe of the atom.

But our vision is blurred, for we enter the new age ridden by anxiety and fearful of the future. The changes have come too swiftly for us to cope with them. We are not prepared for the great adventure upon which, like it or not, mankind is now embarked, and the compelling question Margaret Mead phrased so neatly remains to haunt us: "How shall we, who are so unfit, prepare a generation which will begin to be fit to face the new problems which confront mankind?"

Need for New Emphases

What can the social studies contribute by way of guidance into the new age we are entering? A small boy, as the story goes, had an answer to this question. The boy's father, wishing to read his newspaper but unable to do so because of repeated interruptions from his son, finally handed the youngster a large jigsaw-puzzle map of the world and told him to put it together. Then he settled back with his paper for what he hopefully expected would be a half hour or more of peace. In less than five minutes, however, the boy tugged at his father's sleeve. "I did it," he said. "How did you finish so quickly?" his father asked, looking down at the completed map. "It was easy," the youngster answered. "There was a picture of a man on the other side of the puzzle, and when I put the man together the world was all right."

Unsophisticated though the story may be, it has, we submit, a real point. In Alexander Pope's words, "The proper study of mankind is man." If our commitment to the task of building a decent and ordered world is deep enough to carry us beyond lip service to a serious consideration of ways and means, we will be well advised to plunge into "the proper study" with head, heart, and utmost concentration at the earliest possible moment.

It is not irrelevant to the case we are pleading that the National Defense Education Act of 1958 allocated funds to almost everything but the social sciences. If the NDEA were an isolated example, we could dismiss this singular instance of neglect without too much concern. But it is not an isolated example, and the imbalance between our efforts to manipulate the physical world and our efforts to come to grips with the urgent social problems of our time has become a matter of deepening concern, not least of all to scientists themselves. In a report issued several years ago by the American Association for the Advancement of Science, the authors pointed out that federal support had been "heavily slanted" toward mathematics and the natural sciences. In 1954, they noted, the physical sciences received eighty-seven per cent of the funds; the biological sciences only eleven per cent; and the social sciences a meager two per cent. "Industrial research," the report went on to say, "is at least as heavily weighted in this direction."

In a later report released in the summer of 1960, the AAAS returned to the problem of imbalance. "For nearly two decades," the report began, "scientists have viewed with growing concern the troublesome events that have been evoked by the interaction between scientific progress and public affairs. With each advance in our knowledge of nature, science adds to the already immense power that the social order exerts over human welfare. With each increment in power, the problem of directing its use toward beneficial ends becomes more disastrous, and the time for decision more brief. The problem is not new, either in the history of human affairs or of science. What is without past parallel is its urgency."

Isn't it time we began to take a long, hard, sober look at the urgent problems confronting us? The question is being raised with growing urgency by thoughtful people from every walk of life. Isn't it time we began to try to put the pieces together? Time we began to devote at least as much effort to the search for an enduring peace as we are now devoting to the search for security through armed might and the construction of shelters to protect us on the day of Armageddon? Time we began to devote at least as much time to the study of man himself as we are now devoting to the study of the things man can manipulate with his hands and his ingenious instruments? Time we began to turn increasingly to the social sciences, even as we have already turned to the natural sciences, for help in solving our problems? Time we began to agree that our future depends upon the quality and vitality of a balanced educational program that is as concerned with reaching out for an understanding of man and his relations with his fellows as it is with an understanding of the physical universe?

These are compelling questions. They deserve thoughtful answers from all of us—from the top echelons of government down to the humblest citizen. And if it is obvious that the social sciences have a major role to play in the resolution of the issues the questions raise, it should be equally obvious that an awareness of the issues themselves and the will and courage to tackle the issues must reach the youth of America in large part through the social studies program in the elementary and secondary schools.

The Ultimate Goal

If ours were a totalitarian state rather than an open society, the task of revising that part of the educational program devoted to civic or social education would be immeasurably simplified. In the Soviet Union, for example, both method and content are largely determined by the mandate to develop an understanding of and a commitment to Communist dogma as defined by the ruling hierarchy. We, too, have a mandate, but it has not been laid down for us by leaders either in government or education. Our mandate is rooted in our cultural heritage, the heritage of a free people, and it commits us to what is without question the most ambitious educational undertaking in the history of the human race. American education is expected to take *all* the youth, not just a select group, and by means of twelve or more years of schooling secure their dedication to the values of a democratic society and equip them with the knowledge and the intellectual skills that will enable them to function as effective and responsible citizens.

The task of revising or updating the social studies program is not complicated by lack of agreement on the part of social studies teachers in regard to the large objectives. These objectives, which we propose to discuss in a moment, have been stated again and again, most recently in a report prepared under the auspices of the National Council for the Social Studies.[1] It is true, however, that any meaningful effort of revision runs into trouble the moment it begins to translate objectives into specific courses of study. The difficulty is that objectives, like the terms *good* and *evil*, are susceptible to varying interpretations. And since American schools are in a very real sense "people's schools," being controlled locally, the voice of the public—or if you will, the publics—often exerts a decisive influence over both content and method. This being the situation, it should be obvious that no program of revision can expect to progress very far unless it has the understanding and support of a substantial body of public opinion in the community itself.

The National Council report to which we have just referred begins with the assertion that "the ultimate goal of education in the social studies is the development of desirable socio-civic behavior." Now there are certain implications in this statement that need to be emphasized. In the first place, we have here a definition of the supreme purpose of public education, not only in the United States but in every state, totalitarian and otherwise. To be sure, the term *desirable* requires definition, and this is where a free society can, if it is not well informed and extremely careful, pour itself down the drain.

In the second place, the moment we agree that the supreme purpose of public education is the development of "desirable socio-civic behavior," we are forced to draw a sharp distinction between the social sciences as a branch of human knowledge and the social studies in the schools. To the extent that the social sciences are scientific, they are neutral. The social studies, on the other hand, must be concerned with ethical considerations. This does not mean that the social studies teacher can relax his standards of objectivity. He must, on the contrary, make every effort to meet the highest standards of scholarship in the selection of content and in the methods he employs in the classroom. But in the construction of the social studies program from grade one through twelve, in the development of the courses that compose the program, and in the day-by-day work in the classroom, both the content and method must contribute to the creation of desirable socio-civic behavior. Any effort at updating the social studies that ignores this mandate is doomed to endless frustration and certain failure.

But what is desirable behavior in a free society? And once this question is answered, how can we develop individuals who do in fact meet the prescribed standards? These are difficult questions to answer, and especially so in a world in which long-established ways of life are being transformed and re-transformed with breathtaking rapidity. But difficult though they are, the questions must be answered, if only in tentative terms, tentative in the sense that they are subject to continual reconsideration, for it is obvious that the conclusions we reach will shape the content, the methodology, and the organization and administration of the social studies program. Those who in the name of revision begin the job with exclusive concern for content are putting the cart before the horse.

The authors of the National Council report started with the fundamental questions we have been considering. After listing "the behavioral needs in a free society," they examined in turn "the beliefs of a free people," "the role of knowledge," and "the role of abilities and skills." This breakdown of the ultimate goal into the categories of values, knowledge, and skills is of course merely an analytical device by means of which one can move closer to the practical matter of shaping a social studies program. As such, it has been widely used by social studies teachers, and the existing social studies program —or programs—reflect the search for specific answers to the questions *what* values, *what* knowledge, and *what* skills. The search for answers must continue, and it should be evident that the efforts will be rewarding to the extent that they are able to draw upon the whole body of research carried on in the social sciences; in the behavioral sciences; and by educators concerned with child development, curriculum construction, methodology, and the organization and administration of the schools. Anything short of a completely co-operative effort is inexcusable. Any single group, whether in the academic world or in the public at large, that blandly assumes it is qualified singlehandedly to formulate a social studies program adequate for the needs of today and tomorrow is guilty of unconscionable arrogance. Worse, implicit in the assumption is an alarming lack of awareness of the nature and extent of the dynamics of contemporary life.

We have been bearing down hard upon the need for co-operation. The point becomes clearer when we begin to examine the goals that social studies shorthand has labeled skills, knowledge, and values.

Skills

One can secure immediate assent to the proposition that a primary obligation of education is the development of intellectual competence. It is evident, moreover, that the ability to think critically and reflectively depends upon the mastery of a number of skills. By way of example, and stated in the simplest terms, there are the skills involved in reading, in locating information, in analyzing and evaluating data of all kinds, in formulating generalizations, in making judgments, and in constructing a logical exposition or argument for either spoken or written presentation. Each of these skills involves in turn a number of supporting skills. In the case of analysis and evaluation, for instance, the intellectually competent individual should possess considerable ability in distinguishing between fact and opinion, and in reaching a judgment as to whether a statement is true, probably true, possibly true, or of such uncertain character that any attempt to assess its validity is futile.

The methods by which we learn and the skills necessary for critical thinking have received a major share of the attention of social studies teachers for many decades. Shelves of books and numerous articles in the professional library stand as solid testimony to the continuing effort of social studies teachers to identify these skills and to discover more effective ways of developing them in the classroom. Many of the publications prepared by the National Council for the Social Studies include substantial discussions of social studies skills, and two of the National Council's Yearbooks, one published in 1953, the other scheduled for publication in 1963, are devoted entirely to the subject. No aspect of the social studies has received more sustained and thoughtful attention. This is as it should be. Surely nothing is more important in education today than the development of an informed and intellectually competent citizenry.

But although much is being done in many classrooms to develop the power to think critically, far more can be accomplished when social studies teachers have better answers to questions for which as yet they have only inadequate answers. Take the problem of selecting the skills to be developed and the corollary problem of assigning to these skills some degree of priority in the social studies program. There are many methods and techniques by means of which we seek out and verify and evaluate knowledge. Each of the social science disciplines leans heavily though not exclusively upon certain of these methods. Which of the many are most useful and necessary for the average citizen today? Which will be most useful and necessary in another decade? One can quickly dismiss the highly specialized techniques, such as, for example, glottochronology and carbon-fourteen dating. And, at the other extreme, one can readily accept the need to develop facility in reading and interpreting graphic materials (globes, maps, charts, graphs, tabular data, etc.), as well as that group of skills included in the process of research and verification we call the historical method. But where, if at all, should social studies teachers undertake to develop an understanding of polling and interviewing techniques and the methods of statistical analysis, all of which have become increasingly important in recent years and are likely to become still more important in the immediate future? This is merely a brief sample of one category of questions that call for further study and experimentation.

The determination of the skills that need to be developed

is only part of the problem. There is also the question of how to do the job most effectively. Here, too, the social studies teacher can turn to a substantial body of literature, some of it in the form of speculation, much of it in the form of reports of classroom experimentation. But there is so much more we need to learn. After extensive study of the subject, James P. Shaver of the Graduate School of Education of Harvard University reached the conclusion that "the hunches of the classroom teacher, along with those of his teaching colleagues and his supervisors and academic associates, provide as firm a basis for methodological decisions in this area as does educational research at this point."

Far more difficult questions clamor for answers that can come only from research and experimentation on a mammoth scale. How successful can we be in our efforts to cultivate the rational in man if we fail to come to grips with the irrational impulses that motivate so much of our behavior? On this point, we are reminded of Freud's pessimism. "America," he once wrote, "is the most grandiose experiment the world has seen, but I am afraid it is not going to be a success." Surely a nation that can afford billions of dollars in the hope of exploring the moon can spare the resources to support the studies of human behavior that would, we hope, give the lie to Freud's pessimistic prediction. There is so much more at stake than the study of human behavior. When we deal with behavior we are at the center of the problems of war and peace and the very future of civilization. The larger question we here raise is not one the classroom teacher can hope to answer, but it is one with which, whatever his degree of awareness, the classroom teacher must deal.

In our attempt to build a case for a co-operative effort to strengthen the social studies program, we started with the least controversial of the three objectives of skills, knowledge, and values. Before we leave the matter of skills, it is important to note that the co-operation we have in mind must involve publishers and the general public as well as schoolmen and specialists from the academic world.

What kind of textbooks and other instructional materials would we need if we were to make an all-out attack upon the problem of developing the critically minded and intellectually competent individual? Would we need books constructed largely upon case studies? These are questions upon which, no doubt, all of us have opinions. But we need more than opinions.

And there is the public. In spite of the lip service we pay to the ideal of the thoughtful, responsible citizen, there is alarming evidence that a substantial number of American citizens prefer indoctrination and dogma to a truly liberating education. All too familiar to social studies teachers who have undertaken to develop the intellectual powers of their students is the irate cry of the parent, "What are you teaching my child?" Even as we write, there comes to mind the junior high school that is being investigated for "subversive activities" because a group of seventh graders in a model United Nations Security Council meeting voted to admit Red China to the U.N. In a totalitarian state the directives from the authorities establish the program and provide a security of its own kind for the classroom teacher. In an open society such as ours we must operate with recommendations rather than by directives. If the recommendations are to be meaningful, they must come from the leaders in the social sciences and the social studies. At the same time, the full implication of the recommendations must be understood and accepted by a substantial portion of the citizens in the local community. The degree of support the local community gives depends in large part upon the strength of the endorsement the recommendations receive from a reputable and representative cross section of the educational world.

Knowledge and Values

The case we have advanced for a co-operative effort to develop a social studies program that makes an increasingly vital contribution to the growth of intellectual competence becomes doubly convincing when we turn to the selection and organization of content and the identification of desirable attitudes. Obviously, thought does not take place in a vacuum. It includes knowledge, the exercise of a complex of skills, a generous dose of skepticism, and a cluster of values that, however well or poorly comprehended, serve as a guiding force. Critical thinking moves from facts to evidence to conclusions, and as often as not to value judgments.

Now knowledge, in the broad sense we are using the term, is in Webster's words, "the sum of information conserved by civilization." This, the totality of recorded experience, includes knowledge *of*, or knowledge acquired by the senses, as well as knowledge *about*, or knowledge obtained by intellectual processes. Moreover, as we all know, the sum of knowledge is growing at a staggering rate of speed. For all practical purposes, it is limitless.

Any intelligent attempt to evaluate the content of the social studies must survey as best it can the whole body of knowledge. It must approach this admittedly overwhelming task with two questions: What part of the immense total is most essential for the informed, responsible citizen today? What part will be most essential in another decade? These questions will be answered in one way or another. We can pool our resources and in all humility propose what seem to be reasonable answers. Or we can ignore the problem on the ground that it is beyond human competence to solve and, turning our backs and going our separate ways, leave the answers to the voice of tradition. The latter choice would be equivalent to a decision to commit suicide.

Confronted with such an overwhelming job, where do we

begin? The first requirement is self-evident: We begin by reaching agreement on the principles to be used in the selection and grade placement of content.

Two reports issued by the National Council for the Social Studies contain interesting and significant suggestions for the development of guiding principles. The first of the reports, released in 1957 and called *A Guide to Content in the Social Studies,* outlined fourteen "themes" that might be used as guidelines for the selection of content for the entire twelve-year sequence.[2] The second report, published in 1958 under the title of *Curriculum Planning in American Schools: The Social Studies,* emphasized the impact of the "ongoing and accelerating scientific revolution," the expansion of our physical horizons to embrace the world and even outer space, and the striking advances made by social science research in recent years. After exploring some of the implications of these developments, the report went on to examine the issues confronting American education and to indicate the direction in which the social studies should be moving.[3] Both reports deserve considered attention.

What and where? How much attention should be devoted to the non-Western world—East Asia, India, Africa? How much to Latin America? How much to the Soviet Union? How much to the formidable issues clamoring for attention, among them the challenge of Communism, the rapid growth of population, the growing urbanization of life everywhere in the world, the development of automation, the pollution of sea and air and the reckless use of the earth and its resources? How does one decide which of these and numerous other subjects belong in the social studies program, how much weight to give them, and where and how they can best be taught? And how does one decide what part or parts of the established program can be discarded to make room for the new? There are several ways to answer these and the many other questions in regard to content. They can be answered by each teacher in his own way, or by groups of teachers in each school or school district. They can be answered by legislators, with the answers appearing as legislative mandates or prohibitions. The best way, of course, is to have the answers come in the form of recommendations drawn up by a truly representative professional group.

The success of any co-operative effort depends, however, upon the degree of understanding each member of the team brings to the venture. In this connection, a word of warning from Alfred North Whitehead is in order. Writing as long ago as 1925 in *Science and the Modern World,* Whitehead pointedly observed that the whole is greater than the sum of its parts. "When you understand all about the sun and all about the atmosphere and all about the rotation of the earth," he wrote, "you may still miss the radiance of the sunset." We could in the name of revision improve existing courses in history, geography, economics, government, sociology, psychology, and anthropology, and this would be an important contribution to the social studies program. But it is not the larger contribution we need and have a right to expect in view of the resources an all-out project could command.

The development of moral and ethical standards cannot be divorced from the growth of intellectual competence and the acquisition of knowledge. Indeed—and we quote from the National Council report on *Curriculum Planning in American Schools*—"the fundamental premise upon which democracy rests is the presumption that men and women can be taught to think for themselves and to measure the right and wrong of their actions against freely accepted standards of conduct." No one questions the central role attitudes and beliefs, or "standards of conduct," play in the process of education. Nor does there seem to be much doubt that our basic values are rooted in us during the early years of childhood. If this is indeed the case, we have a convincing argument for an integrated social studies program that starts with the first years of schooling.

Recommendations

In our discussion up to this point we have (1) warned against any inclination to settle for a cure-all prescription for the social studies; (2) directed attention to the nature of the crisis confronting mankind; (3) emphasized the critical role the social studies are obligated to play in a rapidly changing, increasingly complex world; (4) briefly reviewed the goals the social studies seek to achieve; and (5) directed attention to the need for a greatly stepped-up program of educational research and experimentation. Everything we have been saying supports the proposition that a comprehensive examination of what can and should be done to provide the vital social education the times demand is long overdue. In view of the crisis confronting us, it is unthinkable that support for such a project will not be forthcoming.

Several considerations lend weight to the case for a carefully organized and comprehensive investigation of the social studies that produces a firm set of recommendations for the nation's schools.

The increasing mobility of the American people, with something like one out of every five persons changing his place of residence every year, points to the desirability of at least a certain measure of agreement on what should be included at the different grade levels. We are not, of course, arguing for a uniform curriculum established by legislative prescription. We do, however, insist that some degree of consensus on what can properly be taught and where is long overdue.

That any thorough revision of the social studies program must involve the entire sequence from grade one through twelve, and conceivably with reference to the first two years of undergraduate work, is so obviously a necessity that no further comment needs to be made. Equally obvious is the conclusion that the social studies should and must command a larger amount of time. If this means the addition of courses or other organized activities to the daily schedule, no one should hesitate so to recommend. It is utterly unrealistic to assign the social studies to a marginal place in the curriculum and then to expect them to carry a large share of the burden of educating the whole man and the alert and intelligent citizen. Nor is it necessary to repeat—although we do so by way of emphasis and to round out our summary—that revision includes a re-examination of goals, content, organization, and method, including an evaluation of such developments as educational television, team teaching, and programed learning with or without teaching machines.

In an address given at the 1961 convention of the National Council for the Social Studies Howard R. Anderson, then Provost of the University of Rochester, reminded his audience that "the Council has accepted the greatest challenge of its forty-year life. I refer," he said, "to the decision to exercise leadership in the development of a social studies curriculum for all children in the elementary and secondary schools of the United States."

As Anderson pointed out in his report, in a preliminary step toward the development of a program of curriculum revision, the National Council for the Social Studies and the American Council of Learned Societies turned to the specialists whose contributions appear in this volume. What, each of the specialists was asked, is the minimum understanding every high school graduate should have of your particular field of learning? What can geography contribute to the student's understanding of the world and of himself? What can history contribute, political science, economics, sociology, anthropology, and psychology? What can an experience or experiences in area studies, say of the Soviet Union or of India, contribute? In the preceding chapters the specialists have given what, we are sure they will agree, are tentative answers to an extremely difficult but highly significant question that needs to be asked and needs to be answered.

This brings us to the next steps the National Council for

the Social Studies and the American Council of Learned Societies had in mind when they embarked on their joint venture. As Anderson indicated, "These steps follow logically." He then proceeded to summarize the proposals for moving into a comprehensive program of curriculum revision in the social studies.

> 1. Responsibility for the development of a curriculum must involve scholars representing the social sciences, persons concerned with curriculum and the psychology of learning, and classroom teachers at various grade levels. All of these persons need to be involved in the total task. This is not the kind of job that can be done by having each group do its part and then abdicate responsibility.
>
> 2. A university having a substantial program in teacher education and good working relationships with nearby school systems provides the ideal environment for the development of an experimental curriculum, try-outs, evaluation, and necessary revisions. The university and area school systems might underwrite some of the costs of this type of experimentation, but long-term outside support will be needed.
>
> 3. Ideally there should be several experimental centers, each free to use initiative but also fully informed of developments at other centers.
>
> 4. A committee, representing the National Council and the American Council of Learned Societies, should serve in a coordinating capacity, having responsibility for the preparation of publications reporting experimental programs, developing procedures leading to consensus regarding the curriculum, and working with state departments of education, publishers, and other interested parties to insure its implementation.

One would expect that a national commission of the kind here envisioned would assume responsibilities even beyond the consideration of the social studies program itself. We have in mind the obvious need for concern with the education of social studies teachers, both in teacher-training institutions and in liberal arts colleges. We also have in mind the problem of helping practicing teachers to keep abreast of new developments in the social sciences, a task that would certainly involve graduate courses and summer institutes and workshops.

Considering the enormous complexity of the task facing such a commission and the high stakes the entire country holds in the success of such a project, it does not seem too much to suggest that the undertaking be organized on a more or less permanent basis. We can perhaps best illustrate what we mean by calling attention to the Center for Advanced Studies at Princeton and the Center for the Behavioral Sciences at Stanford. If it is true, as we believe it to be, that the social studies hold one of the keys to our future as a nation and to the future of the free world, then any effort to vitalize the social studies program should command the highest loyalty and the undivided attention of all those involved in the work. Perhaps, given sufficient funds, it would be possible to draw representative groups of social scientists, specialists in child development, classroom teachers, and administrators together to work over sustained periods of even a year or more. One would not expect this group to hand down the final words of wisdom. One would expect, however, that its continuing studies, its pinpointing of areas in which research was badly needed, and its recommendations in regard to content and organization and method would supply the schools with a continuing flow of information on which experiments could be based and more effective practices developed.

We round out our discussion with two closing comments. In recent years it has been increasingly fashionable—and in some cases, it would seem, financially profitable—to charge the social studies with just about every imaginable sin. The list ranges from incompetence to organized subversion! At the moment we are especially sensitive to this situation because in the preceding pages we, too, have been approaching the subject with a critical point of view. For this reason it is essential to declare as forcefully as possible that an imposing amount of research and experimentation on the part of thoroughly competent social studies teachers has been and is being carried on across the country. Certainly one of the responsibilities of a national commission would be to serve as a clearing house for the solid accomplishments that the social studies profession, working against extremely difficult obstacles, has been able to achieve.

Finally, although our present concern has focused on the problem of developing a comprehensive program of curriculum revision, this volume as a whole contains a wealth of suggestions for immediately adding depth and breadth and meaning to social studies courses at every grade level. Much can be gained by any group of teachers or by the individual teacher from a thoughtful analysis of the points of view and the specific proposals the social scientists have contributed. Much more can be gained in the future if this, the first step, leads to the creation of a national commission that will carry the project forward. One would hope that social studies teachers across the country will raise their voices in loud and clear support of the proposal.

1. National Council for the Social Studies, "The Role of the Social Studies," *Social Education,* October 1962.
2. NCSS Committees on Concepts and Values, *A Guide to Content in the Social Studies,* National Council for the Social Studies, 1957.
3. NCSS National Commission on the Social Studies, *Curriculum Planning in American Schools: The Social Studies,* National Council for the Social Studies, 1958.